TEN
STUPID THINGS
MEN DO
TO MESS UP
THEIR LIVES

TEN STUPID THINGS

MEN DO TO MESS UP THEIR LIVES

Dr. Laura Schlessinger

Cliff Street Books

An Imprint of HarperCollins*Publishers*

This book is dedicated to the
important men in my life:

Lew and Deryk

Thank you for your love and support

HarperCollins books may be purchased for educational, business, or sales promotional use. For information please write: Special Markets Department, HarperCollins Publishers, Inc., 10 East 53rd Street, New York, NY 10022.

FIRST EDITION

Designed by Alma Hochhauser Orenstein

Library of Congress Cataloging-in-Publication Data

Schlessinger, Laura.
    Ten stupid things men do to mess up their lives / Laura
Schlessinger. — 1st ed.
        p.   cm.
    ISBN 0-06-017308-4
    1. Man-woman relationships.   2. Men—Psychology.
I. Title.
HQ801.S4364   1997
155.3'32—dc21   97-23121

97 98 99 00 01 ❖/RRD 10 9 8 7 6 5 4 3 2 1

CONTENTS

ACKNOWLEDGMENTS

My deepest gratitude goes to the many men who have opened up to me on my radio program and through their incredibly moving faxes and letters. They trusted to share with me what was in their hearts, souls, thoughts, and emotions. Innumerable times, while typing their words into this transcript, I cried in response to their sensitivity, intuitiveness, and depth of feeling. I hope this book will go a long way to correct the undeserved popular notion of men as emotionally "clueless." Writing this book was a revelation for me in that regard. I evolved from the typical female position of smug humor about the universally acknowledged emotional shallowness of men, to a deep respect for their quiet profundity. Thank you, guys, for educating and moving me so deeply.

I appreciate the enthusiastic support of my publisher, Diane Reverend (aka The Reverend Diane), and my editor, Carolyn Fireside (who cheered me on by telling me that editing my work cheered her up).

All of those associated with my radio program have helped me connect to an international audience. First, my crew includes: Dan Mandis, who engineers and orchestrates our music; Carolyn Holt, who produces and screens the calls; Larry Metzler, who is responsible for our production; and Ernestia O'Steen, who takes care of everything and everybody else. Synergy, which syndicates my radio program: John Shannahan, CEO, and Judy Cords, receptionist extraordinaire. Radio Today, which distributes my program: Geoff Rich and Ramona Rideout; and for Multiverse, which sells advertising, David Landau and Ken Williams.

Special thanks also to all the radio stations and to the general managers and program directors who broadcast and support my program—especially at my flagship station, KFI: Howard Neal, GM, and David Hall, PD.

A personal note of gratitude to my dear friends Patti Edwards, Rabbi Steward Vogel, and Rabbi Reuven Bulka— thank you for always being there in friendship and spirituality.

Of course—love to my family: husband, Lew Bishop, and son, Deryk. We work together as a family toward *Tikkun Olam*.

INTRODUCTION

An old Oregon rancher once told me, "There are three types of men in the world. One type learns from books. One type learns from observations. And one type just has to urinate on the electric fence himself."
CARL BARNEY (LISTENER), 1996

The intent of this book is to reach all three of these types of men: the first will learn from reading, the second can learn from the trials and tribulations of other men who have shared their stories in spoken and written word, and the third can learn their way back from personal electrocution!

But this is a book for women too. As my caller Mark complained ever so reasonably, *"It seems that men are constantly being accused of not understanding what makes women tick and perhaps this is often true. As a result, however, we are expected to become scholars of the female psyche or be labeled as insensitive dolts. Why is it that women don't seem to feel the need to understand what makes us tick? Is it any less important in the grand scheme of things?"*

Generally, women are only concerned about those male feelings which involve themselves: Do the men love them? love their bodies? think about them all the time? think about any other woman? think other women are sexy? think about the relationship?, etc. Any attempt at understanding and respecting a man's "feeling" point of view is often met with hostility from some women, as this excerpt from a letter received November 20, 1996, demonstrates:

Dear Dr. Schlessinger,

I have been listening to your program for at least three years now. I agree with most of the advice that you give. Still, there is one thing about you that just makes my blood boil. You may vehemently disagree with what I am going to say, but in my opinion you come across as terribly pro-men. What is my point? That on any given day I can just pick a handful of men and women at random and on average I am darn sure going to find more decent women. Personally, I like both men and women, but I believe more women are going to make it to heaven.

Remember the children's animated movie *All Dogs Go To Heaven*? Well, from this woman's point of view, even dogs have a leg up on men!

When I wrote *Ten Stupid Things Women Do to Mess Up Their Lives,* I dealt with the still prevailing notion that men were responsible for women's problems, failures, unhappiness, and frustrations in life. In hundreds of examples, women, in their own words, clarified how their own weaknesses, fears, impulsive behavior, inappropriate desires, and lack of a value system caused them to victimize themselves. Were the men in their lives faultless and innocent? Sometimes. And other times the men *chosen* by the women were an unhealthy perfect fit: a match made in purgatory.

Nonetheless, when I was interviewed about that book, the interviewers almost always ran to the fallback, politically correct position that whatever women did was out of helplessness because of their oppressed state, victimized not only by bad men but a brainwashing society which trains women to behave . . . stupidly(?).

Incidentally, from time to time I have been challenged (even by a young female clerk aiding in one of my book signings) about the use of the word *stupid*. "Couldn't you have used some other term?" they ask uncomfortably or outright angrily. "Why?" I respond. "What's wrong with the word 'stupid'? It's defining the behaviors, not the person." "Well," comes the typical response, "I just think that with all the problems women have, calling their behaviors stupid is just adding unnecessary stress." Oh, puhleeese. More of that delicate, picked-on women routine. It's fascinating that these women don't realize their own hypersensitivity is what insults and diminishes women, not my calling things as they are.

However, when I've given presentations to audiences across the country in the three years since *The Ten Stupid Things Women Do to Mess Up Their Lives* came out, I never once received anything but wild applause at the notion that there might be a companion book for the men. And the audiences were both men and women! Not only were the men not resistant to the idea of this book, they have contributed more useful, unsolicited material than the women ever did!

In truth, until 1995, I didn't have any real intention to write this book. First, I didn't want to "trade off" on the catchy title of an already successful book; I worried I would be perceived as a one-note exploiter. Second, I was told time and time again that "men don't read this kind of girl stuff (you know, feelings and relationships . . . ugh!); give 'em sports and politics and they're happy."

Let's get back to "first": I could tell not only from the reactions of live audiences, but from requests faxed and written to me, that there was a need and an interest in a men's "stupid" book to parallel the women's. "Second": I heard that same nonsense about my radio program, that "syndication would be difficult in radio markets where men are the predominant audience because they don't listen to a show hosted by a woman dealing with relationships and ethical behaviors. . . . They like yelling about politics or sports." The real problem was that there hadn't been a show about interpersonal issues and morality which didn't come from a politically correct, ultraliberal, man-blaming perspective. No wonder the men did not feel welcome, comfortable, or interested in any significant numbers. My program is different, and in many radio markets across the country my ratings with men top or rival the sports programs and the leading political shows. To steal from the movie *Field of Dreams,* "Build it right and they will come."

So we've settled the issue that men do want to talk about "personal things." However, their typical approach and focus is significantly different from women's. In fact, I'm convinced that if you disguised the voices, I could still tell the difference between a man or woman caller. Simply put, women are more persistently intro-spective, meaning that we can go over our feelings about some problem two zillion times and still be able to revisit it with fresh enthusiasm. Men are more extra-spective; meaning they generally don't look at problems from such a "personal" vantage point, but instead as tasks to be solved. In other words, it's not that men don't have feelings, it's that they don't lead with their feelings—the same way they don't lead with their chins. Or, as one male caller put it, "With men, feelings are something you get over. With women, feelings are something you chew forever."

Just yesterday on my program a newly engaged woman called to tell me that she'd postponed her wedding for six months in the hopes that her man would change and become more expressive about his feelings.

"Expressive about what feelings?" I asked.

"You know," she answered, "how he feels about me and the relationship. How the relationship is going."

"You want him to do continuous commentary on your relationship as though he were broadcasting a baseball game?"

"Well." She giggled. "Yeah, I guess that's it."

"Or you won't feel constantly secure?"

"So," she offered wisely, "the problem is really my insecurity?"

"Bingo!" I concluded.

Mike, a listener, faxed me a long letter containing this small paragraph: *"Men have long been accused by women of not sharing their feelings openly, but I think this is an erroneous and over generalized statement. We tend to share our successes and joys rather than wallow in each others' negative emotional muck and mire (as women typically do)."* That's true, but only as far as it goes. With this book I am going to push much further. For instance, women may "talk" instead of "doing," but men will "do" instead of "talking." While the spoken word can do much damage, or can be depressingly impotent in lieu of necessary action, inappropriate behaviors which occur in the place of important and brave discussions can mess up many lives. This book will focus discussion on the top 10 things men "do to mess up their lives."

Besides mine, there are, of course, other possible top 10 lists. What follows are five out of the hundred or so contributions I received upon request to my radio program. I have titled them based on my interpretation of each author's "attitude." These listener lists are quite revealing about the inner workings and experiences of many of you men.

Cynical

- *When she says "just friends"—she expects you to put your time, money, and effort into courting her, but she is keeping her options open for somebody better.*
- *When she says, "I never think about him [her ex] anymore"—she only has one to three thoughts a day which aren't about him.*
- *When she says, "Money isn't an issue with me"—she means that the lack of money is a very big issue with her.*
- *When she says, "If you really loved me, you wouldn't even mention a prenuptial agreement"—she really means that if the marriage doesn't work, all the household belongings not nailed down will leave with her.*

- *When she says, "My career is very important to me"—she means that she should be able to dine with a handsome coworker or client with your blessing.*
- *When she says, "It doesn't have to be an extravagant wedding"—she means that it'll be in the largest church within one hundred miles and she'll invite everyone she's ever known.*
- *When she says, "I don't want to feel pressured into having sex with you"—she means she's not physically attracted to you but no one else is calling for dates.*
- *When she says, "Maybe we should see other people"—she means she's already been seeing other people for the last three weeks, but this is the first tinge of guilt she's felt about it in her otherwise empty conscience.*
- *When she says, "Eventually, I want to have children"—she means she's not willing to make any sacrifices to take care of them.*
- *When she says, "Relationships should be based on trust"—she means that she expects you to tell her everything, while respecting her privacy not to!*

Confessional

- *Blame others for what they themselves are responsible for*
- *Expect others to do for them what they can only do for themselves*
- *Depend on orgasms to fill the void of what they need emotionally*
- *Treat the bride that they have vowed to love and cherish with criminal violence and abuse just like their parents treated them*
- *Been resisting of help and stubborn*
- *Not in touch with their own feelings*
- *Taken too long to deal with issues until the family was blown apart*

- *Spent too much money on things and gone bankrupt*
- *Tried to do too much too soon—not being patient and careful*
- *Making rash and impulsive decisions without the benefit of the counsel of wise people*

Macho Conceit

- *Confusing macho with courage*
- *Thinking with the wrong head*
- *Needing always to be always right*
- *Running away from feelings*
- *Intimidating, the need to dominate*
- *Choosing the tough and masculine over the creative and thoughtful*
- *Letting "her" handle everything related to the home space*
- *Being stoic and uncommunicative*
- *Being your work*
- *Choosing beauty over character*

Childishness

- *Unwilling to say, "I'm sorry"*
- *Expecting my mate to be my mother*
- *Not taking care of my health, not exercise*
- *Abusing my body with alcohol, drugs, and cigarettes*
- *Holding in my feelings*
- *Marrying at too young an age*
- *Fathering kids too young*
- *Watching television too many hours a day*
- *Neglecting my spiritual life*
- *Choosing mate on the basis of the feeling in my loins, instead of the feeling in my heart*

Caretaking

- *Trying to take an active part in wedding ceremony plans when there are plenty of women in-laws who passionately want to run the whole thing*
- *Not calling your wife when you're out late—or at any time when she would wonder if you'd been in a car accident*
- *Smoking a pipe when it worries your wife, stains your teeth, gives you bad breath, contributes to gum disease, and sometimes worse stuff*
- *Not buying enough inexpensive yet wife-loving things like flowers, which always make women feel special*
- *Not making more effort (arranging for baby-sitter, etc.) to date your wife after having children*
- *Letting her wash the dishes all the time and not helping out more with household duties*
- *Saying anything bad about my wife's family or friends*
- *Not complimenting my wife more about hair, beauty, inner-self; guys forget that women want to be romanced for the rest of married life*
- *Not providing enough foreplay and sexual sensitivity*
- *The male tendency to want to forget miscommunications instead of talking them through; I can hurt her feelings without even knowing it or intending to*

Character

- *Placing more importance on passing pleasures than on eternal values*
- *Thinking "love" is erections and ejaculations rather than choices and commitment*
- *Stopping courting of their wife*
- *Equating personal worth with professional worth*
- *Investing more time, money, and/or energy in hobbies and sports than in family and relationships*

- *Having no purpose in life*
- *Expecting their kids to be as perfect as they wished they had been*
- *Thinking anger, violence, and drug abuse (legal and illegal) are desirable expressions of manhood*
- *Refusing to ask for forgiveness when they know they are wrong*
- *Thinking leadership means total control and dominance*

It seems obvious from these lists (except the Cynical one) that you guys *know,* you are *aware* of, many of the basic tendencies and problems which are more typically male. So, what's the problem? According to L. M. Boyd, a trivia columnist for the *Orange County Register,* "Dr. Pierre Flor-Henry, clinical professor of psychiatry at Canada's University of Alberta, said, 'The male brain is the more likely to malfunction.'" And, as the Cox Communications reported on a book by Michael Gurian, *The Wonder of Boys,* "A boy's brain rests sometimes. Boys are therefore better at doing one thing, moving on, doing another thing, moving on again." Yet another article, by Mark Bowsen for Knight-Ridder/ Tribune Information Services, summarized a report by Ruben Gur, a University of Pennsylvania neuropsychologist: "Women are more inclined to exercise a portion of the lower brain that helps refine the way emotions are expressed. . . . Men, on the other hand, think like lizards."

Nice try, but no cigar! Thirty years of study have shown that the average man and the average woman have about the same level of intelligence, but men do account for a higher proportion of both genius and mental deficiency. So, except for the exceptions, it ain't "smarts" that's the problem. There is something else going on for men and women which leads us to behave stupidly in spite of our smarts.

Throwing my two cents into the nature/nurture battle, I say that that's exactly the problem: nature versus nurture! There are clearly bimorphic anatomical and physiological differences between male and female, there's not much argument about that. The fight begins when we introduce bimorphic tendencies to behavior. Well, friends, we aren't plants and we aren't minerals; we are animals, and with that comes certain biological imperatives or pressures. The amazing aspect of humanity is that we can override biology with a mere decision to do so, e.g., a man staying home as the primary child caretaker, or a man mating with one woman when sexual variety might mean something special to the gene pool. I have come to believe that societal pressures to conform exist not to create something which isn't there, but rather to emphasize what is built into the animal with respect to masculine and feminine.

In the last analysis, the basis of this book is identical to that of *Ten Stupid Things Women Do,* namely, that the "stupid behaviors" of men and women most likely derive from one or more of the following sources: failure to discipline biological urges, immaturity, lack of learned moral/value systems, value systems sacrificed for the thrill or gain of the moment, personal weakness, and, in the words of listener Michael Watts, "failure to admit how stupid I have been."

STUPID CHIVALRY

Men pride themselves on being handy.
So—we go out to find broken women so we
can fix them.
Trouble is we're not equipped to fix anything
beyond a leaky faucet.

DAVID, 1996

During Saturday morning services at my synagogue, an engaged couple in their early thirties came up to the bima (pulpit) to receive the rabbi's blessing. The day before their wedding, it was a lovely and touching moment as they entered into a new level of relationship to each other and to the community. On such a joyous occasion, the congregation customarily responds with song, clapping, and the throwing of candies, representing the sweetness of everyone's joy and the hope for sweetness in the happy, but embarrassed couple's future. Well, somebody didn't buy target-friendly candies, because even the rabbi cringed with pain as those hard projectiles thrown with such enthusiasm pelted him. Without suggestion or request, seemingly by instinct, the prospective groom moved in front of his bride-to-be and shielded her body with his; his back taking the brunt of the hits. When the folks ran out of candy, he moved back to his place beside her and she kissed his cheek, possibly just with joy, but probably also as reward for his thoughtful gallantry.

The rabbi joked good-naturedly about the incident and the man's chivalry, but I was deeply struck by the clarity of that moment: the male's protection of the female is an important part of the biological (and psychological) dynamic between men and women.

The Biology of Chivalry

In the *Weekly Standard,* Chandler Burr describes an illuminating encounter Dr. Laurence Frank, a zoologist at Berkeley, had with a coed after presenting a lecture on animal endocrinology and the way hormones determine maleness and femaleness: "And a young woman came up afterwards and she was shocked, *shocked,* that I would say such a thing. In her view, 'maleness' is just macho posturing 'socially constructed' by society, 'femaleness' a myth created by the Neanderthal patriarchy.' But to biologists, gender is as real as oxygen." And maybe so is chivalry.

Chivalry is the combination of qualities expected of a medieval knight, including courage, generosity, and courtesy. More gender-role specifically, it is the male's obligation to be considerate, courteous, and gallant toward the female, protecting her sensibilities, honor, and person. While biologists don't see much noninstinctive behavior in nonhuman animals which they can label as noble or altruistic, they do see a pattern of male aggression ensuring protection of turf, nest, mate, family, and group—a biological division of labor with the females protecting and nurturing their young.

I was originally trained as a biologist, and I am convinced that the animal part of our nature is the engine of our drives; our ability to reason, to embrace morality, to go beyond the biological imprint navigates the direction of those drives— which is why we can go so haywire! Being "animal" is easy, being an "ascendant human" requires manual override of some of our more animal (food consumption, random mating) as well as our less worthy human attributes (laziness, self-centeredness, etc.). None of this is foolproof or easy; nor can we ignore the potential support or subversion of our important biological selves by societal pressures.

In each era we human beings experiment with gender role behaviors and expectations, and end up discovering more of our unique potential as humans. In doing so, we may sacrifice what is also essential to our well-being and ability to relate as male and female. While both genders have new and incredible opportunities for intellectual and mechanical expression, the way they relate to each other, and want to relate, doesn't seem to change at all! So it seems clear that the expectations, hopes, desires, and needs men and women fundamentally have for each other haven't changed in spite of all the social engineering. I think even *Ms.* magazine has admitted that.

When Chivalry's Just Plain Stupid

I'm convinced it is built into the male to be protective, to be chivalrous. What I worry about is the *blind* Stupid Chivalry which is messing up your lives. According to Selden (a listener), such *blind and stupid chivalry* would be indicated by the following:

- When a woman wants you to "give her a life," you try to do it.
- Try to get a woman to change.
- Stay in a lousy relationship out of a sense of pity (you don't want to hurt her feelings) or obligation (you started this thing, you guess you have to finish it).

Now this is a great start, but there is one central idea you men seem to be blind to: You buy the idea that a woman's situation in life, shaggy dog story of terrible experiences, failures, or problems are *accidents of fate*, or *bad luck*, or *incredible circumstances out of her control*, or *actions of people or persons other than herself*—meaning of course she could do nothing other than what she's done considering what's happened *to* her. I'll give you that traffic accidents, disease, childhood abuse, or adult assaults sadly happen. Yet, instead of observing how she handles these realities to learn about her strength, personality, and character, you determine to step in and heroically take over that responsibility for her.

Worse still, you assume that if she's in distress, there must be a dragon to slay. Dragons are monsters *outside* the person. You need to look to see (1) how heavy a contributor and supporter she is to her own misery, and (2) how hard she works to survive and make things better. Of course, you won't pay attention to these issues if you're off and running after the dragon!

And it's not as if you guys are *totally* blind to what's going on. As proof, a man wrote me this letter, asking for my expert opinion.

> *I am 44 and my new girlfriend is 37. She is unemployed still (for the last 6 years). She is fully capable of working, but lives off her child support money she gets for her 5 year old. She also has two teens, but no support for them. She lives in a small trailer behind her parents' house for $50. per month. Her three kids live with her parents. She has no alcohol problem or drugs of any kind, but does smoke heavily and has asthma. I've seen both of her teens get quite out-of-hand (the 15 year old son had taken her car twice in the middle of the night; her 17 year old daughter has stolen money out of her purse and takes other things from her). Her teens are in Home Study and not even doing good in that. They both use profanity around her and towards her. Her dad is in very poor health. This gal says she loves me very much and doesn't want to lose me.*
>
> *So, Dr. Laura, is this a good woman for me to be in a relationship with or am I asking a very dumb question?*

Reading this letter, I am immediately reminded of a line in the movie *Jerry Maguire*. The girl in love with Tom Cruise is thrilled that he's turned to her in his "hour of need," but her sister appropriately comments, "He'd go home with a garden tool if it showed him any attention."

In spite of all the "garbage," our writer is drawn in by his girlfriend's (pathetic) protestation of love and perhaps made guilty (tweak that chivalry!) by her "not wanting to lose him" (because she has so little).

After one caller, Bob, twenty-four years old, told me he was engaged to a twenty-four-year-old woman with two children (five years and six months) from two men (married to neither one and neither was involved with his child), I said, "Does it cost much to feed your White Horse? You're the hero coming in to *save the damsel from herself,* much less from the dragon." His answer was that he hadn't finished high school, so he didn't know much about knights, and that he had dated too much, and he had known her before all the pregnancies and had been attracted to her. Basically, he had one idea (she's cute, I want her) and stayed with it no matter what.

Oh, by the way, the reason he called me? He was a little squeamish about taking on the responsibility of the kids, since she wanted him to adopt them. There's always a sticky part attached to the "no matter what."

Mr. Fix-It

Some of those "sticky parts" can be deeply painful. Rob, forty-four years old, called about his youngest of three sons (thirteen, eleven, and nine years). Since his wife had had affairs during their marriage, biologically this boy belongs to another man. He worried about the child finding out the truth, since everyone in the family already knows.

After we talked about his boy, I questioned him more about his choice in marrying this woman. I really don't believe personality and character change radically after the garter is thrown at the wedding reception.

"I was divorced from my first wife in my early twenties because I was too immature," he admitted. "I didn't want to be lonely and this lady was very pretty . . . she was smart and everything . . . but I thought I could deal with her problems. She tried to commit suicide a couple of times."

"Rob, let me ask you something. I've talked to a lot of men who will say, 'She was pretty and smart but there were terrible problems of drugs, violence, craziness, hysteria about sex, but I thought I could fix them.' Instead of thinking you could fix her, how come this didn't make you scream and run for the hills away from her? Did you see her magnificent weakness as a challenge for you rather than a failing of hers?"

"Right. I was immature and I didn't have enough knowledge. I didn't know I couldn't fix somebody else's problems. I was silly enough to think that if you feel this terrific feeling of love and companionship that love beats all . . . and that's not enough."

"Rob, this is a big one. . . . If she hadn't been so pretty would you have thought that? If she were suicidal and ugly would you have seen her as a challenge or as a loser?"

"I would have seen her as a loser."

"So, Rob, 'pretty' is enough to have you turn off all your other circuits to your brain centers for reason?"

"It sure was."

"Now you know that pretty doesn't mean that goodness or healthy necessarily lies underneath?"

"That's right, and I promise not to be with anybody who has more problems than me!"

Let's face it, guys, a pretty face and a great body seem to have the magic to dumb you down. You make assumptions about pretty women that ain't necessarily true. While the biological drive for men to pick attractive women with wide hips may have some relevance to suggesting superior health and fertility, projecting your genes into future generations isn't the only consideration in human life: mental health, personality, and character are more important to the quality of your life in your own generation.

Hägar the Horrible, a syndicated cartoon strip, hinted at this truth. Hägar comes upon a beautiful damsel tethered to a post. He asks, "Excuse me, but aren't you a damsel in distress?" "Yes," she answers. Perhaps having been through a sensitivity training course at work he asks before acting, "Would you like to be rescued?" "Yes," she replies, "but only by a *handsome and young* knight in *shining* armor from a *really good family.*" Hägar walks away perplexed. "Damsels in distress are getting more picky every day."

So, perhaps the damsels in distress don't really want your *help.* Perhaps they want you to be their life or to give them a life and take responsibility for them so that they don't have to exert effort to fix themselves. And so that you can be the one to blame when they just don't "feel" better.

No More Mr. Nice Guy?

The "fix-it" mentality is part of the reason that you self-proclaimed nice guys fall into bottomless pits. First, the "nice guy" complaints:

> I am a construction foreman and discussing your topics with co-workers in between their conversations about deer-hunting, woman bashing, and bar conquests would be a real head turner, so I listen in silence. Is it true that the age of the "nice guy" is dead? It seems every time I treat a woman with kindness, respect, and love, I'm constantly told I'm too nice. Friends often say women like to be treated rough and that I shouldn't pay that much attention to them. I am not a nerdy or unattractive man, 26 years old, 6'4", 195 pounds and well built. I do meet plenty of women, but after a few weeks it always comes down to them saying, "You're just too nice, I don't want to hurt you," or, my

favorite is, "You're so sweet, you need to find a nice girl". Please help, because I can see myself slowly slipping to the other side and becoming just another jerk of a guy because it seems that's what all the women want.

And:

I'm tired of being considerate and having it taken for granted. Therefore, I am retiring from the Mr. Nice Guy Club. Seriously, it is a major disappointment that so few women appreciate the qualities of honor, respect and genuine commitment. I am no saint, however, the last five or six years have convinced me which treatment women prefer.

I've heard this pathetic whining quite often in my life as well as throughout the twenty years on air. And it's just garbage. The problem is you!

Here's the real scoop on you "nice guys":

- You use "being nice" as a substitute for "being real." There is a tremendous difference between genuine thoughtfulness and acquiescence in the hope of being wanted or getting some sex. You give her no real feedback and you make no real demands. This fact should have finally dawned on one guy: *"Perhaps what bothers me most is that most women don't even ASK about the choices I've made in my life, or about my background, which tells me that they make THEIR choices based only on superficial things."* That's not all women, just the ones you pick to "work on."
- You give up your "masculinity" to try to become her "best girlfriend" so that there is no threatening aspect to the relationship—another way of trying to "appease the gods." This letter writer may be somewhat typical of this problem: *"I want very much to be in love. Maybe too much. I'm sure I'm probably too desperate for a relation-*

ship. *While I was growing up, I was terrified of my father and relied heavily on my mother to feel secure. What can I do?"* For these voluntarily, self-de-masculinized men, a woman is a mother replacement . . . and how do you act with your mother? Certainly not with any sexual tension or demands.

• You pick women for characteristics *other* than those that would indicate an interest in what you say you have to offer. So it's women who are wild, sexy, adventurous, emotionally volatile, etc. Here's the revelation of one fellow: *"I began to see that I should not care whether or not she found me acceptable because I was the one who was supposed to be **choosing** someone better suited for me spiritually, emotionally and intellectually. I realized that I was mistaking a strong sexual attraction (i.e., lust) for love."*

White Knights/Black Holes

The "nice guy" and even the "white knight" behavior is in part due to the lack of recognition of the important reality that women are actually important to your lives. This issue will be elaborated on in chapter 2, "Stupid Independence," but suffice it to say that the male part of you sees women as essentially peripheral to your lives, while the human man part of you struggles with the frustration that this just isn't true. For example, I remember a scene from *The Bridges of Madison County* where the married but unhappy Meryl Streep is attempting to convince the unmarried but supposedly happy Clint Eastwood that his life is truly empty. He goes on and on about how he loves his freedom and women-in-every-country lifestyle, allowing, however, that women and marriage are the foundation for a man's life, a kind of springboard for all his activities, adventures, and conquests. Of course, at the movie's end, he is desolate that she won't go off with him. Maybe that was because he let down his wall of fear that love and need would take away his masculine, creative powers, turning him into Samson without his long hair.

Until his transformation, Clint's character saw women as pleasant, enjoyable, interchangeable parts on the receiving end of the sex act. Sean, twenty-one years old, probably thought he was just being "nice" when he said, "I see potential in every girl I meet." No criteria? No preferences? No real point to women in your life?

The male-animal part of you men drives you to connect with female(s) for mating. The human-man part of you needs to permit itself to admit to its dependency on a woman's acceptance and support without fearing the loss of the male-animal part.

And you just have to know and believe that there's more that is important about you to a woman than the function of a white knight. Chivalry, as I said before, is a good thing, maybe even a biologically inherent thing. Stupid Chivalry is not only not a good thing, it's a black hole that seems so obvious to everyone around you when you're doing it, yet it's difficult to let go. Why is that? Let me count the ways!

Richard, thirty-three years old, called my program complaining that he always seems to end up with ladies needing to be fixed. I asked him about the "good part" of such a woman. After struggling against the question he admitted, "I guess I'm in control because they depend on me." I asked Richard to describe himself. "I'm kind of a dreamer," he responded.

"I'm not sure what you mean, Richard. Tell me this, why do you imagine that a non-fixer-upper kind of woman might not be interested in you?"

"Well, I'm not really financially secure. I'm a fun kinda guy, but maybe that could seem irresponsible. And, there are things about life, risks and stuff, which scare me."

"Richard, I am impressed with both your honesty and insight. Could it be that fixer-upper women provide less of a chance of rejection for you . . . since they are 'worse off'?"

"I never looked at it that way before, but maybe yeah."

Richard's knighthood was predicated on his need to hide his weaknesses and inadequacies behind the *apparent* strength of his rescuing. Obviously, this is a recipe for no positive growth and change for him, much less for her.

The High Cost of Guilt Tripping

Richard felt unworthy because of how he was living his life now. Another caller, Rod, thirty-one years old, also felt unworthy—but because of past history. Rod has sole custody of stepchildren, ages one and one half and four months, because she gave them to him when she took off to Hawaii with her latest boss! This "damsel" he saved has both a parental and personal history of affairs and shacking up— i.e., it runs in the family. But Rod thought, "You always think if you're good enough to people that they will change." That was a nice sentiment, but I hardly think anyone is that naïve. In fact, Rod wasn't. It turns out that when he was younger and in the military he was into sex, drugs, and rock 'n' roll. He had guilt for these behaviors because, "This was not how I was brought up. I was brought up that I should be married." However, his imagined inadequacy resulting from guilt for his past, first, lowered his sights when picking a woman and, second, made him feel he shouldn't judge and that he could make a difference in the lives of the woman's children, perhaps as a kind of atonement for his sins.

Bill, fifty-one years old and thrice divorced, just never seems to want to get past this inadequacy—and finds a never-ending supply of fixer-upper women to help him avoid having to do so! He called my program asking, "How do you know you're in love with the right one?" We quickly got to his story about the woman he's dating from his support group. "We never had any intention of becoming involved, it's just that we shared a similar past of both of our ex-spouses having affairs. We seem to have the same interests and there was just an emotional high."

Infatuation born of mutual victimhood is probably not the best start for a quality commitment. And Bill's subsequent complaints of a lack of a sustained "high" indicated his need for emotional intensity to verify meaningfulness of himself and his relationship. Compassion, sharing, values, sacrifice, etc., were "lows" in that they didn't spontaneously elevate his being for him. Bonding with a fixer-upper woman to cure your hurts of abandonment is less effective than even an expired placebo.

Jeff was involved with his woman *because* of her mental illness (severe manic depression), not in spite of it. He said, "Our lives are parallel in so many ways—we've both been alone a lot. My love and caring for her illness will cure my loneliness," he offered. I countered with, "But Jeff, if she gets better she will have healthy-woman demands of you that you don't seem to want to be prepared for, and if she never gets better then you won't get the loving caretaking you so obviously yearn for." "I guess I am just not thinking about that," he responded sadly. Jeff must be thinking only that the loneliness of yesterday is gone and his woman's future gratitude will further redeem his emptiness. Which of them really seems more mentally healthy?

A listener named Bill had suffered a terrible blow to his ego: his wife of ten years had left him, taking their three children with her. He wrote:

I was devastated. I concluded that since she had left me, I must be unlovable and fatally flawed. Such self-examination can be a good thing, if it leads to positive steps towards change.
However, in my case, I IMMEDIATELY set about trying to prove her (and, in reality, myself) wrong in this by finding someone whom I could convince to love me. Therefore, I was admitting that I could not objectively assess my own strengths and weaknesses, virtues and faults, and set about making the

required changes. It could only be done through acceptance by someone else.

*Now, one of the ways I could be "valuable" to someone else was by being **essential** to their well-being. Therefore, I found myself irresistibly drawn to a single mother with four boys who was struggling financially. I imagined myself a "knight in shining armor" riding to her rescue. It would be IMPOSSIBLE for her not to value me! (Marriage and divorce and child-custody war followed.)*

*In short, my act of "nobility" was in fact a study in ego aggrandizement. Had I made an effort to work on myself, by myself, to correct the flaws and imperfections that had ended my first marriage, and to gain **self-esteem** the only way it can be gained, within oneself, this fiasco would not have come about, and I would not have yet another child bereft of a whole and healthy family foundation.*

Danger: WOMAN AHEAD!

Now we can move to the intense issues of fear you men have about women. Fearful of women—NO WAY! Yeah, guys, right. As my screener-producer Carolyn Holt informed me with only partial humor, "We black mothers have an attitude about our children if they mess with us. We tell them, 'I brought you into the world and I can take you out!'"

Women give you life, love, support, and nurturance; they raise you from infants suckling at the breast to men looking for some cute new young breast upon which to continue that experience. Your mother has seen you naked with a tiny, pre-pubertal penis, sleeping with your stuffed animals, nervous over some pimply adolescent girl, struggling to grow facial hairs and find muscles to flex, and trying to act like a man when she knew you just wanted to hide, cry, and be safe in her arms.

Perhaps you never got that wonderful mothering, perhaps you got it with too many unhealthy strings attached, perhaps you're afraid that if you want to get that "mothered feeling" from a woman, your penis will fall off—whatever it is . . . you've got fears which make you see a woman as dangerous.

You can readily detect a guy who's afraid of, therefore doesn't trust, women. Ed, thirty-six, and Kelly, twenty-seven, called together. They are newlyweds, having met in December, married in June. Kelly's got three children (twenty-three months, six years old, and nine years old) from three different men (nonhusbands)—and no, Ed's not one of them. Kelly had been heavily into drugs with all three of these sperm donors (none clean and sober, or involved with his child . . . hence, not a "dad" but a "sperm donor"). And, they have a two-month-old child together.

Ed called, hilariously enough, because "issues of *trust* keep coming up." It seems that she's never where she's supposed to be, doing what she's supposed to be doing, with the folks she's supposed to be with. Wow—I'm sure you're all surprised at that. What's the dynamic here? Ed marries slime because his "love shall transform" and then wonders why he doesn't have Cinderella after the marriage ball? No. Actually, it seems that being real close to a healthy woman is threatening to him—the potential for criticism and rejection just too great. Perhaps Ed imagines, or remembers, "having a face (and personhood) that even his mother couldn't/wouldn't love." So, he attempts to transform someone who couldn't possibly judge him (I mean really—look at her!) into someone he can trust to be kind to him. Oops.

These problems with guilts for past transgressions and lifestyles, feelings of real or imagined inadequacies as an adult and/or as a male, fear of the pain of abandonment, loneliness, attempts at ego aggrandizement, fears about women's (aka Mom's?) approval and acceptance, and a fragile sense of masculinity are usually presented as "I continue to choose women who aren't right for me. Like I'm going to help them. But I have no idea why I continue to do this."

When Ray started his call with me saying just that, I

responded, "Sure you do. A knight is in a very powerful position, you're in control. So you don't feel comfortable having an equal in a relationship? We go for what we're the most comfortable with—and you're more comfortable with someone weaker, dependent and needy. The person we're comfortable with tells us a lot about ourselves."

"But I can't seem to find the right one." Ray laughed again.

"What happens, Ray, when you get with needy and dependent people is that they are demanding and overwhelming in their needs. You never get any rest or much back—do you?"

"You got that right!" he said quickly.

"Well, that's the terrible cost of this kind of woman. Let's imagine you with a strong, competent woman."

"Well, then I'd have to be not in control." He laughed again.

"Which would mean what, Ray?"

"That I couldn't be the decision maker all the time."

"If she would be in control then what bad things could happen to you?"

"Well, then her decisions might not be the right ones. I might suffer from this."

There it is. His fear of pain at her hand. "So, you don't trust that a woman could or would make the right decisions and take care of you?"

"Right."

"That's why you pick these little girls. Somehow you have the notion of a woman as dangerous. The only way you can get the closeness and sex and semblance of intimacy is from weak, needy women who you think can't hurt you because they have no power to do so."

"Yeah, Dr. Laura, you got a point there. . . . But inevitably I get hurt anyway because you don't get needs met and you realize that this relationship isn't going to be lasting."

"Nor is she going to give you much back, Ray. What's the ultimate hurt a woman could do to you?"

"To reject me."

To paraphrase Carolyn Holt, one woman brought you into the world, and another woman has the power to emotionally knock you out of it. When your image of "woman" is threatening, you will work around your fears to get needs for companionship and sex met by finding the least threatening woman possible—the "damsel in distress." Problem is that distressed damsels aren't good companions, and sex without more going on gets cold fast. Whatever your fears of your masculinity and/or your mother, or your fears of and failures with women, they don't get fixed when your efforts go into fixer-upper-women relationships.

At least one fellow found that out: *"I think that the biggest mistake I made was to think that I could 'rescue my Damsel in Distress.' I did get her out of an unpleasant situation, but wish that I would have dated her for a few years while she worked out her problems with her family. I could have then been working on making myself feel more confident and important to others by becoming more educated, experienced and mature. Then I'd be chosen because I was good and worthy of love . . . not just as an escape ladder for the damsel."*

Sugar and Spice . . . and Everything Difficult

In all fairness to you men, who, as I mentioned in the introduction, are extra-spective, i.e., outwardly focused and thus don't spend a lot of time ruminating over your motivations and anxieties, let me spend some time going over the typical techniques you use when you're becoming an "escape ladder for the damsel." These techniques of Stupid Chivalry get you into tremendous trouble and pain—so pay attention!

One trait more typical of men than women is taking the opposite sex at "face value." Women are more typically like paranoid shrinks: "What does that *really* mean?" or "What are you *really* saying?" or "What are you *really* feeling?" Whereas you guys, even if you bother to ask for clarification, rarely think much about the response you get. If I were being cynical, I'd say it's because you really don't care very much. I don't believe that's generally true at all. What I do believe is that you men are all basically intimidated by the powerful and seemingly unpredictable emotions of women. You're trying to balance getting along with them with getting what you need from them; if you nag, you lose. Even intimidation is not enough to explain what looks like your gullibility, naïveté, or just plain stupidity.

The missing piece of this puzzle is this: You guys *want* to believe in women's inherent sweetness, goodness, innocence, and vulnerability. So, when you meet a woman with incredible troubles and problems, you assume that the source for the "bad stuff" is outside her: bad circumstances, bad people, bad experience, bad luck. Now you know your place!— you rescue her from these bad people, places, and things.

Wrong.

Richard, thirty-one years old, is a perfect example. For one year and eight months (looks like he's counting the minutes—not a good sign) he's been in a relationship with a distressed damsel coworker who told him she'd been sexually abused by a stepfather from age eight to sixteen.

"She's not dealt with it in a healthy environment, she's dealt with it on her own. I see things in her that I think are a by-product of that—I know I'm not a professional. She has lots of problems in life."

"If you didn't know this abuse happened, are you saying there are things about her which would make you think a second time about a life with her?"

"Yes, it does."

"So, her behaviors make the notion of marriage seem unappetizing to you. . . . But something else hooks you in anyway?"

"Yes."

"Let me guess. . . . It's guilt."

"Yes. But I want to work this through because although she's difficult and negative, I know she is a truly wonderful person. We're best friends and lovers."

"You don't owe her matching up with her because she has a sad story. I can understand your compassion and concern— but marriage doesn't heal all. I bet you feel you can't have judgment, criticism, or requirements of her as a woman because, after all, she's a victim . . . she's been abused . . . how could you possibly require anything of her . . . then you'd be abusive! When you think like this, Richard, you betray yourself and you don't help her improve. Your place is to inform and support. Her place is to take the responsibility of evolving into her best self. She needs your challenge to do so more than she needs you to protect her from herself."

"This is hard. . . . I feel bad for her."

"Is what I said right?"

"Yes. It's just hard."

You men are very responsible creatures and would rather sacrifice than demand—after all, a "real man" can "take it," "do without" in sacrifice to others. That's wonderful in measured doses; but just because you're gettin' sex is not the way to pick a wife.

Feeling inappropriately responsible for "her past experiences" is one way to get hooked into knighthood. Hallucinating that everything that happens in her life is due to moon spots and not her own actions and mentality is another.

Eddie, thirty-eight years old, has been involved with a woman for eight months. According to her she has a long history of abusive relationships and marriages.

"She is a really neat lady," says Eddie.

"How does a really neat lady keep getting into one truly lousy relationship after another?" I ask.

"Guys promise her the world and then blow up on her."

"Your point of view is that this 'sweet, innocent, neat thing,' due to no fault or contribution of her own, keeps getting hooked up with Genghis Khan time after time? Does this really sound possible to you?"

"I don't believe it's her fault."

"Eddie, news flash! She's not an innocent bystander in her own life. Because you don't want to know or see her contribution to her own life won't stop you from getting hit with it at some point. I wonder if you imagine that you're special because you'll be the only good man in her life. I wonder if you imagine that she'll reward you with perpetual bliss?"

"Well, maybe."

Damsels perpetually in distress are the architects of their own miserable prisons and problems. Thinking otherwise is just plain stupid. Lou found this out the hard way:

I am a 37 year old man who has never been married. The price I chose to pay to obtain the financially comfortable and secure life that I now have, was delaying a "significant other." In January I ended what I believed was a potential relationship. For about a year and a half, I was seeing a divorced lady with two daughters. She was in a physically abusive marriage that ended six years ago. Her girls are close in age and were no older than three when she left. I admired her for taking that big step. I believed it especially wise to proceed slowly because there were children involved. There was no sex. In time, I was willing to take on the entire package. I loved her and the girls. I was very good to them and for them. If we were both committed, marriage seemed a natural possibility.

Unfortunately, it was not a match. She practiced some hurtful behaviors that I excused for a while, like broken promises, unreturned phone calls, standing me up and making little time for me. I attributed it to "history," to fear from the awful marriage and a demanding schedule as a single mom. I remained patient. As time passed, the behavior became consistent and increasingly difficult to tolerate. It also became evident that she was not the strong and principled person I believed her to be. I let my pity for her abusive marriage and my admiration for her tough decision to leave a bad marriage be my sole gauge of her character. I was wrong!

I decided the right thing to do was to let go. I truly miss them, but deserve better.

Wow! Am I ever impressed. Lou realized that he didn't measure her by her own actions in relating, but by his assumption that nobility is the inevitable consequence of suffering, i.e., that her worth was inversely related to her past misery. What he finally accepted is that we "are what we do, and do, and do . . ."

Shackled to Chivalry

There are dire consequences to ignoring all of the above in this chapter. Here are some sorry examples:

- Jay is a thirty-two-year-old truck driver who has been married only three months. He's just been thrown out of his own house and had to move in with his parents. He married a woman with two kids, fourteen and twelve. The kids decided they no longer wanted to deal with him, so she asked him to leave. "She was in an abusive marriage and wasn't there for them. They kinda dictate what happens now 'cause I think she feels guilt about that."

   "Jay, would you say that you've always known her to be passive and weak?"

   "Yes."

   "I know the reasons we care about somebody are complex, but what makes a weak, passive woman attractive?"

   "Well, Dr. Laura, I guess it gives you the opportunity to feel needed."

   "But Jay, then you're stuck with a passive, weak woman who behaves that way with everyone and that's why you're out of your house. And, if she changes . . . then why would she need you?"

"Good question. . . . I guess I gotta think about that now."

- Tony just keeps getting "taken for granted." His on-and-off one-and-one-half-year relationship recently got "turned on again" when she admitted that she had made mistakes and was running away from her problems. Tony bought that. Then she began telling him that he was controlling—each time she agreed to go off drugs and didn't, she blamed him for nagging. He felt he was just holding her to her word . . . but you know how guilt-ridden you guys get when a woman calls you controlling!

- Bob, thirty years old, never asks for more so he always gets less. He's a doormat. He hopes that his perpetually and blatantly philandering wife will come back and be true if he is just so "good."

- Dave, thirty-one, tried the Pygmalion thing. He met a woman with a five-year-old child living on welfare. "I treated her like a queen, then she got mean." He's angry because he thinks he did a good deed, a service, and feels he's owed her affection because he earned it!

- Bill, forty-one years old, wanted to give some background as to how his marriage went: *"We were married in September of '92. I was informed that she had about $5000 credit card debt before we got married and I figured that was manageable. However, three months into the marriage, I found the debt to be more than $17,000.! This was only revealed to me after she thought she was going to lose her job. I then had to put a second mortgage on the house I owned before I married her for the next three years. I next went through a jealousy struggle between her and my son from my first marriage. I recently have caught her stealing from my wallet. Before I married her she lived at home with her parents for nothing, she was 32. Finally, the other thing she does that bothers me is that she constantly tells me she loves me, some 20–30 times a day. It drives me crazy because how can she say* *this and still lie and steal money from my wallet and resent my child?"*

- And this from Joe: *"$75,000 in shrink fees and about five years later I woke up and realized that I had a completely NEW wife! My new wife was pushy, fussy, constantly bitchy about nearly everything, antagonistic, spent money like time was running out, hated our old friends, used sex as a tool to get what she wanted, was constantly trying to change me and a few other things. The shrink essentially told me that the 'new' woman was the one who had been bottled up since childhood and I should get used to it. After living through HELL for three more years hoping and working to make life bearable for both of us, I finally divorced her. It was at this point in the marriage that I finally figured out that she had expected ME to make her feel good about herself. When that failed to occur, she blamed me for not being able to 'meet **her** needs.' I think it is totally and completely unrealistic, immature, and un-adult for anyone to expect another person to 'make them happy.'"*

I do too, but it doesn't seem to stop you guys from thinking you can and should:

Dear Dr. Laura:

*I can tell you one of the most stupid things I do. I continue to believe that I can actually **make** my wife be happy. There always seems to be pressure put on the male to provide for the wife's happiness. If she feels lonely it's because I'm not paying enough attention to her. If she is unfulfilled, it is because I'm not seeing to her needs. Why do women have to be so needy? Why do most of us males stupidly believe that we can fulfill their needs? AHHHHHHHHHHHHHHHHH!!!*

You Know, Tarzan Sometimes Did Fall out of Trees

This is a very important letter, but if you take it on face value you'll be way off track! As I've said repeatedly, I believe it is built into the "male" to be protective. In nonhuman males this is basically a physical issue, where the male protects the female against other males so that he can mate with her and ensure his genes go forth and multiply. Okay, so his intentions seem selfish—but that's only the biology speaking.

- Human mating and relationships have the potential for so much more than gene pool enhancement. Our relationships serve emotional and spiritual needs. It's not surprising then that male protectiveness covers those possibilities too. I think it is just natural, and built into male hardwiring, to be solicitous and protective as an end in itself, in addition to the hopes of "winning her favor."

As you've seen in *National Geographic* specials, the males fight, sometimes to the death, to win the opportunity to mate. When you turn into the knight to slay her enemies, you hope to win the prize. However, human behavior and life is more complicated than that of lower animals. For you, it's more than the mating. It's your life. It's okay to be chivalrous. It's totally stupid to be blindly chivalrous and save some woman who is too immature, self-centered, fixated in her "damage," or just plain mean to appreciate the opportunity afforded her.

Here's the magic bullet: **If she doesn't *give*, then she's a lousy damsel.** The problem with you knights is that you either don't realize or admit to what you need and require from a woman in an intimate relationship. Winning her is not enough. Available sex and companionship is not enough. **You need more!** And damsels in perpetual distress are usually wicked witches in disguise. Don't believe me? Well, just cross or disagree or disappoint one—poof! Instant transformation.

"Hallelujah—I Believe!" . . . . Doesn't Make It So

Know what? You guys have the same fantasies about romantic love that women have—just the flip side. Women dream of being princesses; you men get off on the idea of being the hero. Happily-ever-after works only between mature, healthy men and women, not between heroes and princesses, because they inevitably disappoint each other.

Once mucked up in this fantasy, can you escape? Yes! But it takes accepting reality on its terms, and thinking past your fantasies and guilt.

Beau, twenty-one years old, is being emotionally beaten up by a twenty-five-year-old woman who takes out her lifelong disappointments with men on him, all the time expecting him to "be there for her." Although she's broken off with him, she calls him every twenty minutes.

"Beau, how come you didn't dump her?"

"I tried to be understanding."

"Understanding is a friend, priest, or counselor. Why would you imagine staying in a relationship where someone treats you like a punching bag? If you were a woman, you'd probably call her behavior 'psychologically abusive.' How healthy does it sound for you to take it?"

"Oh, it's not healthy."

"Whatever her problems or torments, she gives herself total license to misbehave. Your fantasies of tolerating her abuse in the hopes that she turns into a princess (Handsome and the Witch?) aren't playing out. Perhaps she's doing you a favor with this on/off breakup."

"I felt like a weight was lifted off me. But she keeps calling me."

"'You owe me, you do for me, because I hurt' is not the best seduction, is it? But, the guilt's working on you, isn't it?"

"I told her that for us to get back together . . . it's just too hard to be in love with somebody who doesn't love themselves."

"Separate out feeling compassion for her as a friend, and even a lost hope, but when you think of a partner for life and the mother of your eighteen children . . . does she qualify?"

"No."

"Imagining there is someone or something you can't make better or might not get better on its own seems a difficult concept?"

"Yeah, I guess so."

A Ja came up with these warnings:

1. *Leave Rapunzel in her tower! Let her cut off her own hair and use it as a rope to climb down. She needs to learn to do things herself or you will be taking care of a child in an adult body who will never learn to do it for herself.*
2. *Do not save Cinderella from her lowly financial position! If she never earns her own money, she will never appreciate "your" money or "our" money. She expects you to take care of everything and thinks that money grows on trees.*
3. *Kiss Sleeping Beauty and you will awaken the evil, jealous queen. If you want an ornament on your arm at the party, buy a nice pair of cuff links. They'll stay faithful, won't nag, "Honey, how do I look?" or say, "Not now, I just did my hair (makeup, nails, etc.)."*
4. *Remember . . . Barbie has everything because someone else gets it for her. Where's Ken when Barbie's messing around to keep herself from being bored? Ken's at the office earning the money to afford Barbie's affections.*

From so many of my conversations with men I have gotten the impression that you guys don't think past the "win," i.e., what life is going to be like once you've "gotten her." Perhaps you think it just all works itself out. Perhaps you think she'll turn into your loving mother. Perhaps you think that it's a small price to pay for sex and someone to watch your kids (then she dumps them in day care). Perhaps you think it really doesn't matter because your work is really your life; marriage is just something you have to do so that you're not completely lonely or thought to be gay.

Whatever your "perhaps"—I'm warning you now—you're going to be miserable!

Straight from the Horse's, Oops . . . I Mean, Damsel's Mouth

Through my caller Charlotte's testimony, let me give you some insight into the "other side."

"We've been married over thirty years. In the last eighteen months we've had tremendous stress in our business and personal life. We work together. I have difficulty expressing intimacy and sexuality when bothered and stressed. This is causing problems in our marriage. My husband moved out of our bedroom yesterday. I want to change this but don't know how."

"Is this the first time in your marriage this has happened?"

"No. It's not the first time. I can't be close when something is bothering me."

"And you're mad at him because . . . ?"

(After protesting that she didn't feel mad) "Well, because to me, the need to be intimate and sexual is a selfish act. He wants it to make himself feel better. I can't think about what makes him feel better when I'm upset."

"So, Charlotte, an orgasm never made you feel better?"

(Laughing) "Oh yes, it does."

"An orgasm doesn't make the problem go away, but it can sure give you a better attitude. Charlotte, are you mad at him because he hasn't **fixed** everything . . . so you won't have to feel stress? He's not making everything all better and seems to be getting on with life while you are 'suffering.' Is this what gets you mad?"

"Yes, that's right."

"So, you punish him, to make him suffer like you are. That's why you pull away and stop the sex. You 'cut him off,' so to speak."

"Okay."

"Charlotte, do you still hold on to that little girl fantasy that guys are someplace between gods and fathers and can fix anything, take care of everything, and ultimately protect us from disappointments and frustrations like you have now?"

"Well, yeah, I guess I do want that. Think that."

"That's a tough fantasy to give up."

(Sighing) "I guess I have to talk with my husband and try to work through this with him."

"Yes, you have to stop blaming him for your unhappiness, fears, and life's woes. Instead of punishing him that he can't relieve your pain, that you take some responsibility and relieve it for yourself. . . . And, dear, don't cut off your nose to spite your face. Have some great sex tonight. It's better than a handshake of peace."

What *Healthy* Women Want

Amber, a healthy nondamsel type of woman (don't tell me there aren't any) wrote a lengthy "wish list" for determining Mr. Right. It included the following:

- Treat his mother well
- Protect children and animals and any others who can't protect themselves
- Love God, be spiritual and respectful
- Insist on his children being raised in a traditional home by their parents . . . not a day care institution
- Think his role is to comfort me in rough times and not to protect me from them

You see? There are wonderful women who will appreciate your protective masculinity, while not expecting to be or stay a damsel. You need to have the self-awareness, wisdom, desire, and grit to be worthy of one of those in your own mind. Remember, chivalry is natural and good; chivalry when the only reward is a perpetually distressed damsel is bad.

Danger! Falling Rocks! . . . Aimed for Your Heart

In conclusion, here are Jerry's TOP 10 THINGS THAT TELL YOU THE WOMAN YOU ARE DATING MIGHT BE WRONG FOR YOU:

1. She tells you she has low self esteem
2. She *suddenly* begins to like the same things you do.
3. The period of time between her boyfriends and/or husbands is less than 30 days.
4. She has been with tons of men all with the same problem(s)
5. She is ready to sleep with you after the first or second date
6. Her children don't really seem to matter when it comes to dating you
7. She has a limited number of friends or you never meet them
8. She worries if you don't call every day/hour
9. Tells you she doesn't know what she wants or has no long term goals
10. She's read Dr. Laura's **Ten Stupid Things Women Do to Mess Up Their Lives** and jokes that, "I still haven't done 4 of the stupid things yet!"

2

STUPID INDEPENDENCE

Many men, especially "intelligent" men, are emotional cowards.

DON, 1996

I found him! I found the perfect man—the perfect role model for exquisite, multidimensional masculinity! He's Rod Tidwell, the football player portrayed by Cuba Gooding, Jr., in the movie *Jerry Maguire*. Yes, I know, he's a fictional character, nonetheless, I'm absolutely positive that he already exists in real life, and that he is the potential in every one of you men.

What makes Rod so "perfect"? He's got a big, strong male body (okay—he's an unbelievably muscled hunk . . . that's the biology in me talkin'), he's committed to excellence in his work, he's determined in his goals, and (here's where the *multidimensional* part comes in) even when he's asserting and aggressing all over the phone to his agent about contract and money, he doesn't miss a beat in gently touching his small son's head as the boy leaves the table after breakfast.

He's no coward when it comes to physical pain and endurance (the football scenes are brutal), nor when it comes to acknowledging to himself or his wife, with a face full of tears, in view of worldwide television coverage, that he absolutely loves her, needs her, counts on her, listens to her, depends on her, is fed, supported, and nurtured by her, and finds ultimate meaning in life through her love and their family.

When Rod finally accomplishes his dream (big contract and fan adoration), his ego is gratified only because it is a shared moment with those he loves. He is *not* an emotional coward . . . and I have met no one who thought his character was a wuss or a weenie because of his "sensitivity." Why is that? Why is our perception of his masculinity not diminished one testosterone molecule by his obvious "dependency" on his woman?

Strong and Sensitive *Do* Mix

One reason is that Rod's wife is not portrayed as a ball-busting, castrating bitch, reducing him to a quivering lump at his first sign of weakness. Nope! She is seen as profoundly respectful of his strengths and value as a player, a man, a husband, and a dad. She reminds him of his worth, of her love, and of her affectional and sexual desires for him. She actively supports him when he's "down" or "in pain"—she never degrades him. Be assured that his having her as a wife, and getting all these goodies, is *no accident nor stroke of good luck*. You guys pick your matches!

If Rod had been an emotional coward, he might have picked a weak woman to dominate. Weak women pick *seemingly* strong men (and then later scream "controlling") so that they can feel safe and protected—and are so dependent on that dynamic that they become ferocious and punitive over any display of their man's "weakness" because it threatens their own synthetic well-being. That reinforces their men's phony unidimensional masculinity, i.e., the emotional loner.

Rod, on the other hand, clearly picked a woman who chose to give her love to a "whole male" because she had her own strength. They add to each other, rather than hopelessly trying to compensate for each other's weaknesses.

Another reason we don't see Gooding's character as "weak" or "unmasculine" is that his "sensitivity" is simultaneous with the strength and confidence we generally perceive of as "masculine." It never seems as though he has to sacrifice one for the other, nor does he ever seem ashamed, apologetic, or self-conscious about it. He is therefore masculine in his vulnerability. That kind of confidence is perceived as very "manly," very attractive, and very sexy by healthy, intelligent, loving women . . . trust me on that.

This issue of male emotional vulnerability and feelings has been exploited, demeaned, and confused in most of the pop-psych literature—especially that perpetrated by so-called "enlightened feminist men." In fact, there is very little written about men that in general doesn't sound conspiratorial: "Boys are *trained* to become men who suppress and tune out emotions. Boys are *taught* to be emotionally stoic, tough and aggressive, self-reliant, and to avoid 'feminine ways'" was the conclusion of a psychologist at Harvard Medical School. So, society trains, teaches, warps, and twists men out of their normal and natural emotional selves into mechanical robots? First of all, when did stoic, tough, aggressive, self-reliant, and masculine become bad things? They're not bad things. They are terrific qualities. But no one is truly healthy and capable in life without being able to tend to **all** their human realities—and emotional needs are central to male/female, male/child, male/friend, male/family relating.

So, let's stop saying that "masculine" approaches to life are bad. Let's start saying that part of healthy masculinity is being *un*afraid of your total human self.

Different Doesn't Mean Better or Worse

Much of modern psychotherapy truly is prejudiced against men. The *female* mode of thinking and feeling has become the politically correct norm against which to measure male behavior, i.e., it's rarely assumed that she is emotionally hyperreactive or feelings-obsessed, it's generally that a man is emotionally constipated and withholding.

Not convinced? Watch any professional documentary on the behavioral differences between male and female children. I remember one TV special where they showed how differently two- to four-year-old boys and girls played with a number of toys presented them: "girl" toys (dolls, house things) and "boy" toys (trucks, building blocks), as well as neutral toys (puppets, stuffed animals). No matter what the age, the boys banged the toys while the girls nurtured them. When they put two girls together, they "talked" through their toys. When they put two boys together, they "fought" through their toys. When they put a boy and a girl together it clearly became disorganized and uncomfortable for both children because they didn't have the skills to "cooperate" with their disparate forms of play.

Male and female brains are wired differently, with functional gender differences on various levels, i.e., studies using sophisticated techniques to observe brain cell activity have shown that male and female brains operate differently when performing the same tasks. It has become increasingly clear that men and women do not think alike, but too many academic and psychological research types are so determined to prove feminine equality or superiority, they can't seem to be honest and nonjudgmental about gender *differences*.

Am I saying that society has no impact on the expression of our masculinity and femininity? Of course not! Still, that impact isn't fundamentally as great as many would like to think. Because of our magnificent forebrains, we have opportunities to become competent at a wide variety of skills (men as phone operators, women as caterpillar operators) which may have been arbitrarily or historically categorized as "male" or "female." Yet we cannot escape fully from the pull and push of our biology: it is more typically male to conquer and typically female to nurture. Do we have "will" and "choice," i.e., flexibility in this biology? Of course we do: men can be stay-at-home dads and women can go up in space shuttles. But, is it the typical desire of men to nurture children and women to conquer? I doubt it.

Men, Women, and Emotions

Human attributes distribute along standard statistical curves (bell curves), and for a vast number of characteristics there are separate, although overlapping curves distinguishing men from women. There is a mean for each group. I think that what the society does is attempt, in various degrees and in ever-changing dimensions, to bring the tails of the bell curve closer to the mean—for the sake of conformity. There is a certain relief that human beings find in conformity: expectations are clear and identification with a group is comforting.

You can attempt, as various feminist groups have done, to redefine what the mean should be, but it doesn't work for long because males and females are *inherently different*. Proof? Look in any sandbox and you can see how right from birth, male and female emotionality are displayed differently. More proof? Try calling men to a male/feminist type rally to "learn to let it all hang out" and see how many reasonably healthy guys show up. Call a Promise Keepers Event where the men are urged to live up to their obligations as husbands and fathers (male role assignments), and you can't find a football stadium big enough to hold them.

Men are never going to be just like women. Nor should they try to be. What is unique to each individual should be given respect and opportunity. What is more natural and comfortable to each gender ought to be given equal respect and opportunity. So, within the context of masculinity, expression of *emotions* perhaps is *less central*, but is *not less essential*, to the man.

This letter emphasizes that point:

> *Dr. Laura, I have destroyed my life by not expressing my feelings, denying my fears about losing my wife. I have always had a difficult time expressing my emotions. By not dealing honestly with my feelings of anger, betrayal, hurt, and jealousy, I have destroyed my life and myself. I want to plead with other men not to do the same: Men, if you are uncomfortable expressing yourself emotionally, get help to find ways to get more comfortable. We talk about what's happened to us at the office, at lunch, at the gym, etc. We think that that's "sharing" our lives with our mates. Yes, they want to hear these things, but they also want to hear how these things made us feel. Did that make us happy, angry or sad? Share your heart, not as my wife used to tell me, recite just the "news, weather and sports."*

Before we examine this letter, let's go back to my prefacing statement that "Within the context of masculinity, expression of emotions is perhaps less central, but not less essential, to the man." What do I mean, "less central"? The male (reminder: whenever I use *male* I am leaning toward biology in my thinking) is more "action" and "external" oriented than the female, and this is typical and consistent throughout all human history and most animal species. Human males have always had a typically restless attitude about new adventure, exploit, challenge, battle, etc. Human females with their more highly developed emotional empathy gravitate toward relationships, understanding, and feelings. Given this inherent difference in drive and perspective, it becomes clearer why women have been the civilizing factor for men and society as they strive for family, monogamy, stability, order, and peace.

Therein lies the potential for balance and harmony: men and women, two polarities, each tempered by the unique qualities of the other, a potentially wonderful balance of outer and inner directedness. It only works where there is respect, admiration, and appreciation for what the "opposite" gender has to offer. There is little existing societal respect for men and masculinity.

That lack of respect is one of the reasons men resist being so open about their feelings. They are supposed to be "open" to prove that they are not typical men (now that's some insult) or inadequate creatures (i.e., not more like women). How is such negativity supposed to be motivating?

Winning at Cards/Losing at Life

Another reason men resist being so open about their feelings is that they truly don't see full emotional disclosure as necessarily beneficial. For example, you win more in cards, and perhaps in a number of areas in life, if you have a poker face. Allowing others to know you're hurt or shaken obviously gives them the power advantage. And as peace-loving and solicitous as you'd like the world to be, human nature just ain't so consistently or predictably benevolent. It's just less biologically male to be so emotionally fine-tuned, because it would endanger the male's survival advantage.

That the psycho-biology of the "male" is patently geared for competition was confirmed by a U.S. News & World Report (11/25/96) which analyzed boys' and girls' preferences for video games. "While politically-correct-thinking parents might not cotton to games that feature fighting, simulated flight and combat and lightning action, boys do." While girls "seem to be most captivated by games that offer lots of different activities, social interaction on the screen and between plays . . . they dislike an emphasis on intense competition."

Men, therefore, develop "action empathy," i.e., they

observe the emotions and reactions of others as information for "their next move," while women typically develop "emotional empathy," in which the observations are ends in themselves, serving to enhance contact, connection, bonding, sharing, caring, and nurturing.

Again, it is not that women can't be competitive or that men can't be nurturing, it is that to a greater or lesser extent there is biology to overcome. We humans are phenomenal at learning behaviors which provide new and interesting outlets for our individual, unique potential and innate curiosity. Nonetheless, this ability to transcend our biology doesn't eliminate biology, it just provides variety in its expression.

That means that when push comes to shove, we are more likely to "behave according to type," expressing our innate gender differences in temperament, personality, and goal orientation. In everyday experiences this shows up all the time. For example, one glaring difference between men and women is in the way in which they deal with in-law situations. There are relatively few disputes between men and their fathers-in-law, whereas women and their mothers-in-law are generally built-in adversaries. That's because women tend to personalize and overemotionalize events, actions, words, experiences, and therefore are more likely to have conflicts. Men, on the other hand, tend not to overinterpret and internalize those same triggers so personally. It just seems to mean less to them emotionally. For instance, if a woman's mother-in-law says, "What's the difference between feeding the baby this stuff with NutraSweet, when you drink NutraSweet and are breast-feeding—the baby gets it anyway," the daughter-in-law generally goes ballistic about the mother-in-law being "critical, mean, and overbearing." If a man's father-in-law says, "That's not the best way to get the most out of that 'fraggit,'" the son-in-law will probably say, "Oh yeah? Show me how to get the most out of my 'fraggit,'" and off they go to the garage.

The difference is based on women's intense need for interpersonal acceptance and support and the intense need men have to get the "fraggits" conquered.

That doesn't mean that men can't and don't react or over-react, but that's generally more due to male-animal-oriented threats: life, property, mate, status, which just aren't all that truly "personal." Men, for example, will more likely get crazy if the next-door neighbor trims the part of a tree which extends onto his property without asking for permission first. It ain't personal, however, it is about turf, power over the sovereignty of turf. And it's not accidental that one of the most chilling aspects of organized crime movies is how death and destruction can be wrought so viciously when "it's just business. It's not personal, just business."

To further compare men with women emotionally with respect to relationships: women react to one-degree tempera-ture changes while men wait for emergency weather alerts to be called. Now, I want to be really clear here: neither behav-ior is "good" or "bad." Women need to stop allowing them-selves to get carried away with small slights, perceived or real, and men need to stop ignoring small warnings. This is why I believe that men and women are at their best when they are together, tempering each other's gender tendencies, and adding a dimension of insight and energy which enriches both.

Another reason men resist a lot of openness about emo-tions is that they see it as dangerous or as a distracting alter-native to a call for "action," whereas women see it as mere coffee-time conversation, even an entertaining past time, and/or a call for attention and sympathetic support. The evo-lutionary gender role of males has required some immunity to a perpetual or easily precipitatable emotion. Hesitancy in the acting out of aggression and competition could result in loss or death; hence, stoicism in the face of threat and chal-lenge is of evolutionary value.

The current feminist (and obvious antimale) writers pooh-pooh such a perspective. Now that men can order food through the Internet, they think that male aggressiveness and stoicism should be tossed aside as though masculinity were a nonbiological coat worn out of season. That's just wrong. With our magnificent forebrains, we can channel biology into socially acceptable action—but we can't deny the biology!

When we deny biology, we're lying to ourselves. Women really don't want touchy-feely, perpetually emotive men because they perceive them as weak or emotionally/mentally ill—certainly not the type we can count on and lean on. (Remember the dress designer ads which said, "Klopman . . . a man you can lean on"? He sold a lot of dresses!)

This helps explains the "truth" in men's so-called "nice guy" complaints, that women seem to be drawn to the "bad guys." Well, that's female biology talking! The aggressive, strong, determined, powerful, highly sexual male is the bio-match for the female who needs protection, companionship, and provisions with which to raise young. Throughout the nonhuman animal kingdom, the male has to prove something before he gets to mate: biggest (physical protection), most turf (resources), strongest (good genetics), etc. Females are drawn into the situations with the greatest promise of reproductive success as measured by his abilities to fight, gather food, build a nest, energy and health, etc. The human animal "nice guys," having chosen to divest themselves of "maleness," don't attract women as mates—just as "best girlfriends." Which, by the way, is exactly what women claim they want, but don't select. Just because women have been taught since the sixties to fear and disdain masculinity doesn't stop them from wanting it. What do you think the higher incidence of female affairs is about if it isn't about getting some male sexuality?

I am reiterating and emphasizing the biology precisely because it's being denied and denigrated when it deserves to be identified and acknowledged as an important part of our human animal legacy and identity. Still, as an educated and religious woman, I know that we humans are so much more than our biology. The *Los Angeles Times* (12/29/96) reported a story about the small number of ultra-Orthodox Jews in Israel who are abandoning their faith for the freedom of secularism. One young man who decided to leave the religious life for the license of unrestricted activity and sex said, "My therapist told me that I would live a life with conflict, and he was damn right. It is not easy to leave religion. On the other hand (in Orthodoxy), there is such fulfillment. After you leave, you feel so deserted. Spiritually there is a black hole."

The utter freedom, the animal, is our biology but it is not our totality; the desire for order and for ways to make life meaningful, that is our uniquely human capacity and drive. As with religious life and its obligatory struggle against immediate drives toward self-gratification, so is there a struggle between our biological selves (male/female), which are gender myopic, and our human selves (men/women), which aspire beyond survival to purposefulness. This purposefulness requires intergender cooperation, for with that union, the whole becomes greater than the sum of its parts.

So, do women really want you men to be more sensitive and emotional? Yes, they do. However, they also want it *their way*. What women really do want is a guy who *listens without comment* to their emotional stream of consciousness without a yawn, and who constantly reassures them about his *positive feelings* (only) about the relationship and her beauty, and *never* tells her how to solve the problem or urges her to find some way to deal with it. Don't believe me? Go to almost any psychotherapist with the complaint of a woman that her man doesn't listen. Proof he doesn't listen? "Well, he just tells me what to do about the problem." "What do you want him to do?" "Ohhh, I dunno. Just listen, I guess." The shrink will likely report reprimanding the man for being too much of a man and not understanding enough. Shocked and confused, the man will counter, "But I do care and understand. I listened and gave her advice." "No," the therapist will admonish him. "Caring is not shown by doing . . . but by listening."

The male shows "caring" by action. The female wants "caring" by commiseration. If he dares to "act" or direct her to act, he is condemned for not caring. That's not fair. (Worse still, God help that same man who, when his wife complains about house repairs or money issues, doesn't *act,* just *listens!*)

Women say they want their men to "mother" them (you know, slurp up feelings and emotions). But when, for example, through the conspiracy of therapy, they intimidate these men into doing just that, sexual attraction fades and they no longer feel "in love." The reason for that is the loss of the male-female polarity, which provides tension necessary for the bonding drive.

There is a three-part cure for this gender confusion about the how to be caring/show feelings problem, which I demonstrate and clarify daily with my callers:

1. An acceptance, respect, and enjoyment of what is male and female by both men and women. I am reminded of a conversation my husband had with our son, then ten. "Dad," asked Deryk, whose interactions with "females" were getting to be a more core issue in his life, "will I ever understand women?" "No," my husband told me he responded. "Women are a miracle you enjoy, just hold on tight for the ride!" The New Age feminists would probably have become furious with that statement. I didn't find it demeaning or critical—I thought it was accurate, respectful, and appreciative!

2. Don't let current cultural fads deny you your biological gender birthright. I can't believe how many women, for example, *actually want* to buy the current politically correct (and dangerous to our children) nonsense that institutionalized day care by strangers is equal to or superior to a mother's or father's loving attention and presence. I can't

believe how many men are willing to buy the current politically correct nonsense that being the sole breadwinner is necessarily evil and insulting to women.

3. Look for what is the best in your man/woman and praise it (his strength and her compassion, for example), and look to see how you can use his/her innate qualities to *complete yourself*. I really do think that a married person who accepts his or her gender realities (while, of course, not ignoring her or his own unique abilities and desires) and who realizes that the opposite polarity offers completeness has the most advantage for a fulfilling and happy life.

Another reason men resist going public with their feelings is that it just seems too feminine. In fact, the current trend is to tell men to get in touch with their "feminine side." (Of course, tell the woman saying this that you wish she could get in touch with her masculine side and you'll be hit with a harassment lawsuit and called sexist by the woman as she sobs in confused frustration.) An interesting question is, "Why do men eschew femininity more actively than women worry about losing their femininity to masculinelike behaviors?" While I'm not sure of all the reasons this is so, I have some ideas. You may be aware that until a critical point in embryonic development, all embryos, whether chromosomally male (XY) or female (XX) follow the basic *female* blueprint. At that critical point maleness is imposed upon the "female" brain and genitalia; i.e., masculinity has to be molded from the female clay. If there is a "mistake" at this critical juncture, development proceeds to create female. Hence, the very existence of male requires a moving away from female.

Until our current pathetic veneration (Don't believe me? Check out all your parenting-type magazines for so-called "studies" showing day care to not only not be deleterious— but beneficial!) of institutionalized day care, children were raised by their mothers. At a critical juncture in their psychological development, girls don't have to pull away from mother to identify as feminine, but boys must separate to identify as masculine by more closely aligning themselves with their fathers (before all the single, lesbian, or unwed mothers became more of a significant norm). It is interesting that when there aren't fathers around to teach boys how to be men, the boys most typically *hyper*-masculinize (violence, disconnect affection from sex, etc.) to find their sexual identity. A loving, multidimensional masculine father shows them how to be men without denigrating women or their need for them. A good father, therefore, teaches males how to be men.

It might seem as though I've spent this chapter creating a case that thoroughly excuses men from the responsibility or necessity of dealing with their emotional lives. Wrong! Wrong! Wrong! I've made the case that male emotionality is different from that of women and not as *central* to minute-by-minute existence as it seems to be for women. No judgment, just observation. But don't forget the second part of that sentence, "not less *essential* to the man." Constant attention to one's emotional state, "emotional empathy" turned on high, reverence for feelings over reason and action, are not typically masculine traits. However, a lack of courage and capacity to be aware of his inner state, express it, and get help with it when it results in actions which isolate the man from family and friends and behaviors which are immoral, illegal, fattening, or destructive to self and others is STUPID INDEPENDENCE.

Dependent? Who Me?

The most typical form of Stupid Independence is your unwillingness to admit to your dependency on your wife, but your denial doesn't change reality. The syndicated cartoon *Luann* once pointed out this dependency. The husband is reading the newspaper aloud to his wife. "It says here that men take longer than women to get over a breakup." She responds, "That's because women bond with each other. We have support systems. If you and I broke up, I could turn to Mary Anne or Kirsten or Jeanette. Who would you turn to? Who's your best friend?" He hesitates, and says, simply, "You." She comes back at him with "OK, honey, but see how that doesn't work?"

If you were feeling critical, you could jump on that "best friend" concept. For women, "best friend" means a shopping, whining, and gossiping buddy; for men it's a sports-watching or fix-it buddy. Men compete or cooperate with other men in activities, not emotions. Which is fine *until* you guys have a problem—then you've got to force yourself out of the biology of stoic independence at least to find out if your buddy has information or a common experience, therefore insight and understanding, you could use to help yourself and your situation. You men have to stop thinking that a minor hair trim is the same as having Delilah as a spouse. Dealing with important emotions, especially before you've let your avoidance of them ruin your life, is **not** going to emasculate you . . . it's definitely going to save you from the losses you fear most. Those losses are typically the two W's: your woman and your work. I know you imagine your woman to be a done deal with the marriage—you know, now you have a home base from which to conquer the universe. But, truthfully, a fellow who lives that way is more male, less man.

While you men insist you don't want to be "tied to her apron strings," I know that you know that you do need to know her apron strings are there—even when she's been "bad":

*It has been approximately 3 weeks since I separated from my wife. No doubt this is the absolute **worst** time in my life. I never would have dreamed or suspected something this **catastrophic** could happen to me. Today, I'm about 95% sure I should file for*

*divorce, without consideration for reconciliation. That little 5%
is that part of me that wants to hang on. I don't want to divorce
my wife, Dr. Laura. I want everything to be back to **normal**. I
want all this **bad stuff** to just go away. I want to stay married to
her forever, just like I committed to 17 years ago at the altar.*

I've received so many letters from men who didn't appreciate how important their attachments to their wives were . . . until their wives died or left them. In fact, there is a huge body of research indicating that, especially for men, marriage offers dramatic emotional, financial, and health benefits over both single life and cohabitation. While cohabitation has some, but not all, of the benefits of marriage, married men enjoy better health, financial success, and more satisfying sex—probably because there is more security, sense of commitment, permanence, and interdependency in a marriage . . . safety and comfort.

As my listener Frederick wrote:

*If some men wonder why they have problems with the women
they live with, it is because they don't understand the difference
between being dependent on a woman as a strength versus being
dependent as a weakness.*

*Dependency as a **strength** is when you share your vulnerable
side with someone you love so they can **contribute** to your life.
Dependency as a **weakness** is when you share your vulnerable
side with someone you love in the hopes they will **rescue** you.*

Tool Time

I believe Frederick meant that men want to regard help as yet another tool for them to use as they create, do, conquer, accomplish, etc., rather than as a crutch because they can't hack it; you know, having "Mommy" fight your battles for you. Your wives (assuming you didn't marry a Barbie doll outfitted in dim-bulb attire) are your best tools: men who are alone tend to have higher rates of drug and alcohol abuse, depression, health problems, and behavioral dysfunction. And, interestingly, married men who fight against their innate need for and dependency on their wives tend to get into those same troubles.

The "tool" analogy, while appropriate, also provides problems for some men when they just don't know *how to use* the tool. Kevin, a forty-year-old ex-Marine, called my program after his second marriage ended in divorce. He was wanting to leave the state because he was upset about not seeing his two small children (six and three and a half).

"Kevin," I implored, "you've proven you could take physical pain and face death even with fear. You can do that but you're so afraid of your *hurt feelings*? You really believe that if you don't see your kids you won't hurt from the loss of them? You'd abandon them to protect yourself?"

"Yeah, because I just don't know what to do with . . . how to face the hurt of leaving them after each visitation."

"Kevin, you've got to fight this urge to run—just like you fought it in combat. It's funny, isn't it, that death is less threatening to you than are your own tears of loss?"

In response, he choked up.

Kevin just didn't know what to do with his *emotional* pain. As a Marine he'd naturally bite the bullet and cut off the aching leg! The only civilian parallel he could come up with was to cut off the relationship in order to resolve the pain of loss. I urged him to fight for his visitation and use that time to nurture his children and himself with the closeness they all needed.

"That won't make the pain disappear, Kevin, but it'll sure make the pain seem a small price for the prize of their hugs and smiles. As a dad, you have much to teach them, and that will ultimately give you pleasure and purpose."

Mindless conquest or endeavor without purpose makes life meaningless. And, ultimately, it is the place we operate in the lives of others that makes our lives meaningful. In my last book, *How Could You Do That?!* I included a fax I received from a divorced husband and father who had taken an overdose of sleeping pills to avoid his pain. While he sat in his car waiting to die, he turned on his radio to have company, and on popped my radio program. I was giving some fellow "hell" for abandoning his child and, evidently, this hit a chord in the dying man. He realized that his son would either have nobody or some other man teaching him everything from flying a kite to becoming a "man." He recognized that although he was in supreme emotional agony, he still had a necessary purpose and function to his child. He called 911, got his stomach pumped, and devoted himself to being his kid's dad.

"Just existing" is not the same as "truly living." Lacking a purpose or relevance to others is a kind of nonexistence, a spiritual death. Closeness is the solution. Why do you men avoid it with a passion?

John, twenty-nine years old, called because his girlfriend (with a six-year-old daughter) and he are breaking up—probably—after fourteen months of dating.

"She thought she could change me."

"How?"

"Make me more effusive, understanding, and less self-centered."

"So, what do you think, John, are these necessary or good changes for you to make?"

"Yeah, maybe. I'm used to always doing whatever I please and she's used to having somebody. I don't think we're a match right now. She complains that I don't verbally tell her I care or that she's pretty. I kinda want to stay . . . but I'm not sure."

"John, what do you fear about being 'openly nice' and even 'deferential' to her?"

"I like to be in charge. If I tell her I love her, then she's got power over me."

"It would give her power because it'll show you need her, are dependent on her emotionally . . . and then if she withdraws it she could hurt you. You stay strong all the time to avoid any periods of hurt?"

"Yeah, I don't like giving in."

"You'd rather be totally safe—and for that you'd sacrifice being totally loved?"

"I Don't Need Me No Woman"

Having your women as "mothers you constantly rebel against" or as "sex toys" is a mainstay for male denial of dependency on their women. Having numerous flirtations and affairs and sexual conquests gives you a momentary feeling of the female acceptance you yearn for, which all men need and benefit from, but which you won't admit to in the first place. This cornerstone of denial has sadly been labeled by the psych types as a sexual addiction. To the pop-psychology world, all behavior is an out-of-control, unconscious reaction to somebody or something else; and none of it has to do with character weaknesses: a lack of values at a time when the challenge of fear could be used as a guide in problem solving—not as withdrawal.

Well, unless you're clinically mentally ill, it just isn't so. When you're afraid of something and don't want to face the difficulties attached to dealing with it openly and honestly, you'll look for some other way to satisfy the base need no matter who that hurts or what in your life that destroys. That is emotional cowardice and self-centeredness. That's when you're so tied into preserving the "male" in you that you sacrifice the "man" you're supposed to be aspiring to become. That's when you hurt others to **hide or stop** your hurt; and it's all in vain anyway.

This is my caller John's story in a nutshell. He came on my radio program with a swagger in his voice, announcing that he was contemplating an affair because his wife had one.

"What exactly are you hoping to accomplish with your affair?" I asked.

"For the gratification and the satisfaction that I got her back," he readily admitted.

"Yeah, but to do that you have to *use* another human being."

"True, but. . . ."

"You have to do damage to another human being to create damage in your wife. You'd use one person and hurt another. And somehow that would restore your person—or manhood?"

"No, I guess not, not when you put it that way. I just want satisfaction . . . revenge . . . equalizing."

"There is no satisfaction to be gotten here. You've been betrayed. You've been hurt. This is the terrible pain of this kind of betrayal. It brings up fears of abandonment, concerns about your worthiness and value, upsets an order which you thought was intact and reliable (the home base), distracts you from your life's endeavors, and humiliates you publicly. John, none of that goes away if you find a warm place to put it. All those emotions and realities will still have to be dealt with once the orgasm subsides, don't you think?"

"Yeah, I guess so."

There is a long-standing joke/complaint that men don't "court" after they're married (read chapter 7 on Stupid Husbanding for more about that). Well, if the "male" is to "win the female's attention and mate," the "man" is to bond in obligation and fidelity to the woman. The "female" in women calls for "nesting," and nesting demands ongoing attention. It is just more typical for women to measure a relationship's temperature in an ongoing, sometimes seemingly compulsive way, while the male in men figure it's a given. That's one of the reasons men don't tend to pay attention to daily details and have a barometric sense of what's happening, how it's going, what needs to be attended to. That's also one of the reasons men respond apocalyptically (with behavior that includes violence or self-destruction or suicide and drug/alcohol abuse and perpetual sexual conquest) when their woman strays or dumps them—you never saw it coming because there's just been no attention to detail, and now you are overwhelmed by the loss and affront!

Since I've said it isn't typically male to take the temperature of a partner or relationship every hour, don't think that means you can't or shouldn't think it's important to know when you or your beloved has a fever! Asking questions, having discussions, sharing thoughts and dreams and concerns is not exclusively "female"—it is human, incredibly necessary for the quality and continuity of a personal relationship with a woman, interesting and fulfilling for you, and insuring against relationship loss or destruction. Having her physically there is not the same as "having her." You better remember that.

However, this is not just about being a gardener for some difficult hothouse plant. This is about you having an outlet for natural concerns that come up in the daily order of things. How 'bout lingering in bed some minutes longer to vent about that vulture of a coworker, or about how much you really hate this commute and maybe a simpler life would be a higher-quality one, or about how you're confused between your work and masculinity and your desires for being more central to your kids' lives. I could go on, but I think **you must!**

There is a lot of security and strength which comes from knowing that a woman is with you as you apply your strengths and struggle with your momentary weaknesses. You aren't alone and you don't have to pretend you're the great stone face.

Of course, when you stupidly try to assert masculinity through your bio-male demands, pounding on your chest and giving out that Tarzan yell, you don't become more masculine, actually you become less a man. Chris was behaving just that way. He's been married to Lisa for four years. She is a stay-at-home mom of their one-year-old son.

Lisa offered up that she didn't think that her "husband should be going to Hooters Restaurant with his buddies or his brother. He cannot tell me he won't go anymore. He thinks that I'm being unreasonable in telling him where he can and can't go."

"That's exactly what I said," Chris chimed in immediately. "I just feel that I should just be able to go to lunch wherever I want."

"You're right, Chris, in this country you are free to do almost anything you want. That doesn't mean you ought or should. When you say you 'wanna' you always have to consider that when you're in a marital relationship and there is something hurtful or offensive to your partner, going on the 'I should have a right to do this' road doesn't lead to happy destinations within the relationship. Compassion to the wishes of your partner, especially on issues of relative unimportance like Hooters, should be a factor in your decision. For you it's not. I'll give it to you that it's a little hypersensitive of Lisa to be threatened by a Hooters girl *serving you* while she's home with your baby on her swollen breast. I'll give you that win. But knowing that, still, why would you bother to hurt her? What makes this such a big deal?"

"Because her hypersensitivity is unsubstantiated. She'll let me go to the beach, where most of the girls are wearing a lot less than they do in Hooters."

"Yes, but you're there as a family. Ogling may happen, but when you're with the guys at nudie places or Hooters-type places, ogling *is the intent.*"

"I just think this is just the start of her having major control, the beginning of the list of things I can't do."

"So, Chris, for you this is symbolic of her ultimate control over you. You've gone to war for your independence as a man! Therefore, you're not going to take each situation on its own merit, because now it represents a threat to your borders."

"That's right!"

"So, Chris, is this the paranoia you are going to teach your son about women? Are you going to teach him that the way you assert your independence as a man is to do what you want even if it hurts your wife?"

"This is not paranoia about women."

"Sure it is. You're worried that you're less a man if you sacrifice male things for the sake of your obligation to and caring about your woman. I understand how male sexuality is different from females'. But you have to understand that when a man commits to a relationship and creates a family, his masculinity is defined more by being a man than the animal-independent behavior of the 'male.' This is not about her power over your genitals. You must not have much of a hold over your own genitals if you're threatened by her request to behave less male and more married man."

Sometimes you guys just haven't decided which side of the male/man struggle you wish to be on. The guy who rests on the male side is displaying Stupid Independence.

Now, don't get me wrong, if she gets the heebie-jeebies because you want to do sports or hobbies which are well integrated into your roles as husband, father, friend, citizen, etc., then she's probably envious that you are more a whole person than she is. In which case, give her the companion book to this one: *Ten Stupid Things Women Do to Mess Up Their Lives* and hope for the best, remembering that you picked the flattering and security of a fairly weak, underdeveloped woman.

Escape to Fantasy Island

Some of you men go into fantasyland to hide from the truth of your needs and feelings.

Mike is such a fellow. He met a woman on the Internet, with whom he exchanged photos and a lot of computer talk. He was disappointed that there were so many times "on the

Internet when she called me by other guy's names." Is this the nineties form of commitment, personal involvement, and emotional investment—where fantasies and games become more important than, or worse than, substitutes for real life with its struggles and obligations?

Another form of fantasyland, where you have the guise of closeness (sex) but none of the perks (acceptance and support) is serial or parallel "relationships." Jim wrote something about that:

> *Getting enough of what he needs from the first woman to maintain his self-esteem and such, he will in all likelihood find another. A new woman may or may not actually be better than the first, but that's all relative and based upon his current perceptions. It doesn't matter much that he was just leading the first one on—he continued to get what he needed, which provided him the means of acquiring the next one.*

At least this is sex with another living, breathing human being—this is a step in the right direction. So many of you men sublimate your needs for intimacy because of your fears of hurt and rejection. It is absolutely true that there is a risk of vulnerability with another person whose character and preferences you can't control. So, take it like a man! Don't take it like a male: compulsive behavior and obsessive thoughts about pornography and masturbation. That's about the safe release of sexual drives, disassociating sex from love so there is no threat of rejection or anguish about criticism; but it sacrifices the warmth, acceptance, and closeness you get from opening up to your woman.

Remember, you're not going to get that "good stuff" from just any woman, and probably not from the kind of gal with whom you can engage in sexuality before there is much familiarity with each other. I know the idea of conquest and scoring is attractive and stimulating to your "male" side, but it's going to leave your "man" side much too vulnerable to "silly women." To have depth in a relationship you've got to look for a good enough woman, not just one who will "let you in," so to speak.

Drinking and drugs is yet another fantasy path you may take to try to hide from that struggle between your maleness and your human need for intimate connection. Here's Steven's testimony on that:

> *Dr. Laura, I was an Alcoholic. I blamed my past for my actions and decision of the day. I verbally abused my children through cursing them, and was a totally selfish person. I was happy . . . that is, until you told me that my past was an "atmosphere", not a cause or power, and that my decisions were mine and mine alone and that I could not blame them on my past or on anything else, that with rights comes responsibilities, and behavior has consequences, blah, blah, blah, nag, nag, nag. And, when you told a male caller that "anger is a form of fear", it caught my attention.*
>
> *One month after listening to you, exactly 1 month, I totally stopped drinking, giving it up cold turkey, after drinking for 20 years. I have voluntarily shifted to become the person you wish on people, the one's we really all want to be but are afraid to try. To all your listeners, "It is not hard at all. . . ."*
>
> *I enjoy getting down to eye level with my children and listening to them, actually hearing them, and taking a second to pull out from within myself a response to them—not some protective response for me. Standing on my own two feet without using alcohol as an escape from reality and my responsibilities as a man to my family and my life has meant everything.*
>
> *Is there a way to love someone, not sexually I mean, but as a person who has had a monumental impact on your life? This is the way I see you Dr. Laura, your words and wisdom have helped me find "ME"!*

Stephen's fears were "undefined"—like free-floating anxiety about abilities to perform his obligations well, his sense of neediness and anger that it wouldn't be met. That's the association between men and most of their anger: it's the outward expression of the inner angst of not being good enough so as not to be lovable enough—the fear that your emotional needs won't be met and might be used against you in the courts of life and love.

Risk it. Your fears are usually much, much bigger than reality.

Excessive focus on work is yet another way you guys bury your intimate emotional needs while satisfying your drive for accomplishment and functionality—besides, you tend most to do what you feel most comfortable and confident doing. And sometimes you learn your lessons too well, as David's letter indicates:

> You see, I learned from my father to work, work, work, and hide myself in my work and find all of my self worth in my work and that my work was therefore more important than my relationships. From my mother I learned that "soaps" and "game shows" were more important than me and that I was inadequate of holding any true value. I learned to keep my opinions and feelings to myself so as to not make my parents feel uncomfortable. I have tried to navigate my life around feeling uncomfortable. I have spent many years hiding from myself and my loved ones. I am so grateful to you for showing me how to say what I think and feel and for not letting me get away with "I don't know" and "I'm not sure." . . . I will no longer live my life avoiding that which is uncomfortable. I've only just begun this journey of using my courage and dealing with the truth in my life. . . . I have so much to learn. One thing I have learned is that living is experiencing life as it is in truth. To feel the truth makes for both sadness and happiness. You can't close off the sadness without closing off the happiness too. In the last year I have found in myself so much pain and isolation from others and myself that I've thought I might just

split open. But, I never knew I could feel so much joy too! There is joy in just knowing that I am alive and that I can feel what I am experiencing. And now . . . I'm going to "take on the day"!

It is not true, however, that there is an inevitable cause and effect between early family experiences and how you lead your adult life. Number one: you can change, which means, number two: you made your choice of emotional courage or cowardice to solve the problem of the fear and hurt while causing you isolation and greater pain. Dave chose a different route from his early family teaching:

I am my mom's abandoned kid. After being a loyal listener for quite a while now, it is more evident why my parents and I are not close at all. Since just a tot, I was thrown from babysitter to babysitter, neighbor to neighbor, while both my parents were working together at their own business. I never really had a mom or a dad. When my older (by two years) sister was old enough to babysit and house sit, I grew to resent her, as she tried to be my "mom" (and you know how bossy teen girls can be to their younger brothers under "normal" circumstances!). I worked for my parents for years as a kid and full time after university for a few years. And, after all those years (I am 35 now) I feel that I have been raised by co-workers, rather than parents. Well, the business closed a few years ago, and my parents have memories of the business they "had", and I have memories of the FAMILY I wish I "had". Today, however, I am happily married over 10 years with two great kids. I have in-laws who are "parents" to me, and we have special times like Birthdays, Anniversaries, Holidays, etc., that truly have meaning. And then I have my mom, dad, and sister, where those times don't mean what they should, because the close emotional relationship and relating never happened.

Ken, another listener, didn't make the choice that Dave originally did: to reject, deny, and bury needful feelings. He made sure he married into a family with scads of warmth and acceptance to go around.

Contemplate More Than Your Navel

What you men need is more time for deeper introspective reflection—even though it might not come naturally to you (neither do toilets, as we can all tell from your insistence on leaving the seat up so that it will just look like any other convenient hole in the ground!). It is in this time of reflection you can realize more of your self, your purpose, your pains, your concerns, and your needs. The more you are aware of all that, the less pain you will ultimately suffer, and the more rewarding you will find your life. Next, you need a safe place, hopefully your family, in which to express these inner workings and receive supportive responses.

Finally, you need to think more like Richard, crying while reading his paper out loud for his English class about his eight-year-old son's MRI for a suspected brain tumor, who responded to another "male" student's question of "Why are you being so sensitive?" with:

"I'm sensitive and it has no negative effect on my masculinity, in fact, I am probably more masculine because I can share my feelings!"

No emotional cowardice here.

3

STUPID AMBITION

A lot of men scratch, bite and claw their way to the top of the ladder, working the extra hours, being the "team player."

Once they get to the top of the ladder, however, they come to the staggering realization that their ladder has been leaning against the wrong wall.

SCOTT, 1996

Stop the presses! Incredible revelation! A *USA Today* survey of gender priorities in life choices shows males and females have differences! Can it really be true that after thirty years, the women's movement has not *yet* reached its *(unrealizable)* goal of creating unisexual beings with the same feelings, thoughts, drives, ambitions, attitudes, desires, preferences, and satisfactions? Guess not. And I don't even believe that gender differences are inherently bad. But now let's review that survey—The Wirthin Report statistics measuring gender priorities in:

- Having a rewarding career (males dominate)
- Achieving financial success (males dominate)

While females dominate in:

- Developing personal relationships
- Finding deeper purpose in life
- Growing spiritually
- Making a difference in world
- Raising a family (and *this turns out to be the most significant priority* recorded for either gender!)

What?! Raising a family is still a woman's number one priority!! After all these years of consciousness-raising, women are still motivated by the "natural drive" to mother, to nurture, to live for others (note: "live for" is not the same as "live through"; the former is magnificent, the latter is underdeveloped).

What? Raising a family is also the number one priority for men? How can that be when males are supposed to be so self-centered and object oriented? Could it be that men value family, but struggle with how to be a part of it? That mystery, and how to solve it, is exactly what this chapter is about.

Doing What Comes Naturally

Now, about these "gender differences"—and how threatening they seem to be to the "feminists." The feminist mentality, separate from the worthy and noble ideals of equal respect and opportunity, has severely warped how each gender views and values itself, much to the loss of what is precious to each and desirable to the other. This has been accomplished in part by a diminution of what is considered "natural" for males (i.e., ambition, sexuality, providing, physicality, individuality) unless those qualities are being exercised by a woman. Similarly, what is "natural" for females (i.e., spirituality, feelings, nurturing, verbalizing, interpersonal bonding) has been devalued, unless it's adopted by a woman engaged in a more male existence (corporate

CEO), or adopted by any man who's eschewed a male lifestyle (he's home with the kids). Tricky stuff.

The angry feminist (redundant?) philosophy preaches that men are inherently not interested in marriage, family, children, elder care, etc., and are, therefore, *less human*. According to Christopher Caldwell in the *Weekly Standard,* "The Feminization of America" (12/23/96), "Men in every society have always wanted these things, and they've done their part by earning a good living and protecting the home. Taking care of the ill, the aged, and the newborn has historically been a collaborative effort of male providing and female nurturing. [The feminists'] subtle trick was to exalt nurturing as the *higher* of these two virtues. Henceforth, the female virtues would be the 'human' ones, while the male virtues were merely backward remnants of the not yet 'humanized.'"

Simply because a quality tends to be typical of a specific gender doesn't mean (1) that it is nonexistent in the other gender (except for the issue of reproduction, we "humans" are really not so distinctly either/or creatures), (2) that it should be valued as better/worse (versus "naturally" different), (3) that there is no personal choice or variability (humans can override the "natural" to take care of necessities, unique preferences, and opportunities), or (4) that expressing and enjoying a quality more typical of the opposite sex automatically cause you to gain/lose in the gender struggle (gender is but one aspect of our complex "humanness").

That there are gender differences is simply a fact. That the genders are "designed" to merge so as to elevate and complete each other is an understanding that philosophers, romantic poets, and religious types have had since before the beginning of recorded time.

What's true for metals and magnets is true as well for males and females: polarities attract. Attraction is necessary for humans, but not sufficient for a quality life together. A quality life requires shared commitment to values, goals, mutual well-being and expression, and an ability to appreciate how the gender differences of the other are a blessing and a joy (if not an ongoing perplexing mystery), instead of seeing those differences as a curse or threat.

You truly can be "all you can be" without enlisting in the Army. *Within* the context of your maleness, you should be able and willing to explore the possibilities which elevate you males to men. It is therefore not a toss-up between "male" or "human," but how to be *your* optimum blend of "human male," aka a man.

I deeply believe that your ability to be this "human male" (man) absolutely requires femininity—not in yourself, however (so don't get all in a lather about that "female side" that's supposed to be lurking somewhere in your psychic innards), but instead, in your partner. Your expedition from male to "human male" is taught by other men, but tempered and civilized by the significant women in your life: your mother and your wife. For example, it is more likely that your father taught you to "take it (or dole it out) like a man," whereas your mother would more likely care-take your hurt feelings and suggest a more compassionate view of whoever was your nemesis. Neither approach is right or wrong, but both are necessary. Your father would take you out to share adventures, while your mother would teach you about the fulfillment found in attachments at home. Here again, neither approach is superior, but they both are truths to be reconciled as your "male" and "man" aspects struggle for moment-by-moment supremacy.

And I know that you men do struggle. Stephan, twenty-eight years old, called my radio program because he was torn between a personal life versus a Fortune 500 job.

"The job is long hours, lots of money, power, prestige, and status."

"And the point of a personal life is . . . ?"

"Having something outside work."

"I guess baseball could do that. You don't seem to see much value in a personal life, other than a break from your real life."

"Well, okay, personal life, personal development, meeting people."

"Even love and family? . . . I'm having to prime the pump here for you, Stephan. It's all too typical that this question is more easily answered right after the man's first heart attack—that's assuming he survives it. Generally, it's the men with rich, fulfilling personal lives who are less likely to get the attacks, or more likely to survive them. But, at twenty-eight, you're probably still into seeing yourself as indestructible."

"Yeah, that's true. Well . . . you've given me a lot to think about. Hmmm. You've given me a bit of direction here."

"Really? And what is that?"

"That I've got to force myself to make time for the personal side."

"Whew, *force yourself*. That sounds so negative, mechanical and pragmatic. But, Stephan, maybe that's simply what a good start in the right direction often sounds like in advance; you can't discover and enjoy the beauty along the road if you're not on the right road. And, I guess it is possible to be unwilling and unsure of your desire to be on the right road, and ultimately still come out at the right destination. It is wonderful to have incredible talents and great ambition, but enjoyment and deeper meaning from those comes in a complex mix of context, purpose, and sharing."

"Got it."

"Good. Now, Stephan, would a Fortune 1000 job be so bad?"

(Laughing) "Maybe not."

Your Road Map Gives Choices

Does it sound like I, a woman, am telling you, the men, what the "right road" is? Possibly. But, I am not arrogantly dictating your appropriate destiny. First, as Jim Phelps of the original *Mission Impossible* television program would say, "It's your assignment, if you choose to accept it. Good luck."

Second, you can read the maps of other men who go before you:

I told myself that I would return to school as soon as the opportunity arose, but the moment never seemed right. I passed up the chance for advancement because it would mean spending time away from my family, and I soon settled into the grind of a 9 to 5 job that I really didn't enjoy. Another daughter came along three years later.

 Eventually, I stopped thinking about my photography degree. That didn't stop me from complaining about my job or whining about the sacrifice I was making. I felt as if my family was all I had going for me. I felt like a loser. Somehow, I still missed the point.

 It came to me one evening as I sat at the supper table with my wife and two daughters, one now 13 the other 10. At first, I was simply watching them engage in the daily ritual of relating their day at school and thinking to myself how beautiful they were as they laughed. I realized that two happy and well-adjust kids sat before me. My wife and I had done something right in getting them to their point in their lives. I was suddenly filled with a deep sense of contentment and accomplishment.

 I knew at that moment that I had been doing something worthwhile all those years and it was more worthwhile than anything else I could have been doing. In the process, I had found what many men never find. I had not found it in my work, or the kind of car I drive, or the house I own. I had found a sense of contentment through my family.

 I never finished photography school, although I may someday. I continue to shoot photos as a hobby, and feel that my best shots are those of my wife and daughters.

Signed, Tom

Ambitions are wonderful, exciting, motivating, and even necessary to a fulfilled existence. Stupid Ambition embraces those efforts which strive solely for personal identification, ego gratification, acquisition, power, and challenge *in spite of* the reality of all your other needs and means of gratification which requires you to move from the wholly *personal* into the *interpersonal*. Don't worry—your "self" will not be lost, it will be perfected!

But, boy oh boy, do you ever have rationalizations and excuses to defend what is ultimately Stupid Ambition. And, as you will soon see, if you don't pick the right women, the wrong one will help you stay STUPID by punishing you when you start getting SMART.

"To Get Ahead": American Dream or Nightmare?

One age-old defense of Stupid Ambition is the so-called ideal of "getting ahead." One dad mailed me the editor/publishers column from the *Energy Times* (10–11/95) because it enraged him. It reports on a basic day for the editor and his working wife: Their alarm goes off at 5:45 and by 6:45 they're downstairs for breakfast. Between 7:00 and 7:30 A.M. their two-year-old comes down to greet the nanny. Mom and Dad have to catch the 7:48 train to work. Somewhere about 6:30–7:00 P.M. Mom gets home to "relieve" the nanny and Dad comes in sometime later. Dinner is prepared and consumed by 8:30 P.M. and the "ritual" of putting a two-and-a-half-year-old to bed begins. Mom and Dad are exhausted. Mom is eight and one-half months pregnant. "I don't know how we are going to do this when the new baby arrives."

Forget the "how"—ask yourself "why?" Their rationalization: "Getting ahead and wanting to give your children more opportunities than you had is a cornerstone of the American Dream."

The editor does give some lip service to "balance": "But remember, balance is the key to good health and happiness. So make sure you always set aside time for your children, your spouse and most importantly, yourself. The time you miss today with your family can never be redeemed, so make the most of what you have now and live your life to its fullest."

I have to bring your attention to three issues: time, focus, and balance. Look at the schedule—what time have they allotted for family? The nanny is their child's primary emotional relationship. Their colleagues are their primary relationships. And, I'm frankly astonished that "and most importantly, *yourself*" is actually admitted. Doesn't this editor realize that Mom and Dad's schedule choices *are exclusively for themselves?!* Or do they actually believe that a two-and-a-half-year-old child is warmed and comforted today by the future financial opportunities afforded by inheritance? Who are they kidding?

I am flabbergasted at how the concept of the American Dream has become distorted to apply only to wealth, status, and "self-actualization" with the notion of obligation being the new ugly sin. Let's be more honest here—you *want,* not *need* stuff, just want it. And, you've bought into the new American religion of ego and acquisition, where family is just a . . . a . . . what is it?

Troy, thirty-three years old, was just about to figure this out.

"I've been married a little over five years. I'm trying to find a way to build a relationship with my wife because it's not as strong as it should be."

"As it should be or as it once was or both?"

"Both."

"Why do you think that's so?"

"Well, we're both heavily involved in our work occupations so we have little time, less than we used to. But also I think it's that we've allowed ourselves to get to the point of using harsh words more than we should."

"Do you have any kids?"

"No."

"Is that on purpose?"

"To this point, I would say, 'Yes.' In my opinion it is because my wife is wanting to be more secure, and in my personal opinion it's because I'm wanting to make sure that this is the person I want to stay with. And, I'm not sure that's the case yet."

"So, after a commitment and five years of marriage you're not sure she's a 'keeper'?"

"Unfortunately. But, I do think she has qualities that merit the effort . . . "

"Okay, Troy, would a Martian coming down to observe the two of you imagine for the moment that you were two people putting the effort into the family?"

"No. We'd need to have communication, quality time together, sharing interests and hobbies together. From the outside we look like everything should be okay. From the inside, it just isn't."

"So, you guys don't put effort into being a family."

"Yes we do, but truthfully, it just isn't enough."

"Well, maybe you two are too much focused in on consumerism and ego."

"That's very possible."

"That's counterproductive to a family. Your life philosophy is way off—you're both focused in on yourselves, what you can gain, how you personally feel. How can you be a tennis player without focusing on tennis. How can you be a family without focus on that. You're not family—you're colleagues cohabiting so you won't be completely lonely."

"How do we make subtle changes?"

"Why 'subtle'. . . ? Don't want to give up too much of what *you* got *or are*? What are you afraid of losing and why don't you more value what you could gain? It's fine, I guess, if you're a single person to focus in on personal gain and goodies, but it doesn't work when you take on a family. The reason you're 'annoying' to each other, is that you both feel that the other is in the way of 'what you wanna do.'"

(Laughing) "Sounds like you live here!"

"Troy, I think you need to sit down with your wife and tell her that you believe that the two of you are working too much and considering the wrong things important. For example, you might say, 'We consider security to be money, and not the loyalty and love of each other.'"

"I know that that's true and I feel I've been betraying myself because of exactly what you're saying."

"Stop betraying yourself."

"You're right."

The very next day after Troy and I had this dialogue, I received the following fax from him:

I just wanted to thank-you for the privilege of speaking with you today. I appreciate the straightforward approach that you use with all of your callers, including me.

Having both of us be ego-crazed and self-centered has been very destructive in our relationship, to say the least. You hit it right on the head, we annoy each other.

Cars, boats, big houses . . . I used to believe that if I had the love of the woman whom I loved, that we could live in a teepee and be happy. We've got some work to do. I will take to heart what you said yesterday, and give you our progress as we go.

A Balancing Act

Now that we've tackled the issues of "time" and "focus," let me take on "balance." Well, first let Ramzi take on the concept of balance from the most familiar perspective:

*I just heard you talk to a man who was having a hard time deciding between work in a Fortune 500 company, and a personal life, and you mentioned the work **balance**. Balance is the key!! I work for a Fortune 2 company. That's right, it's #2 on the Fortune 500. My company preaches balance. Among other things, they encourage us to take our vacations, they help us with flexible work schedules, offer wonderful part-time work schedules and benefits for working moms, they offer paternity*

*leaves for dads, etc. . . . basically we all have a very active
personal life.*

*I truly believe that the caller's main problem had nothing to
do with Fortune 500 companies, but rather a fear of setting
priorities which may conflict with those required by the job. I
think the callers course of action should be to **set life's priorities,
and then find a job to fit those, and not visa versa.***

Now that sounds all well and good, but when you're young,
hot, and ambitious, life's priorities are set by your blind
energy, and anything more spiritual or familial is dismissed as
only the musing of old men, right? So, you put yourself where
you're sure you ought to or want to be, only to find out later
that the sacrifices were too great. Bill served in the Navy for
thirty years and admitted to me it had become the overriding
factor for everything he did in his life. He realized early on that
being in the military is a commitment that must be honored
before anything else. He doesn't regret being in the military or
the commitment he gave to it, but he does regret involving
other people (wife and family) in that commitment. For the
first time he sees there was probably no way for someone outside the military to understand completely his need to be gone
so much, and involved so completely. He writes:

> *There is an excerpt in the military code of conduct that talks
> about giving your life for your country. Now I realize that
> doesn't mean just that you might have to die, but that you give
> up your life in increments. I would like to tell other men that if
> you make a commitment to a job, or a way of life, ensure that
> others who may be involved with your life know that it is the
> primary concern in your life and they will be secondary.*

Interestingly, Bill doesn't express personal loss, he
expresses compassion for the losses of those close to him
because of his commitments elsewhere. It is so typically male
to express this "balance" in terms of obligations and not as

necessary personal resources or desires. I realize that you male types do tend to *try* to attain a sense of well-being primarily through work (aka combat and accomplishment). Have you thought about why that is?

Terry, forty-nine years old, has an interesting perspective:

In 1969, I went to Viet Nam with the Red Cross as a non combatant. I was by myself about twenty five miles from the Cambodian border and my primary job was to find and tell servicemen that their parents, wife or child had died in the United States. I was 22 at the time, married for a year, and feeling like a boy dressed up and doing a man's job. When my boss and mentor put me in charge when I was the youngest, and I showed myself to be competent, I felt that I moved from "boy pretending to be a man" to a "man". The downside to this story is also a "guy" thing that unfortunately we "compete" with damn near everything we do to "prove" that we are a man, and it never works because there is always someone better in any aspect I choose to measure.

Here it is, men, the fulcrum of the seesaw between establishing male ego/identity via externalities (competition and combat), which is mostly "male," and the human male, i.e., "man," aspect of your being is expressed in Terry's closing paragraph: *Sooner or later, if we truly make it to being a decent man, we develop our own internal yardstick based on our own chosen values and have the discipline to organize our life around our values.*

While ambition helps you to define an important aspect of your maleness, it just isn't really enough to bring a deeper level of satisfaction and meaning to your life. In my conversation with a caller named Jerry, I felt as if I was giving men more respect than he was!

Jerry is a currently unemployed paralegal staying home with his kids while his wife goes to work. He was literally tossing softener sheets in the dryer when I put him on the air.

He has an opportunity to go back to school and is torn between the careers of law and speech pathology.

"Law would take up all of my time. I'm afraid I wouldn't have any family time at all. The kids would be in day care. I feel bad about that. However, in the long run we might be financially better off."

"Jerry, since when do little kids care about 'the long run'? My kid comes in eighty times a night for hugs, kisses, cuddling, and conversation. He never comes in to discuss annuities. I don't know what it is about kids . . . they just like us there *now*."

"That's true. I get that now. But, it may give us a better chance for my wife to be home instead of me."

"I'm okay with whoever takes care of the children, so long as they're called either mom or dad—so, if you two want to work out an arrangement where she is home, that's wonderful. But you having *no time for family* is a great loss for you and for your family. Please don't reduce yourself to sperm and cash—if that's all you're worth, your wife could have gone to a sperm bank and then found herself a once-a-month sugar daddy and she doesn't need to be married. Well, my beloved Jerry, I seem to have more respect for a man, husband, and father than you do!"

The Lifestyle Trap

When you guys distill yourselves down to *only* provider status, you diminish yourselves to your "biology" of male provider. It's an easy trap to fall into, ultimately unfulfilling and unsatisfying but easy—made especially easy by our love of lifestyle concept which usually means "things." And you can fall into this lifestyle trap of things for seemingly even the right reasons, as Ken relates:

My wife and I enjoyed a very nice lifestyle as we both held respected, well paying jobs. We knew we wanted to have a family and had tried to "build the nest" as best we could before our children arrived. In the process of building this nest we had grown accustomed to being able to purchase what we wanted when we wanted it. I really believe that too many people (myself included) expect too much from life in the way of material possessions. Time with my children is a commodity that cannot be bought or sold. Time with my children is the most important investment I can make for both my future and theirs.

Ken stays home with his children! He and his wife forfeited one half of a handsome income because he felt that being at home with his boys was far more rewarding in an emotional sense than any material possessions could be.

Incidentally, when people first find out about a father being a stay-home dad, there is always a "Mr. Mom" stigma attached. At first this bothered me somewhat, but now I no longer attach any importance to the comments. I no longer feel the need to explain to others my decision to stay home. Those people who truly need it explained would probably have the concept lost on themselves anyway.

So, the term "provider" can mean more than sperm and cash? You mean, there's more to Dad and Husband than sperm and cash? Like what?

Paul was a general manager of a small business, working sixty hours a week at the office plus two to three nights out per week. He was "excusing" this time at the office and for business trips by pronouncing that they were for "the sake of the family." In his words:

No one knows the financial pressures on families as much as I do, and there is unquestionably a responsibility to provide for one's family, but a family needs a Dad at home, and a wife needs a Husband at home, and no amount of money can substitute for ole' Dad. My wife had not worked outside the home except part-

time during the hours when the kids were in school. Finally, we
as a family—Dad, Mom and three kids—decided I should take
another job at 33% less pay where I was home every night by
5:00 PM and did not work weekends. We have never regretted
the decision. We have a wonderful well-adjusted family, and I
have some terrific family memories and relationships with my
wife and kids that I would not trade for half of my former salary.
I could share more with you, but I have more day to take on.

So, men, don't sacrifice what you *mean to* and *need from*
family relationships under the guise of "helping" the family
by providing sperm and cash. Not that I really believe you're
necessarily being all that altruistic. For some of you, the
almighty job is your way of hiding from life's realities, risks,
and challenges behind excessive work. For example, you
realize that getting married was not an end point; that there
are ongoing demands and expectations attached which con-
fuse, scare, challenge and even annoy you. Your children
don't just "do it all right" as you remember you did. Then
the relatives push and pull with their shenanigans. The neighbors are a pain. The dog is too destructive and your birds
keep dropping dead. "I'm sorry, dear, I'm busy providing you
with all the things you want and need—I don't have time for
these things" is the typical cop-out.

Why You "Stray"

Then there are those pesky "internal" realities. You want the
status and the toys to make up for perceived or real personal
shortcomings. You "provide" because you want to please
and be loved. You believe that the only way to have people
care about you is to provide them with material possessions.
And when none of this brings the satisfaction you hoped
you'd feel you become hurt—not admit to hurt because that's
not "masculine"—which turns to anger. In your anger you
withdraw, become demanding, work even more, drink and

eat too much, and/or find some honey who'll *really give you what you want and need.*

Scott's contribution elaborates this concept:

The very thing (work) that the man sees as his primary way of contributing to the family (things make happiness) is what ultimately destroys the family, or at the very least, makes it an unsuccessful, unhappy household.

A man rationalizes his long hours at the office, his being out of town when his baby takes her first steps, his finishing that contract on the weekend instead of the family outing, etc., by saying to himself, "Someday, they'll thank me for it. They may gripe now, but if they only understood how much better their lives will be after I get this promotion/raise/contract, they'll be happy about their 'small' sacrifices."

Now, segue into the man's realization that his family "doesn't understand" and "isn't happy" about his long hours and their "small" sacrifices. Nobody understands his altruistic self, tied to his desk like she (the new woman) does. His family, ungrateful as they are, certainly don't. His wife, well, all she does is nag and complain about his never being home, his never being at the kids' sporting events, his forgetting (again) their anniversary. Not once has she said, "Honey, I know you put in all that extra time at the office just for us. I thank you so much for the 'long run' of things, etc., etc. You are a dream come true, you hard-working breadwinner. We know you're home in spirit and that's what counts, dear."

No, he hasn't heard that. Instead, he's misunderstood and hen-pecked. How's he to survive? Of course, he'll have an affair—who wouldn't. In fact, his wife and demanding, rebellious kids are the ones who drove him to this. He never wanted this, oh no. They're the ones to blame.

His family and marriage have broken up (maybe his second or third by now); he winds up in the hospital (again) for quadruple-bypass surgery; he topples from the ladder's top (although he's sure he's been pushed) and no one is around to

*catch his fall; he's on his deathbed evaluating his life and is
struck by the fact that no one's last words were ever, "My only
regret in life is that I didn't spend more time at the office."*

Fortunately, not all of you men end up that way. Stanley
believed that work was more important than his family. He
used to work for a large company and was always gone. He
missed the early years of his children's growing up because he
was always traveling. After eleven years the company left
him! He was laid off cold for no reason other than they
wanted fewer employees.

*And now I work at home. I see my boys off to school each
morning and am here when they come home from school. I
volunteer at their school and drive them to their sporting events.
I would never trade it for anything—for I see my children
growing up before me is everything. I am my children's Dad, for
my work world is now second to my personal world.*

Face the Facts, Sir

Let's get back to this issue of balance, which can have a negative side. Sometimes, your attempt at balance is yet another
excuse for not facing up to the facts of your messed-up priorities and disintegrating family life. This kind of negative balance generally means that you find some position on that
seesaw that gives you more of what you want and less of
what you don't. However, all obligations and responsibilities
are necessarily under the "want" column, and you have no
right to diminish the time and effort you put into them when
they are definite "supposed to's." Values must supersede
wants if you are to be a man, not merely a male.

Sometimes, too, this negative balance comes from a revision
of truth and values. This usually results in someone else paying
a price. For example, day care. It used to be considered a
tragedy when a child had to be institutionalized because par-

ents couldn't/wouldn't take care of them. Now, it has become a given that stranger care is equal to, and perhaps even better than, a mom or dad. After all, work makes Mom and Dad "happy," and if they're not "happy" then how good can they be for anyone else? A simple revision of truth and values and you're free to do "what you want" under the guise of balance.

Positive balance, on the other hand, means that you take control and make rules and limits. For example, you determine your hours and projects. These self-imposed limits may cut down on rewards and ultimate accomplishment and you may constantly feel you're having to explain why you're not doing more or better. Your life, albeit more modest, will now have the quantity time in which quality moments can happen.

Beyond Time-Management

For other men, the very concept of "balance" seems absurd. Robert B. Reich, the *voluntarily former* Secretary of Labor for President Clinton, quit. Why? Because he felt that there was no way of getting work and family into better balance. He "gave notice" through an article he wrote for the *New York Times* (11/8/96) entitled "My Family Leave Act." He wrote, "You're inevitably short-changing one or the other, or both. You're never able to do enough of what you truly value. Don't tell me to improve my time-management skills. I've done that, and I'm scheduled to the teeth. Teenage boys don't need you on schedule. A spouse doesn't share intimacies on command. Work doesn't always present new opportunities or crises just when you block out time for them."

Mr. Reich then makes a point I try to drive home daily on my radio program: "In the end, you simply can't do more of both. There's no room for better 'balance.' The metaphor is all wrong. You have to make a painful choice."

He concluded with "I have the best job I've ever had and probably ever will. No topping it. Can't get enough of it. I also have the best family I'll ever have, and I can't get enough of them. Finding a better balance? I've been kidding myself into thinking there is one. I had to choose."

You might be upset with Mr. Reich seemingly saying that "You can't have it all." That's anathema to the promise of the American Dream! Well, guys, you can *and* you can't have it all. Yes, you can have both satisfying work and a meaningful home life. No, you can't have it all maximally, simultaneously, or single-handedly:

- Maximally. Remember Bill, thirty years in the Navy? Admittedly, his oath to his country superseded his marital vows and obligations to his family. Day-to-day choices were not his—they were the military's. There was little time, energy, or commitment left for family. You just can't commit 100 percent of yourself or your time to "work" and expect balance. Won't happen. You can commit 100 percent of your attention to your work *while you're working;* but those limits have to be under your own power, and you must not be resentful of the trade-off. You've got to see your personal life more greedily; as something you need and want, not just something the wife and kids nag you about.
- Simultaneously. Building an empire at the same time you're building a family usually won't fly because empire building is 100 percent time-consuming and ultimately not nearly as satisfying as building toward family. However, sequentially with overlap does work. Therefore, once you've committed to the family, you need to temper the empire building. Jeff, thirty-six years old, got this point, albeit the hard way:

My family has been going down hill ever since I opened my own shop ten years ago. In that time I have spent entirely too much time trying to be successful and not enough time developing my children's character and family harmony. I regret this has happened and am now committed to make every sacrifice necessary to obtain the goal of raising self-disciplined, confident, responsible, balanced and happy children and harmony within our family.

- Single-handedly. You can't "have it all" without a good woman. A good woman is not a princess (waiting for your kisses and daring-do to make her be alive); she is not androgynous (declaring that, "since women can do anything a man can do, she should be doing everything her man is doing," thereby having no polarity or team effort in the home), she is emotionally and psychologically healthy (she can be flexible and adapt to the unexpected events and crises of the moment without attacking you for not keeping her "safe"; she is proud of her femininity and of being a woman (doesn't perceive life as an evil empire dominated by men for the exploitation and oppression of women and small animals); and she appreciates the inherent differences between the male and female temperament (which elicits both humor and compassion).

Change or You're Toast!

Sometimes you can tell a good woman by the ultimatum she gives you. The notion of an ultimatum from your lady *should* make your hackles rise only if it is unfair or selfish, but I would offer that her laying down the law is generally about civilizing you . . . bringing you home from hunting. Steve got such an ultimatum:

> *My day started at 3 AM, driving 182 miles round trip to the job site and returning home by 8 PM. I then would have a quick dinner, followed by a lesson plan for my children (my wife and I home-school our kids) and then off to the basement to build gadgets (for over 7 years I've been developing and building a product for external communication with industrial computers) til 11 PM.*
>
> *One evening when I came home my wife said to me that I had three choices:*
> *1. The marriage goes*
> *2. The job goes*

3. The gadget goes . . . "You choose!"

I couldn't see throwing out seven years of developing and making a product that is better than what multimillion dollar corporations have to offer. I knew that my company would be making me work out of state soon. If my wife thought that she didn't see enough of me now, she definitely would see a lot less of me being out of state! So I did what any other husband who loved his pregnant wife and five children would have done. I gave my boss two weeks notice!

It has been over thirteen months since I left my job. We are a family of eight now, and live on about $1200. Gross per month. We do not receive food stamps or any assistance from the department of Social Services, nor do we want to. So the next time you have a caller who says that "he can't", tell him he can. My family and I have living proof that it can be done.

When the Princess Strikes Back

Now, if you didn't get a "good woman" you'll be cut off at the pockets when you want to get smart about your ambition, or when life forces the point. That's what happened to Eric:

After 13 years I lost my 52K per year job through no fault of my own. My wife insisted that I not tell anyone. She continually made sarcastic comments to me. She even made comments in front of my children (then 16 and 12) that we were broke and they would not be able to eat and go to activities as we previously had, because dad . . .

Needless to say I was totally devastated. It was bad enough to lose my job, but it made it much worse to have my wife kick me in the teeth while I was down on the floor. This was probably the most important point in my life and I need the love and support of my wife . . . and she failed.

Fortunately a month later I found a good job for more money! However, I will never forget the way my wife treated me. I am considering leaving her when my youngest graduates

*from high-school. If I do, this incident will probably be the
deciding issue.*

Now, I don't know if Eric created this monster for himself
when he married a princess type, and/or when his Stupid
Ambition limited his domestic presence and significance. It's
also possible this wife was thrust into such insecurity and fear
when Eric lost his job that she displaced her worries from the
challenge at hand to punishing him because emotionally she
didn't know what else to do with her feelings. However, if
Eric is just going to "sit on this" and wait out his time "till he
can justify leaving," then his willingness to communicate and
deal with personal issues of fear and disappointment seems
very questionable—and may more critically be the problem
than the miserable way his wife is treating him.

Perry, forty-four years old, also had decided to end his reign
of Stupid Ambition. When he informed his wife of his desires to
change work to be home and more involved with the family, she
attacked him as "a loser," took the two children, and left her
third marriage! As long as life together was "charmed," she was
loyal and content. The minute change or challenge reared its
ugly head, she got disgusted and took off. Now that Perry
thinks back, he remembers that his ex's leaving her first two
marriages followed a similar pattern: he changes, she leaves.
Perry must have thought he'd be a more consistent prince for his
princess bride than her other husbands.

Excuses Are a Lousy Defense

Bottom line to this chapter, for your own well-being and sense
of satisfaction in life you need to see family as a source of joy,
not just as maintenance work. That doesn't mean that you
have to give up masculinity or ambition, but it does mean that
you have to recognize that a total protein diet without sugar
can be a bitter life, for you and those you hope to please and
be bonded to. Christopher Matthews wrote in the *Tennesseean*

(12/29/96) about a former US senator and failed presidential candidate's tragedy of a daughter's alcoholism and ultimate early death. "Later, after she was gone, he discovered in notes she made in her personal journal 'the hurt and sense of loss' she felt as her dad's political ambition kept him away from her." She wrote, "Nothing any of us children did to get his attention, to get him to come home and be a father, worked. In his ego-omnipotence, he thought he could sweep back into the family and change things from the outside in. He never got it that the trouble was in the hearts of his children."

Sadly, this famous father "got it" too late, but he got it finally, and, according to this article, had this to share: "Both her life and her death have taught me that life is not only precious, it is fragile and uncertain—and that we need to love each other more."

Mr. Matthews concludes his article with: "To the wife and children marooned at home, it matters little whether the absent father is spending the night at the White House or at the taproom around the corner."

He's right, you know; all the excuses in defense of Stupid Ambition are ultimately found to be useless or outright lies.

Smart Ambition Can Be Scary

I know, I know, there are lots of insecurities attached to getting "smart," and lots of *potential* limitations which you experience. I say "potential," because they are not truly determinant or immutable, because you always have choice and attitude. Dave, forty-two years old, is in the process of working on his relationship with his wife and family. He knows he has to change his job, because skippering a fishing boat keeps him away from the home for months. He's concerned about the obvious: the change in lifestyle (kids in private school) and what career he'd change to (has only fished his whole life). These are realistic concerns, but not ones which can't be worked out. Dave's main problem is feeling so lost about the idea of giving up work for family concerns. "I grew up in a family where men worked. It was a working family, and I didn't learn much more than that."

So it isn't just the downsizing of the work which causes the angst; it's how you fantasize interaction with the folks at home once you're there! Change, like anything else, is a learning process—and that's where men's groups can come in handy.

You can get yourself so worked up over your feelings of inadequacy, confusion, and discomfort with "family stuff" that you simply horribilize yourself to death to avoid making any change at all. Randy lost his wife of twenty years and two children because he couldn't (really wouldn't) move past those fears of change and the unknown. As a quick aside, it seems sad that so many of you men see "relationships" with your wives and children as an "unknown." Nonetheless, what is on the top of that next mountain is also an unknown, but you naturally tackle it anyway; so, treat personal issues with that same courage and openness.

But, back to my conversation with Randy:

"Dr. Laura, I'm what I've heard you describe as one of those pack mules—one of those men who works to support and take care of his family, and does such a good job of it that he neglects things at home."

"Did you and do you see that as an either/or enterprise, as though your 'heroism' in supporting and financially taking care of your family gave you a signed slip excusing you from the participatory aspect of family?"

"Well, maybe. Well, I'm gone for long periods of time."

"That's a choice."

"Yeah, well, when you become a certain age it becomes more difficult to break out of that mold."

"Maybe so, but you've had twenty years of ages to tackle that. First you're a hero, now you're too elderly. Boy, do you ever have excuses. You're defending yourself instead of owning up and making the changes you need to hold on to your family."

"Well, she made the decision to divorce last weekend."

"First you are heroic, second you're too elderly, now it's too late. What will it take to get you out of your rut?"

"I guess I just don't understand what she wants."

"She wants you—imagine that—you."

"I can't see how to provide that without giving up everything else, then how would we eat or live?"

"Heroism, elderly, too late, impossible. Boy, do you ever make it difficult. You're going to be alone and that's sad, for your two kids who need a dad, your wife who needs a husband, and yourself, who needs more out of his existence than being a pack mule."

"I guess I just don't know how to pick between the two. I've just tried to keep the money coming in."

"You don't pick losing your family and you don't horribilize yourself into inaction."

"Dr. Laura, you've stressed that a person's duty was to take care of children."

"Yes, but I never said that was purely an issue of money. I stress the intimacy, love, affection, attention, involvement . . . "

"I agree, if you're not there you can't provide those things."

And then he said the underlying and profound truth: "I guess I equate money with my prestige, my barometer of how I'm doing. I hate change immensely."

There it is: my friend Randy is the poster boy for Stupid Ambition and could lose everything over it. I told him to sit with his wife and talk these truths out loud and work something out . . . for the best of each and all of the family.

Phil, forty-six years old, has been divorced for three years after an eighteen-year marriage. The divorce was caused by his "marriage to his business, the love of my life." His wife wanted him more than she wanted the money. Now he's shacking up with a honey who wants him to work more than he does; she clearly wants his money more than she wants him. Think Phil believes that at forty-six he's in a better place?

Many of you men, especially since the women's movement, want your women to go to work—especially when you feel insecure financially. This way you can have the "things" and not have the "burden of sole support." Joseph is thirty-one, and his wife of four years is thirty-two. They own their own home and have a son of fifteen months. Since the birth of their child, his wife has not held an outside job. Joseph made a discovery this week about "division of labor":

> *My income allows us to maintain our day to day necessities, however, does not address our credit card debt. When insecure, I want my wife to get back into the work force. However—this past holiday season, my wife was struck by the flu. Fortunately, my company takes the two holiday weeks off, allowing me to become the primary care giver to our son. I would like to say that I can not think of any more important function than raising our son. I have had the most wonderful time this holiday season with my son and ill wife! Our financial situation did not allow for many store gifts this year. But, this has been our best holiday to date.*
>
> *I have opened my eyes to the importance of the primary care giver and the family unit. I have heard you for so long take this position. Now, I have experienced it for myself. My wife does a fabulous job, and but of course, I have the most wonderful son—all thanks to my wife.*

Enlightened Choices

When you guys want a family life, don't get caught up in the guilt about having your wives actually be involved in that. One fellow who called my show was dating a brilliant young medical student. Since their respective work schedules were so demanding, they spent very little time together, and he was agonizing over how they would make room for family.

"Well there is a full-time nanny or a day-care center, then a house-keeper to shop, clean and cook, vibrators and videos for sex . . . you see . . . there are ways to make up for the lack of each other."

"But, I want a real family."

"If you marry a woman with serious ambitions and commitments to a demanding career, you either seriously rein in your expectations, ignore your better sense and desires, or volunteer to be at home. You can't have it all ways. You have to choose."

I'm a working woman, so it might seem heretical for me to talk about traditional families—yet mine basically is. Because my husband, Lew, and I didn't want anyone but us raising our child, we rearranged our lives to accommodate those values. Lew became my manager and began working from a home office. I do my radio show while our son is in school, and plan any personal appearances around his school schedule so that "business trips" become family adventure. It's all in the values, the attitudes, and the ability to accommodate to what you might not have expected or fantasized, but what is necessary and profoundly more important.

Beacons of Progress

And you're never too young to be aware of the importance of these choices, and have the courage to make them. Ted Roberts in the *Wall Street Journal* (10/3/95) reported on a six-foot-seven-inch, 340-pound offensive tackle for Brigham Young University. He had a 3.5 grade point average and was judged to be the third-best senior offensive tackle in the NFL draft. His dilemma: "He could sign up with the NFL, play ball on Sundays, and fill his lifespace with Rolls-Royces, suburban Taj Mahals, and Brooks Brothers suits, or he could teach math for $25,000 a year and honor the Sabbath. The answer to the BYU student's ethical equation was honor the Sabbath and wear chino pants with a nice Wal-Mart shirt."

"But, Eli," Ted Roberts asked, "what about your family and an 18 month old daughter, who some day will cry for designer jeans and, later, maybe a $40,000 wedding?"

"Well, Eli says, his family will do just fine, and maybe a blessing from above is better than a bank account. Eternity is so long and life is so short, you know. Hey, you can't be a beacon if your light don't shine."

Another "beacon" is Mandy Patinkin, the Emmy-nominated star of CBS's *Chicago Hope*. He begged out of his five-year contract three and one-half years early.

Pete Rosenthal reported on his interview with Mandy in the *Daily News* (July 25, 1995). According to the article: "I won't be as famous and I won't be as rich. But I will have my kids and my wife, and that's all I wanted."

Mandy relates, "I have a friend whose father was a very, very, very famous television star. That friend said, 'If my father, only once, had NOT canceled a family vacation or a family event because of a job, my life would have been different.' I pray that this would have some kind of major effect on my kids, to know that they came first, and not my career."

And, as I warned you, Mandy had married a "good woman": "My luck is that I'm married to Kathryn," he is quoted in *Parade* magazine (7/14/96). "She fought for what the family needed. She has taught me how to be a better father every day of my life."

I conclude with Dean's letter:

> As a recent law school graduate, I was faced with the prospect of going to work for a large law firm. Such a choice would have greatly increased my checking account, but left little time for family, personal development and other things that you, Dr. Laura, among others have convinced me are more important. After a long search, I was offered a job teaching at a local university. I will be less wealthy, but will have time to live a balanced life.

My friend Dean is not giving up the "guy thing" of "slaying dragons"; he's just picking his dragons wisely, recognizing that any good hero requires the sustenance which home, family, and love give him. This is *not* Stupid Ambition.

4

STUPID STRENGTH

*A Male
Becomes a Man
When He Learns How to Always Be
Gentle with a Woman*

OTEY, 1996

I'm home today, flu ridden, watching a marathon of really bad sci-fi monster movies on the Sci-Fi channel. Here's the scene which, with very little variation, appeared in just about every one of these movies: the monster is about to gain the power to decimate humanity but *he* (the variation is that it is sometimes *she*) comes up with a "hopeless-but-what-else-is-there-to-try" idea, while *she* (no variation here) warns, worries, and sobs that he could die, but *he* (no variation here either), with seemingly no such concern, submits his very person to "save the day." *He's* the hero, gaining the gratitude and respect of all . . . and getting to have sex with the *"she."*

That innate male protectiveness, the courage to push back fear and reflexive self-preservation, the grit to endure pain, the focus to parry wits with the enemy, the potency to prevail . . . ohhh . . . *very* masculine, and to women, *very* sexy.

Whether or not modern women join increasingly antiseptic

and computerized armed services, it is still the guys who seem to have invented competitive combat. Anyone with small children can attest to the fact that little boys can be sitting right next to little girls and virtually OD-ing on *Sesame Street* and *Mr. Rogers,* where there is no physical aggression or depiction of weapons, can turn right around, create imaginary swords, knives, guns, and cannons, and commence to battle. Indeed, contest, competition, and conquest punctuated by art, poetry, music, and philosophy summarize much of male/human history, with religion as the bridge between.

Unlike the cynical feminist rancor toward "men and civilization," what I say is without any inherent negative judgment: while one war may be a genocidal "killing field," another is to stop a "holocaust." The "male" tendency toward domination and rule is a fact; the benevolent possibility of such power being uncorrupted by evil is only an option.

Words such as *power, vigor, force, might, potency, control, authority, strength,* and *control* are seen as "male" simply because they *are* primarily male characteristics, not only because "society *says so.*" Has "society" "said so" throughout human history accidentally or coincidentally? No, of course not; it's because strength and power issues are more typically a male reality—applying not to all men, nor excluding all women (don't forget the bell curve of distribution of characteristics discussed in chapter 2)—but still, it's *more* of a *male* reality.

Now the problem is that *all* men don't *want* to have to be *so strong* all of the time. Yet they often don't know how to act instead or even how to reconcile the temporary dropping of the martial colors. Many men are also frustrated by the inconsistency of women's criticism which seems to rail against "male strength" on feminine whim or convenience.

For example, women may demand a successful man who competes aggressively at his work (financial rewards, power, and status), but call him an abusively controlling chauvinist if he tries to "run things" at home—or self-centered and uncaring if he leaves it to her to "run things." What's a guy to do/think/say/be?

Well, fellas, some of the problem is your own damn fault. Here's how it goes: First, you don't pay any attention to what you *need/want,* just what you think you're supposed to *do.* Next, you don't *think* about what place the heart and hearth fill in your life and psyche, just that they're something to have. Third, because first and second are true, you don't realize that the kind of woman you pick is crucial to your emotional health and well-being and happiness. . . . Yikes!!! Did I say *emotional?* Whoops, sorry. I realize that "emotional" is not a male ideal, but as I've said repeatedly, "male" is only your foundation; you are a human man. If you forget your humanity and value and focus only on your "male" aspects, you will make yourself horrid to others and miserable to yourself. Granted, your emotional needs may not be your sole or even favorite focus, but if they're disrespected and ignored, this eventually will be your downfall.

This chapter is about male tendencies to power and control; and there's good news and bad news. The good news is that this aggressive drive has put men on the moon. The bad news is that this aggressive drive can also take the form of domination and menace. It is an obvious disaster when the latter occurs in the home or community—and that's Stupid Strength.

You Can Overdo a Good Thing

This problem of overcontrolling can actually come from good intentions. We all applaud a strong sense of responsibility, that is, the willingness to carry the burden of obligation. Obviously, if a man is in a position of accountability, he has to make decisions he has to defend as well as honor. That is "control," and the right to control is "authority." Therein lies much of what "being a man" is supposed to be about.

However, once in partnership with a woman (marriage), some guys, in responsibility overdrive, just don't know how to share that authority. Dana's letter is an example of good intentions and the Highway to Hell:

> *Why do men like to "control" others in their lives? Well, I feel a deep sense of responsibility. I feel it strongest for my children, then for my wife, then for me and others. This sense of responsibility leads me to want to take action where I see problems. I want to fix things that feel or appear wrong. I WANT to do the right things, the correct things, the proper things, all the "shoulds" with my children. If something is wrong and nobody is doing anything about it, I have a strong desire to step in and take some corrective action.*

Here are some of the problems and dangers of Dana's "good intentions" going awry:

- Some situations are made worse by immediate intervention; time often mellows the participants and/or eventually reveals the solutions.
- Not all situations require/benefit from solutions. Sometimes tolerance, acceptance, and coping are more appropriate responses.
- Imposed solutions may be intellectually solid, yet fail because others who didn't participate in the process resist implementation.
- What you see as "needing fixing" may indeed be someone else's preferred behavior.
- When your solutions "don't work out," your determination, shame, or frustration often become rage directed at the very people you've been trying to "save."

Protect and Serve

Many men truly intend to be good at their "role" as man of the family; but when that role becomes too threatening or confining, they resort to escape (a "honey" on the side for which he is an easy and instant "hero") or fight harder to do a better job (get dominating) instead of getting comfortable with flexibility and adaptation (the cornerstones of mental health). So, it's not at all that the "role" is a bad thing. It's just that you guys need to put yourselves on dimmer switches so that you can modulate your determination to take action with what is feasible, necessary, appropriate, and appreciated.

If you don't go on "dimmer switches," your anxieties about screwing up can make you downright wrong and ugly. Bob confirms this in his letter:

Since way back when, society has expected men to be providers, leaders, problem solvers, etc. The problem comes that notwithstanding female demands for equality, it's still expected by most. Many men feel pressured to fulfill this thankless role (in their opinion) and their feeble attempts (absent of true confidence and self-esteem) results in their being "too" controlling. They think they have to be all knowing, have all the answers, fix everything, "make it all better." Consequently, if a man can't be the genuine article (hero) in either his woman's eyes or in his own honest conscience, he nonetheless feels compelled to play the part. So, men becoming "too everything" can sometimes reflect their fears, insecurities, unhappiness, pressure, stress . . . whatever.

To summarize, an aspect of male controlling behavior fulfills the biological destiny to create and defend your life and reproductive "space." Another aspect compels you to take the full burden on yourself—even when teamed up with a competent human female with whom you need to confer and share that burden. Consequently, you don't permit yourself to ask for input, direction, or support when that burden gets too heavy, which in turn results in affairs, addictions, and abuse, right? Right.

The Mr. Spock Syndrome

What makes it so hard for you to admit . . . shhh . . . *weakness*? Well, the obvious answer is that weakness and masculinity don't mix. While that is true, oil and vinegar *still* make a damn good salad dressing.

Mr. Spock, the beloved character from the classic *Star Trek* television series and theatrical movies, is half Vulcan and half human. Vulcans have evolved into a culture which deplores emotion and celebrates only rational thought. They believe, for theirs is a "religion" of severe self-control and discipline, that in all dealings logic is superior to human emotion, including intuition, compassion, fears, and love. Spock's struggle is with his human side. While we are impressed with his obvious strengths (no hurt feelings, self-doubts, or fears), we only are intrigued when that passionate human side peeks through his rational armor.

According to a listener named Alan, the Spock type would be men's ideal:

> *We men are like we are because we value logical response to questions and problems over the emotional. It seems like it is a higher mental ground, so we are sometimes (okay, usually) unable to compromise and therefore we control, show our frustration through anger and lack of patience. But, we do love you ladies anyway!*

This argument has a lot of truth to it. You guys have two struggles going on at the same time: the first, to minimize your own emotionality; the second, to juggle the emotionality of the women in your life. Since emotions are not your specialty, you may feel inadequate handling the emotions of others. That plus avoiding your own emotions leads you to "overcome," i.e., compensate, by controlling.

If that's the disease, what's the cure? Is it even possible to incorporate something from which you are constantly running and find degrading in others? The core problem is in your Spock-like all-or-nothing mentality about emotions. While Spock was half 'n' half, he denied his human (emotional) side, as though he "logically" believed that *some* automatically became *all*. That's as stupid as thinking if you put cheese on a sandwich the bread will disappear. Ever hear of "seasoning to taste"?

Many of you men—so severely stifled in your acknowledgment of your own emotional content, so fearful of your loss of masculinity should you "give in" to any of your emotional yearnings, so frightened about the consequences of any emotional display—blow your emotionality way out of proportion to its true reality. In other words, what you struggle to avoid naturally grows in magnitude in your imagination.

So, the key is to:

- acknowledge the (obvious) truth that you have emotional needs and reactions
- not wait until your emotions become overwhelming to examine and discuss them
- realize that having emotions is as natural to all human beings as testicles are to males
- understand that emotional experiences are sometimes the whistling teakettles which alert you that you're boiling over
- recognize that emotions are also an integral part of your heart's appreciation of life's joys
- realize also that your emotions are simply information from "within," as uniquely you as your fingerprints, and without which there would be little texture or dimension to your life

- determine to respect your emotions as valuable to your identity, experience, and actions in life—over which you can have control *only* if you accept these truths

Emotions are not facts; they are not necessarily rational; they are often unpredictable; they are often confusing, fleeting, and changeable; emotions, while universal, are experienced egocentrically. That is why on my program I stress ethics, morals, and principles over mood, ego, circumstance, and the emotional when deciding a course of action. I have often been accused of not caring about emotions or not thinking they have any importance. That's the black-and-white mentality of those who skim across the top of a shallow pond. Values are more reliable than feelings with regard to direction of action. However, laws without compassion can be cruel; while compassion without laws is a chaos of unaccountability. Together, however, they are sublimely human.

History records the efforts of men throughout the ages to conquer and change the world. There is at least one arena where that simply won't work: women and relationships.

Male Alchemy

The wizards and magicians of the Middle Ages promised a method for transmuting base metals into gold. So many of you men act like emotional alchemists when you try to turn situations and people of little merit into objects of hope and satisfaction. Here's Ben to tell this story:

> After two marriages, and other now dead relationships, I have learned that (a) you, Dr. Laura, are correct when you say love is not enough, and (b) I have been quick to label as love something that isn't. Considering how wise, educated and intelligent I think I am, that is quite an admission. So now it is a bit like looking at accident photos and shattered autos, to attempt to find the causes. Only, I'm looking at memories and people.

*For me, the quick answer to why men are controlling and critical is frustration, for example, my attempts to **overpower disappointment**, and the realization of how poorly I made decisions about myself and the women I've "loved".*

*When I have gotten too critical, too controlling, too domineering, it has been in part because of profound disappointment in marriage. In both marriages, we didn't know or value the other's core visions and beliefs. We thought we did, but we deceived ourselves. Each of them had little clue as to what I value, what I have as a vision of life, or even an idea of truth, common sense, or justice. I didn't do the work of finding out about them. I ignored all that I suspect. **I thought I could overcome it.***

Criticism and attempts to control outcomes can be justified, but only with large amounts of tolerance and understanding. I guess that's where the love really comes in. I choose not to divorce, which would do her great economic and perhaps emotional harm. I had my innings. The game is done.

It's ironic that men seem to marry out of "emotional" versus "practical" motives. The emotional motive is that she makes you feel good because she's pretty, nice, gives you sex, and you should be married by now or everyone will think you're gay. The motive should be you two share common values and goals, whether she is someone with whom you can really be yourself, and whether you can really count on her to take on life with you as a true team. But you guys marry for the (limited) emotional appeal, then try to turn it into gold. The snag is that sand stays sand, and it's hard even to build a sand castle if you've not taken the time to contemplate the floor plan.

Eric's letter gets right to where the only real control over "people" lies:

Through your wise, moral, ethical, no-nonsense cut-to-the-chase advice, I've learned to take care of myself at the age of 31 . . .

finally. My therapy has also been a life-saver. I can't control my wife who's had two affairs! I can only control my own behavior and leave her to stew in her own justifications. It's her responsibility. If she can own up to her own character defects and handle her own problems, I can respect her and maybe love her again. If that doesn't happen, I know I deserve better. I'm on the road to being a whole person.

Eric has come to understand that even the laying on of heavy male hands can't match up to the power of someone else's will to do right or wrong. You can't change reality, you have to face reality. And, the best time to do that is before the wedding—although that would mean putting as much effort and attention into the issue of relationships as you do into sports and work. But, that's for a later chapter ("Stupid Matrimony").

Not all control is about tilting at windmills. Some control is about getting what you want, when and how you want it.

King Baby

One anonymous fax outlined this intent:

My expectations are not as high as they once were. I find that when I am critical, angry, or controlling, I am actually scared. I am scared that I won't get what I want, how I want, when I want. Or, I am scared that I will lose something I already have and don't want to give up. Thank you for allowing me to fax this to you. My wife has spent all her life giving because I was taking. Now we both know how to give. Critical of my wife?— not anymore.

Well, there it is, and it couldn't be more succinctly put. Many of you men are controlling (via criticism, put-downs, sarcasm, demands) simply because you haven't moved past the baby stage of screaming incessantly for your mother's breast. Boy oh boy, isn't that difficult to admit without see-ing yourself as a sniveling mama's boy? Fact is that every man wants some mothering. Fact also is that every woman wants some fathering. For there to be a good relationship both of these needs must coexist. When either party wants to stay *only* in the baby mode, you'll have little mutual sat-isfaction.

Think it through. If your wife is to be your omnipresent "breast" (feeding you a perpetual sense of importance and being wanted and feeling secure), then two main problems are immediate and predictable:

1. The reality is that she can't be a perpetual mothering machine. Therefore, you *will be* starved and frustrated quite often.
2. When #1 occurs you will feel unimportant and insecure. This generally leads to a greater demand for "feeding."
3. When #2 occurs you will diminish her desire to feed you and you'll grow more starved. This will lead to greater demanding behavior . . . which will lead either to increased threats toward her or to alcohol/drugs to self-medicate the hunger pangs.

No one is ever assured of getting all he wants. And you must remember that most of our satisfaction in life does not come from a full "stomach," but from feeding others.

Nonetheless, some of you are fixated at that baby stage, yearning for the breast. These are men who don't truly want the "milk," just the "breast." It's not, therefore, what they can give and take in the relationship that is important; it's not how having a woman in their lives will complement, complete, or help fulfill them as people; it's not having some-one with whom to share the struggle of life . . . it's actually an avoidance of all of these important endeavors. It is as though securing the woman, the prize, implies or appears like or actually creates the whole reality of becoming a man.

I'm here to tell you that it doesn't work. But that doesn't stop some men like Tom from trying.

"I'm confused about what it means to take responsibility for something. I feel bad because I got arrested and convicted for something I did."

"Which was what?"

"Misdemeanor stalking of my ex-girlfriend."

"Oh, you did a scary thing."

"It was not scary."

"It was to her!"

"I know. I know."

"The first thing about accepting responsibility is to realize that you did something which hurt someone else. And, you did it on purpose to satisfy some feeling. Justifying it, even explaining it, is not how you take responsibility. Admitting that you intentionally hurt her, scared her because you wanted her back to feel better about yourself, is on the road of taking responsibility."

"I feel like crying."

"For whom?"

"I guess for me."

"Because you got dumped, caught, and convicted, or because you understand the pain you caused her? Do you just feel bad for you?"

"Yeah."

"Maybe that's why she left you in the first place—because she sensed being used as a 'part,' not joined with as a 'person.'"

"I guess I'm still kind of girl crazy. I like meeting a lot of women."

"Girl crazy means you don't have much purpose in life. Conquest, which is constant motion, becomes primary when there is anxiety about inner content. It's like *winning* something actually means you *earned* and can *sustain* it. But, you know that's not true."

"I guess I just haven't been enjoying life very much."

"Well, Tom, making sure you keep any woman just won't build you a happy life."

"Mmmm."

Acting like the authority by stalking, threatening, or demanding doesn't make you an authority in any true aspect of life. It generally gets you feared, hated, dumped, and even incarcerated. I know, I know, most of you don't go that far with women when you're trying to define or assert your importance to the world. An intermediary behavior is feigned stupidity ("Gee, I didn't know that's what would happen"), more commonly known as passive-aggressive behavior.

Trent's call was a classic case of passive aggression. He and his wife both choose to work full-time, despite having small children. After the holidays, they both had to get back to their regular schedule. His wife left early, while he waited for the baby-sitter to show up. To "kill time" he decided to do all the laundry and fold the clothes. "Inadvertently," he ruined all her delicate sweaters by washing them in hot water and drying them under full heat. She came home and had a fit, claiming that he did this on purpose.

"Would you say that you have a history of doing some unpleasant things and not quite owning up to them?" I asked.

"I would confess to that in a variable sense," he admitted (?).

"Variable sense means a lot of times yes, right? Then she has some reason to assume that you 'stuck it to her again'?"

"I think there is some grounds for that. But, what frustrates me is that I can look her in the eye and say that I didn't do that on purpose and she won't believe me!"

"Gee, Trent, that seems to surprise you."

"Yes, it does. I'm a well-meaning husband frustrated that I can't get to work because the sitter has not shown up when my wife's already gone to *her* job. . . . "

"And you're feeling angry about that and you 'even it up' by ostensibly doing something good and accidentally doing something bad."

"Well, there was some underlying hostility, but my primary motivation was to do some good with the time. My wife thinks I'm frustrated because she's working and not at home taking care of these things. We have a child with autism and I have a wife on anti-depressant medication and I have a lot of pressure."

"Trent, the issue with this passive yet aggressive behavior is that it is an attempt to deal with powerful feelings like hurt, anger, and frustration without bringing them to the fore. Whether it's because you think you can't because your complaints aren't really reasonable, because you're afraid to admit that you're simply overwhelmed, or because you can't see how to make anything better so you're just trying to 'get by' instead of making serious changes."

Frankly, Trent is reasonably overwhelmed by problems worthy of producing that exhaustion. It is too typically male to try to "make it all happen anyway"—you know, don't complain and full speed ahead! Well, in addition to the aforementioned addictions/affairs/abuse, there is also striking back without it being too noticeable so that you can get one shot in without paying for it. Is that moment of veiled revenge worth the loss of potential to do something more substantially positive? I hope not—that's just plain babyish behavior.

I'm Not Squeezing Your Neck—I Just Have to Hold On to Something!

Then there are those times and circumstances when your "manly need to be in charge" is simply your last-ditch attempt to feel like any kind of man at all. In other words, whatever you've used to define your manhood, be it health, wealth, power, activity, or importance, has vanished, and now dominating those who are available and unaware is your ticket back to potency, their ticket to hell.

Mike, forty-five years old, called about his problems with

his second wife. He began with this incredible background: He has a twelve-year-old son, whose custody he fought for in the courts for seven years, and won a year ago. Seven months later his ex-wife died of an overdose of illegal drugs. A month before her death, Mike married a thirty-five-year-old woman with three boys of her own, ages seven, nine, and twelve.

"They were all without a man in their lives for five or six years," Mike informed me. "I guess they're not used to having a man around, for discipline, and I kind of run a tight ship. Since we've been married, the in-laws and my wife tell me that I'm showing partiality to my son and being harder on her kids. They punch and push each other."

Well, it turns out that Mike's son has been acting like a "show-off" at school, stealing from stores and playing dice on school grounds. Mike said he "knew nothing" about all of this, and only last night confronted his son, who confessed the behaviors. Mike has had his son in "grief counseling for six months," and said that that's also when he first noticed a subtle change in his kid's attitude. Maybe, he suggested, he was more lenient on his own kid because of the boy's grief over his mother. I reminded Mike that in the same period he married a woman with three boys around his son's age and that was an added adjustment challenge for the boy.

So far, this call does not seem to make the point about Stupid Strength through inappropriate controlling, does it? Well, something remarkable happened at this point in the call with Mike. As I re-listen to a tape of that call right now as I write this, I'm not sure what told me to take Mike for a sharp U-turn with my next line of questioning . . . but, it was pay dirt.

"Mike, what do you think is the source of your anger?"

"I don't know that I am angry."

"Well, assume I'm right for a moment that you are angry. What's it about?"

"I'm angry that they [her boys] don't treat each other better and show caring and appreciation to each other."

"I don't think you'd be angry about that—try again. You're a forty-five-year-old man and this is where you are in your life. What are you angry about?"

"Maybe myself because I've been disabled for a year and a half and I'm trying to be rehabilitated. I've lost my vocation and I have to be re-trained. Maybe that's what it is, I think. I have a back injury. Maybe I'm a little disturbed with myself. Could that be?"

"Could be. It's not unusual for men who don't feel functional out there slaying dragons to feel less important and less powerful and try to muscle kids and wives, everybody, to try to 'feel' a sense of power. Of course, trying to get three boys between nine and twelve to stop roughhousing is like trying to hold back a tidal wave with only your nasal passages."

"Yeah."

"Instead of trying to muscle in concrete ways outside yourself, I think you need to sit down with your wife and admit to being Genghis Khan, but tell her that the reason is that you don't feel like a man, you don't feel whole, you don't feel powerful or important, nobody listens to you, and, 'I'm of no value and I'm going a little crazy here! I need help with this!'

"Mike, the whole family will rally to help you. But, if you hide the truth of your feelings and instead try to compensate for your feelings by being overbearing, they're all going to reject you. You're acting out just like kids do. Men and kids are similar in this regard because kids, who are not necessarily clear on what their feelings are, behave in impulsive ways in response to those feelings. Men, who won't permit themselves their feelings, also act out in indirect ways to try to fix or avoid those painful feelings."

I further suggested that Mike could help his son by clarifying that parallel between men and kids—for instance, telling the boy that he sympathized with his struggles (with divorce, mother's death, dad's remarriage, and stepbrothers), because he too was trying to cope (with divorce, custody battles, and single parenthood, ex-wife's death, remarriage, and responsibilities and a serious physical handicap). By showing his son that they were "in the same place," Mike could make a good connection with his boy. By admitting to his own inappropriate ways of handling the emotional stress, he could be a role model of coping skills for his son—and everyone would win!

Chris, a listener, came to this realization too late—his wife left him. This is what he had to say:

> *In recent years I have been domineering, overbearing, critical and controlling. Four years ago I experienced some financial upheavals. Two and a half years ago I got laid-off from a company I had been with for eight years. Then, last June I had congestive heart failure and almost died.*
>
> *I felt like I was losing control over everything: my finances, my job, my health . . . apparently I was. I was becoming angrier and angrier and my controlling behavior intensified. I think now that I was trying to control (my wife) because that is something I **still had control** over. What an idiot. I realize that this was just causing her to want to get away and now, ironically, there is one more crisis in my life.*

Don't *use* your loved ones for immediate gratification when life seems to "let you down." Do *use* your loved ones for support as you pick yourself up; they can help you accept and cope with some inevitable and painful realities of life.

It Ain't Me, Babe

However, you don't pick yourself up by stepping on the backs of your loved ones. That's what you do when you don't want to accept responsibility for your own weaknesses, mistakes, stupidity, wrongdoing—or don't realize that catastrophes are provided to everyone by life.

My listener, Ken, faxed me his "just in time" revelation about just this sort of blaming behavior:

We began to grow apart, so to speak. Listening to you made me take an important step before doing anything rash. . . . I decided to take a look at myself, instead of trying to just blame my wife for everything. Much to my chagrin, I realized that in fact, most of what was going on had more to do with me than with her! Once I took responsibility for what I should have been doing to keep the marriage healthy, a very productive dialogue ensued, and a much more cooperative and loving environment resulted.

Ken was "man enough" to accept personal responsibility for being a co-architect of the monumental mess his life had become. That realization and that admission, along with his obvious "heart," gave him the power to change things.

Then there was the fax which truly disappointed me. This man (unsigned) clearly hadn't made a leap in maturity, courage, or heart:

I heard you say something on your show recently that has really appalled me. I am a man. I am so disappointed in you, I feel like crying. I feel hopeless that women will ever understand men. I mean, if you don't understand this, what woman will? My stomach feels like lead.

The situation in your call was that a woman in her upper twenties was engaged to a man in his mid thirties. She went on a trip and before she did she asked him to reassure her that he had stopped using the internet "chat" rooms (to talk to women, etc.). He did use the internet chat room, and her fears became reality (she checked the computer and found evidence that he was "relating" to another woman).

His wanting to meet someone else was about as predictable as the sunrise! She had no right to forbid him to use the chat room. Don't you, a psychotherapist, know that the number one thing a man needs from a woman is trust? He needed trust from her, but she treated the thirty six year old man like a child.

I have no problem believing this man is a completely trustworthy man before this incident. Their relationship is probably over, as it should be. This woman will never meet this man's needs. He would be crazy to marry this woman. Yet, you made him out to be the bad guy.

She will meet another man and do the same to him, and the next guy will suddenly turn out to be "untrustworthy" too. Look, she has the problem. She is not trusting. He will, I'm sure, go on to find a woman who trusts him. She will never find a man worthy of her trust. Why? Because it is impossible for a man to be worthy of her trust if she has no trust.

I remember the television comic Flip Wilson playing a character determined to get his own way and do whatever he wanted. When caught, he would proclaim, "The devil made me do it!" What makes the above letter scary, is that the writer seriously implies that the behavior of pseudo relationships and anonymous flirting via the Internet was somehow *caused* by her lack of trust. Amazing deflection of responsibility. The truth is, the guy got caught.

It is pathetic at best when anyone betrays his spoken word in a "real relationship" and runs to the convenient anonymity of a "computer relationship," where he can type in any reality he'd like. The man's wife was right not to trust him. She was only wrong in trying to change him. Our letter writer is also wrong if he seeks to shift responsibility from the man's own fears and weak character to any behavior of his wife's.

So, men, enough of the "I wouldn't have done it if she

- "trusted me"
- "believed me"
- "didn't upset me"
- "did what I wanted"
- "was nicer/loving/sexual, etc."

You do what you do because you choose to. It's as simple as that. And, even assuming your woman hasn't been "ideal," you are not entitled to revenge, reciprocal hurt, breaking of vows and covenants, or breaching of morality. No disappointment, rage, frustration, or hurt removes your responsibility to be the best, most honorable man possible.

Don't use women as a scapegoat for your inadequacies.

"I'd Be Okay If You Were Better"

Not all our reasons for choosing a mate have to do with kismet. Too often you pick a partner *because* of an urgent need to feel better about yourself, when you just simply aren't entitled to! For example, I've asked many a caller with "low self-esteem," "What have you done which is of value? Which you admire yourself for?" I'll get back some nonsense about how smart or good-looking they are. I then remind them, "That's genetic. What have you done on the face of this earth which would make another human being grateful you're here?" I'll get back, "Well, ahh, nothing, I guess." "Then," I'll challenge, "why should you have self-esteem? You haven't **yet** (hint, hint) earned it."

Instead of "earning it," some of you men get weak, young, naïve, sweet, etc., women to dominate and criticize—poof! Instant superiority? Hardly. Read this fax:

> You mentioned on your program today that you wanted to hear from men who were critical of their spouse, and I had to laugh because you were talking about me. I married my wife at age nineteen, she was eighteen. We had a darling boy six months later (I do not say that proudly). I always criticized my wife. I only saw the bad things in her, and magnified everything she did as a bad thing. There was not a thing she could do that made me happy. I am now in a 12-Step program because I was an alcoholic, drug addict, and later progressed on to being a wife

beater. Now, I've found that I had my glasses on backwards. (It was me.)

In this same context, I took a call from Chance, twenty-two, married with a one-year-old baby. He called complaining that his wife has gained weight and he's starting to abuse her verbally and doesn't want to go anywhere with her because she doesn't look good anymore. Initially, I went in circles with him about the superficiality of some younger men wanting "hot chicks" on their arms in order to look masculine and studlike. (You know, the woman other men see you with somehow projects the size of your penis.) I talked about "mature love" which accepts changes and challenges. Blah, Blah. Somehow, it didn't feel to me that we'd discussed the "real problem"—so I kept probing, and finally:

"Chance, what are you *really* unhappy about in your life?"

"Well, we only make minimum wage and life is such a struggle."

Bingo! Chance felt frustrated at "not having more success/money/status/power." The struggle of adult responsibilities wasn't "fun" either, and he was "striking out," not at life, but at his wife. He didn't feel like a "man," so to compensate he told her she was less of a woman. Ouch.

It is also true that even when things with your woman are good, that her "appearance" makes you feel less than other men who have great-looking babes. Jeff, thirty-six years old, is married and has a two-year-old daughter. While he admitted to loving his wife, and feeling good about the family, he was still struggling and suffering with something. He was bemoaning having married "beneath his station" ethnically and culturally. He said he felt angry and hurt.

"Jeff, how do the differences between you hurt you?"

"She's not living up to my expectations."

"She's making you *look* bad?"

"Ohhh. Mmm. Yeah, I guess that's true."

"Jeff, my man, you might be sacrificing what truly makes you happy inside as a man for the rest of your life based upon what you think you're supposed to have to compete with other men."

(Long dead silence) "Ahah!"

Guys, don't get caught in that trap of sacrificing what really makes you feel good by believing that it is through how your women "look" that you derive competitive standing with other men—and thereby become "more of a man." Other men aren't bearing your babies and taking care of your soul . . . are they?

To zero in on the main concept threaded throughout these stories: When you draw on your *anger strength* instead of your *vulnerability strength* you create your own minefield to dance through. First of all, anger isn't really strength; its defensiveness, fear, uncertainty, immaturity, and hurt posing as something seemingly strong—and additionally, it's only temporary. Criticism, yelling, and violence are ultimately poor, ugly, immoral, and illegal substitutes for inner strength. Vulnerability strength is the willingness to face personal shortcomings and fears (real or otherwise), and in so doing to gain the ability to get and be better. Don't give up that long-term opportunity for short-term pseudoglory.

Without owning up to vulnerability (fears, needs, dependencies), the world can become an ever more scary place. Listen to this from Nick:

> I am overbearing or controlling (whatever) because it seems like I have to keep on the top of everything because I don't want to give the devil an opportunity. The funny irony is that I would generally very much prefer to get along with everyone, but it seems like things come out of the woodwork unexpectedly when it comes to interactions between people, and sort of like physics, actions not only cause reactions but also seem to demand reactions.

A fear of or discomfort with people and the unpredictable challenges of life is normal! But thinking the only way to face that fear and discomfort is distance, isolation, and relying only upon yourself leads, as Nick's letter ended, to a sense of life that *"seems like some sort of cruel joke, that to me doesn't really seem all that entertaining."*

Men, don't go it alone, and don't go through it like a puppy dressed up in a grizzly bear costume. There's so much more you could be, do, and enjoy. Don't hide the truth of who you are and what you need behind Stupid Strength. If you do, no matter what woman you're with, you'll feel profoundly alone.

Yeah, Well, That's Easy for You to Say!

Perhaps this all does sound somewhat "easy to say, impossible to do." But that's only true if you don't engage your thinking in the possibilities, and if you aren't willing to take any risks or suffer any discomforts in making a transition in your current style of dealing with issues of "appearances" of strength, to the truth of your situation and need. Here are two major guidelines for making the transition successfully.

GUIDELINE 1: AVOID UNNECESSARY COUNTERATTACKS

In work, in public, in friendships, and with family, you are confronted with situations which annoy, anger, or threaten you. What you have to decide with each and every challenge is how to respond, how to protect yourself, fight back, overcome the enemy, and score the final victory. One letter from a retired Marine officer gave more subtle focus to this concern. He wrote, "I always ask myself: is this the hill I want to die on? Man, if that doesn't ever give you incentive to pause and reflect on the ultimate importance of the 'potential skirmish at hand.' I'll bet that more often than not, your answer will be 'no.'"

John, a listener, confirmed my assumption with his letter:

This letter is to say, "thank you!" I wrote you a couple of months ago with a dilemma about my father and his ex-wife (not my mom) and girlfriend. Well, to make a loooong story short, he passed away two weeks ago. I had doubts about going to his funeral, because of the very ill feelings about his behaviors and the ugly pressures I'd gotten over from various family members because I refused to have a relationship with him.

The day of the funeral I decided to go, not to be there for "him," but to support the pain of my siblings. Before we left, my wife asked me if I were nervous. I told her, "I wasn't going to pick any fights," and that I was going to pull a "Dr. Laura, by just being polite."

I met with the entire family at the funeral, and didn't go in with a chip on my shoulder, but instead with a "wait and see" attitude.

The looks I got from some people could have "killed," but I just decided to not let it bother me. And the people who did come up to say snide remarks were in shock when I simply said, "I'm sorry you feel that way. But, I did have my reasons and feelings about this matter and I would rather not share them with you at this time."

Normally, I would have jumped down their throats and taken a bite! But, I was glad with the outcome of "just be polite." Thank you for that tool, Dr. Laura. It was the best thing to do.

Men, choose carefully the "hill you want to die on." You don't always have to exert your strength.

GUIDELINE 2: MOVE YOUR LIPS FOR OTHER THAN WHISTLING OR YELLING, I.E., LEARN TO TALK IT OUT.

You men don't like to be caught with your proverbial "pants down." If your woman sees you struggling or failing, your narcissism (founded in a fear of not being admired or loved if you aren't perfect) causes you to lash out. My listener Glen's father would "slug" his mother when she wanted to help him with his frustrations, or asked him to "talk about it."

While I'm not the least bit impressed with Dad's solution (so much so that I haven't talked to him in five years), Mom would still have her teeth if she would have shut up. Surprisingly, I've seen the same sort of thing brewing between my wife and me. I'd be working on my semi-tractor or on the computer and something would go wrong. She would then start talking to me about it (which is just what I didn't want to do). I'd tell her it was no big deal. However, after seeing me take the sledge hammer to my truck, needless to say, she wouldn't believe me. She wouldn't drop the subject. Before long I would start yelling at her.

I was a little surprised yesterday when during one of these outbursts my dog approached me for a hug. I gave him one, told him he was a good boy and scratched his belly. Then I went back to yelling at my wife. This really made her mad ("You love your dog more than you do me!") Later, after she went to bed in a rage, I was able to reflect on the matter. I don't love my dog more than I do her. But, my dog never forces me to talk about things I don't want to talk about and think about things I'd just as soon forget.

Today I explained this to my wife. She listened. It's been a great day and I've really enjoyed being with her. Only time will tell if it continues, but I sincerely hope it does.

What Glen's insight lacks is the admission of his need to "look good" in his wife's eyes (whereas he knows his "dawg" doesn't make such judgment), and of his allowing her to "minister" to him when he knows he's being a baby/jerk (her "helping" just emphasizes his silly behavior to himself), as well as an acknowledgment that he is restoring his personal sense of power, strength, and competency by "taking off after her."

Once you're aware of your narcissistic weaknesses, however, it is fair to explain them to your woman (at a quiet, less emotionally charged time) and let her know that you will talk when you're feeling less nuts!

N.B., your woman isn't judging you by your computer prowess; she is judging you by how you treat her!

Calling AAA for Help Is Not "Auto-Castration"

What do Rambo, Terminator, 007, The Saint, all fictional male heroes, have in common? Simple. Not one of them ever calls 911 or the Orkin Man. They always have the knowledge and ability required to win no matter what the circumstances. Howard, a listener, admits to a more profound truth:

> *My behavior of choice is to be blaming and judgmental. I notice that when I am "out of control" with something at work, with a friend, family member, my weight, etc., I tend to not allow myself to be "out of control" by doing nothing or letting things just be the way they are. Now, when I use the phrase "out of control," I don't mean typical raving lunatic male obnoxious behavior. What I mean is that I know inside that I have no power over an outcome or situation that is in front of me that day. I am frustrated that my own resources are limited. What I have found is that I am usually only powerless until I use other resources outside of myself. In other words, I have to ask someone else how to handle a situation that I know very little about resolving.*
>
> *It is in that moment when I have made that mental decision to either utilize the resources I have, or get new ones if needed, or—be frustrated, confused, angry at myself and turn on my wife with my judging and blaming her for behavior that is not any different than, say, yesterday. But, yesterday I wasn't faced with my inability to solve a problem on my own.*

Gosh, guys, even the President of the United States has a Cabinet of experts to use as a resource. What makes you think/feel that the only way to masculinity, love, and respect is solitary perfectionism? You may have painted yourself into that corner by choosing a princess (notice how these princess women are "helpless" yet relentlessly "demanding"?) for your wife, one who gives you grief when you trip or fall because her "comfort level" is being threatened.

The incredible irony here is that it is *only the women* in this style of relationship who are seen as *dependent*. In truth, you men who play these excessively or unilaterally controlling and responsible roles are actually revealing *your* overly dependent natures! You figure that if you have a woman who cannot function without you, and to whom you supply all needs, wants, and relationship interactions, you will be safe from losing her—safe from being abandoned, rejected, or alone.

Maybe, if you could admit your need for a woman's companionship and assistance through life, you'd be better prepared to develop yourself into a truly attractive (in terms of behavior and spirituality) man able to attract a truly wonderful (competent and feminine) woman. But, therein lies the "rub": in "locker room mentality," isn't admitting to needing and wanting a woman for other than a good *schtup* kind of admitting to being a wuss or a momma's boy? "Real men" don't need women except for sexual release, right? Wrong. Be careful about living your life through the eyes of the wrong kind of men.

A woman's love, companionship, comfort, support, and cooperation give your life purpose and meaning, depth and satisfaction. That's just a fact. If you think denying that reality makes it go away, you're wrong again—wrong and running on empty.

Warning: Don't Try This at Home

There is yet another behavioral area where Stupid Strength gives your weakness away: when Stupid Strength takes the form of verbal intimidation and/or physical violence. This is because while you're afraid to admit to your "need" for your woman, that need is so great that you live in fear of losing her and disintegrating. What happens when you need her, won't admit it, and live in terror of losing her? You may try to demean her, and discourage her from doing things or having people in her life which might pull her away from you. You may strike out with physical violence, projecting your self-hatred outward onto her, and terrorizing her into not leaving you.

Men, there is an immeasurable difference between simply not leaving you and actually loving you. You can be a tyrant to avoid the former. You have to be lovable to gain the latter.

Dr. Amy Holtzworth-Monroes, a psychologist at Indiana University, having extensively reviewed existing studies on battering, concluded (in the *New York Times*, 6/22/94), "The majority of men who strike their wives are violent only once or very infrequently." She also noted, "These men are frequently dependent on their wives and fear being rejected. Their fears can lead to intense arguments, but if they become violent, they feel bad afterwards." Her report continues by stating that these men could benefit from ordinary therapy and don't want to be violent.

The second type of men are "hypersensitive to signs of abandonment, and become very jealous and preoccupied with their wives. . . . Any sign that she'll abandon him triggers violence." Such men "need intensive therapy to change deep-seated jealousy and abandonment fears."

The third type, the "antisocial" men, "were among the most vicious in their brutality, the most emotionally abusive and most calculating in using violence to instill fear in their wives." These most violent of abusers are generally beyond repair, and are not likely to be reading this book.

It is only fair to point out that many hands-on therapists report scenarios other than the stereotypic "big bad man." Valorie Gibbs, a social worker, wrote in the *Detroit Free*

Press (August 1, 1996), "I have worked with thousands of families, and only twice have I seen the one-sided male/female relationship in which a terrorized, defenseless woman is beaten into helplessness and submission by her partner. Usually, the reality is that both partners are equally aggressive, verbally and physically. . . . I expect my daughter not to tolerate being abused, but it is equally important that she not verbally belittle or hit anyone—not even a guy."

Nonetheless, men are bigger and can do more damage. Additionally, you cannot blame your behavior on the inappropriate behavior of others. Chris, a listener, is now separated from his wife and three children. He accepts responsibility for his battering:

> *I would rationalize it as my wife's fault. I have learned through group and individual counseling that I chose to react to negative situations; it was not my wife's fault for the abuse. I feel that I cannot reconcile with my wife, as it would be an unsafe atmosphere because of the way my wife handles stress: she yells, pounds on the table, stomps around the house, slams doors and drags our kids around by the arm. I cannot be around that, as it could be a temptation for me to do what I know is wrong; and because I love my kids and wife, I cannot be abusive again. In part, my marriage is over because my wife feels she is blameless. In my case, almost all of the abuse was intimidation and trying to gain control of my life, and now that I have control, I have no family. That is very hard for me to take, but also a consequence. I hope that women can take responsibility (for their own behaviors and for reacting the first time male abuse happens so that help can be gotten) and that men do the same and own up to what is abominable behavior.*

Bill Sherman, a listener, who is fourteen years in recovery as a batterer and has been working with battering men for over seven years, says that

*Violence is clearly a choice or decision, one of which men use to regain their loss of control, authority and services. It is my experience that **men's violence is not a matter of learning how to manage their anger, so much as to learn how to be intimate with their other feelings, such as being afraid or sad.** (Anger is more familiar and "masculine"?) Violence is learned behavior and can be replaced with assertiveness, communications, feeling and impulse management, and acceptance of the reality that we do not have the right to control others.*

To the Victor Go the Spoils

In talking about "services" Bill brings up an important concept—that is, a sense of "male entitlement" which demands a certain "treatment." Historically, when a battle is over, the soldiers steal the gold and rape the women, sometimes in the drunkenness of conquest, sometimes to humiliate the indigenous population to keep them in control (as the Bosnian Serbs did to the Muslim women).

Well, some of you men, guarding your obviously insecure masculinity and importance to the world, think that dominating women and children establishes your kingdom. You therefore feel superior to your mate, demanding services from her (domestic and sexual), while not treating her as an equal, nor respecting her needs, thoughts, and judgments, thereby ultimately dismissing her. You guys know who you are . . . and remember . . . despots are not loved, are generally undermined, and are eventually disposed of when the time seems right. Is that the destiny you wish to write for yourself?

Read this checklist, paraphrased from the Project for Victims of Family Violence, Arkansas, to see if there are any characteristics which seem familiar from your own behaviors:

- Pushes for quick involvement (instant intimacy just isn't possible; an immediate sense of attachment and belonging is a sign of unhealthy dependency needs)
- Jealousy and controlling (constant contact and inquisitiveness about activities; keeping the money/car; demanding she ask you for permission for activities)
- Unrealistic expectations (she must be perfect and meet all your needs or you're disappointed and angry)
- Isolation (you must be the center of her universe, a universe with no other planets allowed)
- Blames others for problems and mistakes and feelings (only others mess up your life or cause you to do or say the things you do)
- Hypersensitivity (easily bruised or insulted)
- Cruelty to animals and children (often seen as gross impatience with normal child or animal behavior and characteristics; 65 percent of spouse/partner abusers will also abuse children)
- Verbal abuse (critical, degrading, cursing, blatantly cruel and hurtful things said, ugly names, etc.)
- Threats of violence (intimidation with threats of physical violence and death directed at spouse or children . . . often later dismissed as temper)
- Rigid roles (dictating of wife/husband responsibilities without mutual agreement)

You don't need to be doing all or most of the above list to benefit from checking your behavior against an honest inventory of your behavior, especially under stress. These are all acts of Stupid Strength.

Sometimes a woman will "kiss you off" early on, which could be a terrific wake-up call. Peter, a caller, got a "Dear John" letter from such a woman. She lives only five blocks from his house, but has informed him that she doesn't want to see him anymore because he's been oppressive and smothering with his needs, which have "bordered on coercive and pressure and has caused her stress." She was polite (more typical female posture even under threat) in her letter, and to let him off "gently," offhandedly suggested that she might feel differently in the future, but as for now, the situation was "nonnegotiable."

Peter called me because it hurt him to see her with her kids and not be part of them anymore. "I don't know how it got to this. Everything was going great."

Can you imagine. This woman was distressed enough to call Peter's behaviors oppressive, coercive, and stressful, but he thought everything was going great? How is that possible? It's possible when the mutual well-being is of no interest to you, and only your own need for attachment counts; when you don't care to look and accept the truth of your impact on others, whose needs and feelings are of no real importance to you.

"Peter, you ignored her. You have no empathy for anyone other than yourself. You ignored her needs and feelings. You ignored and denied her feelings of dismay with your behaviors. You were so afraid of rejection and loss that you believed that what you didn't see, know, or respond to would simply stop existing. You were wrong. And now you're alone."

"I want to tell her I've changed. I want to call her."

"Peter, you haven't changed. First, nobody changes their personality and mental health status quite so spontaneously. Second, she argues that you are oppressive because of your needs. Your answer is to oppress her with your needs. See? Nothing has changed. Take this as a warning or wake-up call. No healthy woman is going to tolerate your behavior, and an unhealthy woman is only going to descend into darker depths with you. Please, Peter, get some professional help."

Your family is your foundation. When you attack (abuse) or retreat (substance abuse or silence) from your foundation because you fear ridicule, rejection, or abandonment, you lose the very core of what you need as a man and as a unique individual who can survive and live a life of joy and fulfillment. Don't be that stupid.

Finally—Not So Stupid

In conclusion, I offer this letter from a forty-eight-year-old male, married, a father and a grandfather:

I have a reputation as being impatient, loud and insistent upon my own way. Pretty much a red neck.

I've never understood this behavior on my part. My wife is terrific, and there are no "buts" following that statement. She just is. My sons are loving and trusting. I have most everything a man could want from life.

Today you made a statement on the radio that I heard in passing. It was as though you had reached out of the radio and slapped me. My eyes literally stung and teared so badly I had to pull over (I was in my truck, leaving a service call at the time).

That statement was that, "Anger is usually the expression of fear." It was as if someone had allowed me to see for the first time. It wasn't a sudden revelation. Over the period of most an hour, I thought of things I've said and done to everyone in my life and I now realize was an expression of fear.

Fear is the last thing anyone who knows me would think me capable of. I now realize it's probably the way I feel most of the time.

Now, thanks to you, I'm going to have to do something about it. Once again, you have forced someone to face reality and put aside the B.S. This is a tough thing for me to do. I'm sure my wife and kids will like it when I eventually work it all out. They liked it when I quit drinking eleven years ago. They like it when I stopped smoking at the same time—but neither of these things were easy.

As you say, though, the right thing is seldom easy. Somehow,

I fear facing my fear more than the bullets in Vietnam, being on my own at 15, or anything else I've ever done.

If there is anything I can say in my defense, my fear has never taken the form of physical abuse. I've handed out lots of emotional abuse though.

Thanks for getting me started.

5

STUPID SEX

Q: Why do many men tend to give their penis a nickname?
A: They wouldn't want some of their most important decisions to be made by a complete stranger.

ANONYMOUS

I'm female. I never had brothers. Nonetheless, I remember being curious about "what boys had" ever since I saw a piece of artwork depicting one naked. When I was in second or third grade, I brainstormed with girlfriends about what boys did with "it": Was it rolled up or accordionlike when not "in use"? (At this point in my development, "in use" only meant urination.) I was the one elected to ask, so I randomly picked out a male classmate and boldly went where no other girl had dared to go before—he freaked, turned bright red, and ran away.

The only comparable curiosity that men (and women) have about the female anatomy revolves around the vagina being a "potential space," not an actual tunnellike canal, i.e., like a flattened mitten, the vagina has internal volume only if something goes inside it. Now when we girls first learn about menstruation and tampons, this space concept is a big issue: the diagrams literally show a canal into which the tampon is inserted. While this may be an interesting curiosity, the vagina simply does not hold the fascination for women that the penis holds (pun intended) for men.

Once when my son was about two years old, he noticed that I, his momma, did not have a penis: gasp! He grabbed himself, worrying aloud about what happened to mine and would the same thing happen to his! Oh no! Panic! I thought this remarkable, since he was not yet aware of his penis as a "sexual organ" or a symbol of power and potency. Frankly, I thought that at the tender age of two, the penis must be a navigation and balance tool, boys are always holding on to it while they walk.

I asked my girlfriends about their daughters' responses to noticing that a dad or brother had a penis when they didn't. Universally the little girls' reaction was one of mild curiosity, with no concern at all that they didn't have one, nor any requests to get one. No concrete evidence for penis envy there!

My next mother-toddler penis event was when my son first became aware of an erection. He proudly came running out of the bathroom, pointing excitedly at his penis and crowing, "Look, Mom, penis tricks!" He thought it was wonderful that this thing changed sizes, sometimes tickled when he was in an elevator, and generally felt good to just hold when in the tub or going to sleep. I began to see how very central this small (oops, don't mean to be insulting) percentage of a man's total body was to his existence, well-being, and identity.

This fact is highlighted in Berkeley Breathed's syndicated cartoon *Outland*. He depicts several male "creatures," all hanging out with beers telling dumb-woman jokes: "Hey, how do you know if a woman has been working at a computer?" "How," asks one of the other males. "There's 'white-out' on the screen!!" he responds, as they all howl with laughter. Having overheard the joke, an approaching woman calls, "You dumb hypocrites. You mock the half of humanity that makes your graceless existence bearable. *Men should pause for one moment and take another long hard look at the very thing that brings meaning to their meaningless lives,*" she snarls as she walks off. The men are first frozen in their tracks. Then, in unison, they all check their pants.

Most mothers teach their sons to call their penis a pee-pee partly as a reminder of what and where and how they are supposed to use it so they won't wet their pants anymore; partly because most people can't handle the correct names for things; and—not so incidentally—because they're putting off the notion of their sons becoming the sex-crazed young men they themselves had to fight off as young girls.

The penis's dual-use reality (urination/intercourse) is a real kick to try to explain to a five-year-old boy. It was at that point that I started to explain biology, love, marriage, and reproduction (note the order of things, please) to my son. When I got to the "penis goes into the vagina to deliver sperm" part, my son became concerned about how a "pee-pee" could know which job to do when. I explained that his brain and nerves would make the right choice without his having to give it much thought.

How *IS* a Man Different from a Bug?

Face it, the biology of male sexual functioning doesn't require much conscious thought. The biology of the system works for small bugs, bison, and bullfrogs—none of which have ever had to call a sex info line for directions and suggestions. The complexities for a man (as distinct from a male) come from these *facts*:

• Whereas biology calls for simple sperm (genetic) dispersal, developing human beings require persistent, intense relationships with the male parent to thrive as confident and constructive members of a community and society.

- Whereas biology calls for immediate relief and gratification of sexual tensions, human beings develop greater self-respect and sexual regard for others when they feel they are masters over their urges, not the other way around.
- Whereas biology calls for immediate relief and gratification of sexual tensions, thoughtful men consider the consequences of inappropriate emotional attachments (hurts of the heart—hers as well as his), sexually transmitted diseases (hurts of the body), and unwanted children (hurts to the innocent).
- Whereas biology provides the beauty and excitement of sensual and sexual pleasures, men ultimately realize that the real thrill comes from the love and acceptance from a woman in a committed relationship.
- Whereas biology provides the initial feelings of rapture and infatuation, men, by virtue of their obligation to their woman and their children, determine to trade serial rapture for the satisfaction of having someplace to feel safe, wanted, and valued for more than what their penis can supply.

Moving away from the biology does take thought; it also takes self-discipline, morality, values, and a courage to withstand the pressures of a male culture which is more biologically entrenched than is truly good for the being and soul of men. Sexual behavior which is not supportive of your being and your soul is Stupid Sex.

"Yeah, right," you're probably saying to yourself right now. "This woman [me] has lost her bean. A *real*, normal, healthy male is a constantly available erection looking for a place 'to happen'; a perpetually alert penis looking for new, exciting opportunities; a mere support system for an organ that'll lose its rhythm if it don't dance; a creature who doesn't really need a warm place to belong, just a 'warm place to put it.' That's a man!" That's a man? No, actually, that's an immature, out-of-control, erection-and-ejaculation-fixated guy who could only be a hero to those with no depth to their lives—or to other men excited by passion devoid of obligation and connectedness, i.e., who are drawn to their more animal male side.

Let's talk about that animal male side. First a letter from Bob, who took me to task about this very dichotomy between male (animal biology) and man (spiritual and civilized potential):

> On your show you dwell on the moral and religious aspects of human relationships, but ignore the most common laws of nature. Those of us who adore our dogs and cats sometimes use the expression that, "pets are people too!" Many of us must realize that, "people are animals too!" It's no accident that women are attracted to big, strong men with lots of money. Likewise, men are attracted to women with large breasts, a slim waist, and nice hips. Dr. Laura, it's called natural selection, replication of the species, and survival of the fittest. Didn't you take Biology a lot in undergraduate school?

I loved this letter, because it actually helps make my point! Yes, of course humans are animals, and in some ways are driven by built-in information with respect to sexuality. However, Bob's "expression" about "people being animals, too!" misses the point that animals *are not* people (no religion, culture, laws, morality, rationally conceived free will), and people, while not being plant or mineral, are certainly more than animal (in that we have the capacity and potential for philosophy, altruism, compassion, sacrifice, obligation, justice, etc., which is not a function of pure instinct, although, for obvious reasons, I often wish it were).

Instinctual behavior is difficult to change because it's "hardwired." Well, what may be natural in terms of male sexual behavior (fidelity, monogamy, promiscuity) isn't unchangeable. Any student of sociology and psychology can attest to the tremendous flexibility of the human mind and the powerful role of experience, learning, and values, in guiding each individual toward potential behaviors *in spite* of the drive to be and do what is *natural*.

Time magazine's August 15, 1994, cover story discussed the conclusions drawn from evolutionary psychobiology concerning human sexual behavior and love. The author, Robert Wright, says that men "are also more inclined toward the casual fling. Men are less finicky about sex partners. Prostitution—sex with someone you don't know and don't care to know—is a service sought overwhelmingly by males the world around. And, almost all pornography that relies sheerly on visual stimulation—image of anonymous people, spiritless flesh—is consumed by males. Many studies confirm the more discriminating nature of women."

A Sperm Is Worth a Thousand Words

Most scientists attribute this raging, impersonal male libido to men's nearly infinite potential rate of procreation. A female requires nine months to gestate, followed by a couple of years of breast-feeding and weaning, followed by a dozen and a half years of more nurturing till college and out of the nest! The male's single "biological" imperative is depositing sperm in as many available uteri as possible to increase and extend his gene pool possibilities into the future generations.

According to Mr. Wright, this lustful urge to intercourse and DNA insemination is magnified with male success. "The ultimate purpose of the wealth and power that men seek so ardently is genetic proliferation. Thus, it is natural that a rising corporate star, upon getting a big promotion, should feel a strong attraction to women other than his wife. Testosterone—which expands a man's sexual appetite—has been shown to rise in non-human primates following social triumphs, and there are hints that it does so in human males too. Certainly the world is full of triumphant men—Johnny

Carson, Donald Trump—who trade in aging wives for younger, more fertile models."

In other words, the more alpha males (successful, resourceful, powerful, dominant), due to testosterone-injected instinct, are biologically driven to procreate with younger, more fertile females to keep their "exceptional" genes going on and on. And, conversely, these are the guys to whom the young, fertile females are most receptive, also for biological reasons (resources to protect and provide for her offspring).

This is an area where biology, though true, significant, and powerfully driven must duel with morality. When what "is natural" is deemed "good," the fabric of lives begins to unravel: repetitive divorces and remarriages (serial polygamy), where men and women perpetually search for that "perfect love," doesn't necessarily produce perfection for themselves. And it definitely doesn't produce perfection for the children, whose lives grow fragmented and disconnected when parental bonds are destroyed. Think of the pain caused by the constant change and challenge offered by: visitation with parents with new spouses, children and extended families, and inattention of custodial parents lost in their fresh romantic love experience.

Evolutionary psychiatrist Randolph Nesse wrote that natural selection does not work toward overall social welfare, that much of human nature boils down to ruthless genetic self-interest, and that people are naturally oblivious to their ruthlessness.

Whew, *ruthlessness* is such a negative way of talking about sexual gratification, curiosity, and drive, isn't it? Maybe not. The next time you're feeling discontented (sexually or otherwise) with your spouse, and wonder what that other person might be like in bed (in car, on floor, in closet, in apartment or motel) think about the emotional, psychological, familial, financial, and social shrapnel-bomb whose fuse you light with an orgasm. One would indeed have to be ruthless to trade those moments of personal gratification for all that destruction.

The old saying that "men give love to get sex and women give sex to get love" actually has some foundation in the "biology." On the woman's side first: Giving "sex" to a man inspires the "hope" that this availability will keep him near; that when he produces children he'll feel "connected" enough to protect and provide while she nurtures. On the male's side: He talks of love to gain the opportunity to play Johnny Appleseed with his DNA. So what leads to **monogamy**, which as I wrote about earlier, **is in the best mental and physical health interests of men** (whether or not they wish to believe it).

Neither love nor sexual attraction is enough to ensure monogamy. Feelings of love and sexuality wax and wane with your blood sugar, moon spots, job success, hairline, etc. Although the current societal mentality doesn't support "hanging in there and working on it" during a period of "wane," partners in healthy and happy relationships discover that a deeper love and attachment is found in weathering those storms, not just setting out for a new place to anchor.

If love is therefore "not enough" to ensure monogamy, what does it take? Commitment. And that's where society, religion, and the state have let us down. Marriages are too easy to make (six to nine months mandatory premarital counseling should be the rule), and divorces are too easy to get (no-fault decisions leave spouses and children abandoned), and "shacking up," affairs, and promiscuous sexual relationships (even when small children are involved) are no longer severely stigmatized or critically judged.

What, you think I'm unrealistically cutting into your possibilities for fun? After all, you have a right to happiness and pleasure, don't you? Let me answer you with two points. First, surveys show men who are married and monogamous express more satisfaction with their sexual lives than single guys; and second, what may be your right isn't necessarily the right thing to do, and exercising your rights doesn't always build toward a happy, quality life all the way around.

Okay, enough "goody two-shoes" morality stuff. What's a guy to do with all those sexy thoughts? Over a dozen folks have faxed me a 1991 cartoon (by Jennifer Bemb) depicting "Thought Frequency as Pie Charts," comparing men and women. For women, relationship thoughts occupy about 70 percent of time, while the remaining 30 percent of thinking time is devoted to the following subjects: trashing men, aging, having to pee, things they shouldn't have eaten, food, pets, and sex. The men's pie chart had a distinctly different pattern. About 30 percent of thinking time dealt with career, another 30 percent with sports, another 30 percent with sex, and the final 10 percent was distributed between going bald, aging, and strange ear and nose hair growth.

While perhaps a bit silly, this cartoon does point out some real differences in "thinking issues" between men and women. No surprise here. But what do you guys do with all that "sex thinking" if it doesn't or can't lead to "sex acts"?

As Bud put it:

I find that adventurous sex is not responsible, nor very likely to happen for an average looking slim fellow who studies physics and computers (me). Without a physical outlet, a "healthy" man represses the desire for sex, and "hopefully" converts that energy into his work. Yet, I find that the longer I go without sex, the more I want it, to the point of creating neurosis. Dr. Laura, you wouldn't be blond, slim and looking for a new man in your life, would you??? I am trying to avoid—narrowly—the typical male action of turning his radio-counselor into a harlot. . . .

Oops, now, now, Bud, watch that! So, some of you men take those "sexy thoughts" and sublimate them: in other words, you use them creatively in "work" ways. But, my listener John's letter informed me that, especially for young men, restraint (male virginity is not prized) or sublimation (how much sports can you play or talk about?) isn't so easy:

> As a young man, I just turned thirty, I thought I'd clarify something from the male perspective. Young women believe that their boyfriends are "different"—that although the reality is that most 19 year old guys are uncontrollably horny, hers isn't. I think I can explain why she is mistaken:
>
> First, she must understand that in my years I have talked about women and sex with easily hundreds of teenage men, and I have to tell you, getting laid is easily the most common concern. To paint with a broad brush, the reason is two-fold: 19 year old boys are walking hormone bags, driven to scatter their seed as far and wide as possible; this is just basic biology.
>
> Second, 19 year old boys live, eat, breathe, and play with other 19 year old men. I guarantee that no matter what these boys actually believe and feel, they also compete with each other. Sex is one of the competitions.
>
> A decade ago, I swear, not a single one of my peers would admit to anything as damning as virginity (although I'm sure that the condition was secretly pandemnic). When a person pretends something enough, they begin to incorporate aspects of it. Nineteen year olds pretend to be studs.
>
> A third factor is that 19 year old boys are convinced on a number of things, which add together to make promiscuous sex a stronger probability: #1 is that they believe they are men. #2 is that they also believe that they will live forever, and that whatever they do is actually with the best of intentions and will have good results, etc., etc.
>
> Therefore, my direct statement to young women is this: he will tell you whatever he needs to in order to convince you to have sex with him. I guarantee it. It is also reasonably certain that he means every word of it when he says it. However, he has a secret master, and it lives between his legs.

Dennis, another listener, once lived that script and got a lot of action, but discovered something deeper about himself and life along the way:

While promising the moon, stars and anything else required to accomplish the task at hand which was sexual gratification, I continually lost sight of the most important things I should have been watching for: mutual respect, goals and ideas which combine well with spirituality, honesty and integrity. I have paid well for the sins of the skin and immediate gratification . . . and the pain I caused (others).

Lory, still another male listener, wrote me a lengthy letter, which gave further clarity to what is behind those "sex thoughts":

I think that men approach love-making similar to sports. I am not a fan of sports, but in my opinion, men enjoy the challenge, the conquest, and the triumph. Women approach love-making as an "environment", a "feeling", and consequently they need romance (to produce that environment). I think that men, especially when they are younger, just need "a warm place to put it." Then we like to go to sleep.

Men's sexual biology is compelling, and as we will see in this chapter, a profound struggle with respect to making the "natural" more "human" and the "banal" more "sublime."

Before I move on to issues such as promiscuity and affairs let's consider my listener Tom's contribution to the Ten Stupid Sexual Things Men Do to Mess Up Their Lives:

1. *Believing that the woman you meet in a bar has the potential to become the woman of your dreams*
2. *Basing the entire relationship on sex*
3. *Having sex without protection*
4. *Having sex without compassion*

5. *Having sex without commitment*
6. *Having sex without being in love*
7. *Having sex with the sister or best friend of a past partner*
8. *Believing that men and women think the same about sex*
9. *Not bothering to get to know her so you believe that she's someone she's not*
10. *Having sex without making them breakfast the morning after!*

Yeah, yeah, I know what you're thinking: "What's the harm of a little fun, a little thrill here, and bit of excitement there . . . if nothing bad comes of it?"

Well, guys, let's now explore the truth that sooner or later something bad always comes of it:

- spiritually
- emotionally
- medically
- socially
- legally
- financially
- embarrassingly

Too Little, Too Soon—Too Many Surprises

Jeff, a regular listener, recently sent me this fax:

> *I recently had an opportunity to become sexual with a woman whom I barely knew. With the little angel of Dr. Laura on my shoulder, I opted not to, and boy was I glad! Within another couple of days I found out she was a liar and a major flake. Of course, I made this decision based on the sense given to me by "Mother Laura". Thank you, dear friend!*

So what is my point here? It's not okay to "drop anchor" just anywhere *only* because you don't know what's infesting the waters? If she hadn't turned out to be a "liar" and a "flake," all would have been right with the world? That's like saying it was okay to steal because there was no chance of getting caught. Clearly there has to be a more profound basis for making decisions about our behaviors—and that basis is morality. The interesting reality about morality is that it is basically *pragmatic*. The interesting problem with morality is that its inherent pragmatism takes time to reveal itself.

Pain Has Long Fingers and Much Patience

First, here's Brian's song:

> *My promiscuous teen life has been haunting me all of my married life. At about the same time I committed morally and spiritually to my wife, I received a phone call from a former girlfriend from high school. She never came out and stated the facts, she simply danced around the possibilities of what we could do together with each other and **the child**, who was then two years old! Torn between my love for my wife and the high probability that this was my child, she made the choice easy for me by not saying out-right that the child was mine. I still feel that it is my child, and as promiscuous as I was I can only pray that there aren't any more. The liberal upbringing I had will not be duplicated with my legitimate family.*

No matter what you men proclaim about women's responsibility for birth control, the availability of abortion, or the possibility of adoption, when you create children with a hole in their heart where a "dad" ought to be, something "bad" *has* come of it—although the pain is someone else's to suffer. Brian evidently feels "relieved" at "not knowing" if this is his child; the child will never feel relieved at not knowing who his dad is. It's crucial to remember that the pain you cause doesn't disappear simply because you decide to put it *behind you.*

If Brian had decided to follow through with paternity tests, child support, and visitation schedules (assuming the child is his), his life with his new family would be directed by that "past." For example, he wouldn't be free to move away; the family income would be subdivided; holidays and special occasions would become more complicated with the "two" families; the "legitimate" children would have to share time and emotional resources with the "other" child; the extended families would have to broaden their established boundaries to include the "other" child; his new wife would have to accept that her husband has another responsibility aside from her babies for her husband's and her attention.

That moment of mindless, passionate sex has the potential to dictate the rest of your life—if you are a responsible man. If you are not a responsible man, then you just desert and destroy. Which m.o. can you live with?

Don't give me arguments like, "She lied about birth control," or "She's a slut and it didn't mean anything so why should I have to be responsible?" or "She could have had an abortion," or "I always told her I didn't want to (1) marry, (2) have kids," or "It's not fair that the woman has all the power to decide birth, abortion, etc., so if I have no power I shouldn't have any responsibility!" Listen up, men. None of that is relevant to the requirements of the new life you created. When you "make a baby," it's the welfare of the child which matters, not petty, angry exchanges between the egg and sperm donors.

One of the most obnoxious "organizations" in this regard is the so-called National Center for Men (Fighting for Fairness and Equal Rights), centered in Old Bethpage, New York. Here is a quote from their press release dated December 11, 1995: "But men are routinely forced into parenthood. A woman has choice . . . a man has none. He has no voice and he is often forced to be responsible for her choice. She has control of her life and his. He has control of nothing."

The author of the above, Kingsley G. Morse, Jr., is upset that women can choose abortion or birth and that men are choiceless in that regard. With my double-barreled shotgun, I'd like to take both Mr. Morse and the pro-choice types out right now: the time of choice is intercourse. Both men and women choose to risk the possibility of conception at that moment. Once a man ejaculates in a woman's vagina, he's voluntarily entered the "made a choice zone"; and now nature determines the result. That the woman can legally terminate that life on a whim is a great sadness for humanity. That the man wishes to run and hide from his obligation to the child, wanted or not, is also a great sadness for humanity—and a tremendous disaster for that child (see chapter 8, "Stupid Parenting").

Ignorance Is Parenthood

"The lack of male involvement in birth control," according to a 1994 report published in the *New York Times,* "contributes to unplanned pregnancies, estimated to account for 40% of births." A Harris Poll for the Kaiser Family Foundation of Menlo Park, California, discussed in the same article, determined that "73% of the women said men were 'not responsible enough' to choose a birth control method, and nearly 70% of the men agreed. Both sexes said men were uninvolved because they 'don't care' and because they considered birth control the 'female's responsibility.'"

Teena, a listener, responded to a call I aired with this account of a young man who didn't want his girlfriend to abort their child:

I couldn't help but remember a similar discussion I had with my brother last week. You see, my brother has difficulty finding a girlfriend who is a "keeper" and at 32 he has that settling-down urge. His latest girlfriend started with hardly a day's conversation and they were in bed together. I told him that was his first mistake and I wouldn't consider having sex with a man until knowing and dating him for at least 3 months (he was flabbergasted and amazed)—and now, thanks to your sound statements on your radio program, I won't partake in sex at all until I'm married.

Anyway, I asked him how he could have sex with a woman when he's taking the chance of fathering a child. He said, "Well, I won't date a girl unless she's pro-choice." I said, "So, you won't have sex with a woman unless she's willing to abort your child?" He said, "Yes."

I think I was about to be sick and my heart sunk thinking my brother was so selfish about "putting-it-in" instead of more important couple behavior.

"What if she says she will abort and changes her mind after getting pregnant?"

He had no comment.

I told him I thought he'd better tell his dates his "let's have sex and then abort" policy.

He had no comment.

Thanks for encouraging me to think and act morally.

"Morally." There's that archaic concept, "morals." Why archaic? Because my caller Greg told me it was.

Greg had a "good-looker" girlfriend for four years. They recently broke up because of an ongoing problem: she thought he spent too much time with his jerky friends instead of alone with her. He recently started a new relationship with an easygoing woman who keeps herself busy so she doesn't mind his doing things with his buddies. However, she's not as attractive as the old girlfriend.

"So, Greg, you're finding out how superficial you are."

(Laughing) "Yeah, could be true. I have a hard time when we sexually get together."

"We're doing that already?"

"Actually, we've been dating for four months . . . so . . . yeah."

"Oh, gee, that's a long time."

"Well, I think in today's world that is a long time."

"That's sad. That makes the sex virtually meaningless."

"Maybe that's true . . . well, it isn't *that* meaningless. I guess the sex to me isn't that important. It's just part of the relationship, kind of like going out to dinner is part of the relationship."

"I think it's sad when sex gets demoted to that."

"We're not having children or anything like that."

"Honey, babe . . . next month you might!"

"Anyway . . . I just can't get as sexually excited about her as I did with the other girlfriend because she's not as pretty."

"Well, Greg, if for you the sex means nothing—it's just sex, then if the situation isn't very horny, you're just not going to 'get off' with as much enthusiasm. For people with a deeper, profound feeling about their partner, and a deeper meaning about sexuality, the sex comes out of the deep sense of love, affection, mutual experience, bonding, closeness— the turn-on then becomes the depth and quality of the relationship including the sexual relationship."

"So, you think I need to do a little maturing with regard to this thing?"

"Yes. When sex is not an expression of anything between you and your woman, then it is totally dependent upon impersonal issues like her attractiveness, wine, and fantasy."

"So, if I cut off the sexual relationship and try to develop what you're talking about I think she'd have a fit and say, 'What do you mean you're cutting off the sex?'"

"Do you want to develop yourself or not?"

"I want to develop myself."

"Then you have to tell her that at this point in your life you'd like sex to mean something. She'll deal with it whatever way she does and so be it."

"But how do I become less superficial?"

"The more that you think of sex in 'that way,' in other words, the more time you formulate your ideas in terms of purpose and meaning, and the more you direct your behaviors toward that end, the less superficial you will become. That's what morals provide for you—a sense of purpose and meaning, and a direction away from emptiness."

There is something wonderful about considering sex in a more "holy" or "moral" light. It gives the act greater magnificence, depth, and ongoing satisfaction than just getting horny and getting off.

It was Greg's last question which brought focus to an important concern:

"Do you think you can have as good sex when it's sort of an emotional thing like you're talking about versus when you go out with somebody who is a *Playboy* centerfold type?"

"Greg, when you go to a ball game or the mall, how many folks do you see who rate that level of attractiveness?"

"Not many."

"Do you think that they and their partners automatically aren't happy with their sex?"

"No, I guess that's not true."

"No, Greg, it's not true. Just today I received a fax from a man, married thirty-nine years, who describes his wife as 'not just my friend, but my best friend and lover. I have a love for her that is more to me than life—to me she grows more beautiful each year.' Greg, I doubt he said that because after thirty-nine years she looks more and more like a *Playboy* bunny."

After Greg's call, I wondered whether we had missed another point. You see, he had great sex with the first girlfriend—maybe not just because she was "attractive," maybe because being with him mattered. This new one is truly independent and doesn't much care how much time he spends away—maybe the lack of sexiness isn't from her less attractiveness, maybe it's because she doesn't seem to care as much. Yes, guys, having somebody care about you does matter to you.

One of my listeners, Tony, revealed that truth to me in this fax:

After years of "dating," infatuation, lust, one-night stands, failed relationships, etc., imagine my surprise one day while reflecting upon my "purpose" in all those exercises to find that all I wanted was to be close to someone. The more I thought about it the clearer it became. All that sex stuff was my way to get intimate (close) with someone (by the way, no children or STD's given or received—boy was I dumb lucky).

Now I know that all that superficial "closeness" is not what makes a good relationship. A friendship, with trust and respect, is what makes a good relationship. And that can't be developed instantly by jumping into bed. I'm 48 and it took most of those years to understand this for myself.

So now I see that many of those guys in many of those bars, picking up women to have sex, are really looking for the intimacy and closeness that sex seems to allow. And, for some of those "real men" tough guy types, sex is probably as close as they'll allow themselves to get to someone.

The secret is out! You men do need closeness, comfort, and the other blessings of intimacy. And, frankly, without them you are just a male, not a man. James, a listener, wrote to me about how developing the ability to be lovingly close was responsible for his transition into manhood.

James had his first sexual relationship in high school. He describes himself then as manipulative and self-serving, getting sexual gratification from his girlfriend on demand because she was dependent on him for self-worth. When they were freshmen in college, she became pregnant and aborted. He realizes now how difficult this must have been for her, especially since she was the adopted child of an unwanted pregnancy. After the abortion, James broke off with her and became self-destructive, involved with alcohol and promiscuity.

The last week of his senior year in college he met "the" woman. They dated long distance for two years.

We have a relationship based on trust, love, honesty and respect. She had the courage to say no when I was my worst, and somehow turned me into a man. Because of her respect for herself, her morals, and her ability to let me know that I was very important to her, but not worth losing herself over, I fell in love and gained great respect for her. Because of her strength she stayed a virgin til we married. I can only wish I could say the same.

In an age when society says that it's OK to have sex freely, that morals are for the radical fringe, and where living only for ones self seems to have no consequences, it's important to know that there is always a price to be paid for one's actions.

My high school sweetheart is still recovering from the trauma of the abortion I helped cause. I pray that she finds peace and someone to love and respect her as she so deserves. Oh yes, my child would have been five last May. I'll never forget.

I frankly rue the day female sexuality was "liberated" and the "double standard" became a sexist notion. Truth is that, all through the rest of the animal kingdom, the male has to put on one helluva display in order to convince a female to permit him to mate with her. When human females decided that there was no point being as choosy as a lowly guppy, humanity lost something.

A listener from the Midwest confirmed this concept:

I was careful not to father any kids or pass along diseases. I also drew the line to keep my displays of affection out of range of a woman's children. It ticked me off that some women didn't worry about this last point. I refused to bed an extremely lovely brunette once for this. She had four kids by three different men and her youngest (age two) asked if I were her daddy. How sad!

Thank you for encouraging your women listeners to return to a sexual "gold" standard. But, we guys need to also!

Yes sir, I do vote for that return to the gold standard for both men and women. It's interesting how many men are only now revealing that after the sexual feast comes emotional famine. David Maloof wrote in *Redbook* magazine (1/94) that he'd never "Move in Again": "Living together is just a modern, self-indulgent non-solution to an eternal challenge. It promises nothing—and it delivers. For living together's undeniable foundation is conditional love, and conditional love is not love—it's as oxymoronic as 'temporary permanence.'"

Truth be told, you guys need more than sex. You need love. You need caring. You need purpose and direction. You need connection. You need belonging. Don't settle for a quickie—that's stupid.

What I Need Is the Love of a Verrrrry Young Woman

At the beginning of this chapter I talked to you about the biology of the successful males (lots of resources) going after the fertile females (DNA dissemination centers). Well, for human males, with complex human psyches, it's even more complicated than that. To quote journalist and humorist L. M. Boyd, "Many a man who thinks he'd like to get rid of his early wife really wants to get rid of his early self. What such a husband seeks, says one matrimonial savant, is a partner who doesn't know him so well."

Let's face it, men, when your weaknesses, failures, unmet goals, personal shortcomings, and disappointments in life finally dawn on you, one quick-and-easy solution is to "fake it" by mesmerizing a silly young thing who thinks you're something else simply because you've got character lines on your face. She's so naïve, she thinks those character lines were earned, not just too much sun, booze, and age!

When a forty-seven-year-old man says he has a lot in common with a twenty-three-year-old girl, it means he's voluntarily retarded. Older men seek out younger women to impress others and convince themselves that they are something they aren't. It's a quick-and-dirty way to bring excitement into your life—proving that all your problems aren't truly "yours," because some young thing just adores you. Problem is that after a while the truth seeps through.

A listener, Jim, pointed that out:

"She" was 27, had a 5 year old daughter, hard worker, great mom. I was 47, 3 much older boys, 2 still at home, and fresh back into the dating game. What was I thinking . . . and what with? That part of my anatomy had a mind of its own for a while. Then I realized, where was the communication, the feed back, the common things we should share? I'm over the "shell-shock" of it all now. For a while I would have rather gone back to Viet Nam for a year than try to get a date—at least I knew what I was facing there.

That tendency toward escape and pretend is also the stuff affairs are made of.

Remember the "Never" in Neverland

During one of my newsbreaks in 1994, I received the following fax—which became the subject of my next hour's opening monologue:

I'm in my mid 40's and have known my wife for 17 years. My problem is that I think I've fallen in love with someone else or have I just fallen out of love with my wife? Am I going through that strange male 40's thing?

The girl I've fallen in love with is someone that I've had strong feelings for over many years. We've been good friends and flirt with each other but she doesn't know how I feel.

Nothing can happen because she is also married.

Sometimes I wonder, did I ever love my wife? We have a one year old baby and I feel I must stay in the marriage because the baby needs a father. My feelings say, "You no longer love this woman, run, get out, go somewhere!"

I married my wife because of her personality. I never had that great, heart thumping, infatuation for her. I thought our love would grow and that looks didn't matter. Such a noble thought, but I'm not sure it worked.

I need that heart thump and I need someone that has the heart thump for me.

Any ideas are greatly appreciated.

After reading the fax in its entirety, I described my recollections of the motion picture *Switch* with Ellen Barkin and Jimmy Smits. Initially, the main character is a rich, successful, blond, great-looking guy who lives on serial and parallel "heart thumps" by having exciting affairs whenever, wherever, and with whomever. He's having a great old time until . . . he's shot dead, presumably by an unhappy heart thump. However, God decides to give him another chance to get into heaven, by recycling him back to earth as a woman—played by Ellen Barkin. The deal is that, retaining his memories of his "former self," s/he has to make a woman love "him"—when that happens, s/he'll earn eternity in heaven.

This movie is basically a comedy, so there are the expected and hilarious scenes of his/her adjustments to a female body and lifestyle. S/he even tries a lesbian relationship in order to get a "woman" to love him/her, but ends up being used for business or physical pleasure—nothing personal (what a lesson!).

Jimmy Smits, who had been "his" best friend and has been told about the new arrangement (although he has trouble truly comprehending it), ends up falling in love with him/her. After a night of emotions, talk, and a few drinks, they have sex—and "s/he" gets pregnant. Sadly, the physicians inform them that s/he can't go to term with the baby without sacrificing his/her life. Ellen has a choice: abortion and life; birth and death. Fascinating choice, don't you think?

Ellen and Jimmy marry; Ellen chooses to go to term, recognizing the miracle of giving life to the world.

When the newborn *girl* (remember God's "deal"?) is placed in Ellen's arms, Ellen realizes a love and bond s/he had never experienced or dreamed possible. As the baby looks up at him/her, Ellen says, "Look. She's staring at me. I think she loves me."

So—it was the process of connecting to, and sacrificing for, another life, not the thrills of orgasms or infatuation, which changes him/her.

Does this story relate to the "heart-thump" fax from John? Yes. We as human beings can be so self-centered and stupid about what really has meaning in life. When you're forty years old and you imagine that perpetual heart thumps and hard-ons are what's going to make your life meaningful—that's small thinking. After a while, by the way, ennui will set in with the new heart thump, and you'll be left with the same dilemma—who to have perpetual heart thumps with now! Human beings have evolved with values and morality to carry them over these realities of life—and among them is that familiarity breeds *comfort,* which is reassuring, but not always that exciting (novelty gone, your creative enthusiasm is required—see chapter 7, "Stupid Husbanding"). This is where values come in—they help you appreciate that connectedness to people who accept you and care about you is an incredible miracle of life.

Insecurity, immaturity, and self-centeredness are what generally lead folks like John to test the greenness of other grass. But, I wouldn't have gotten this fax if John weren't struggling with the issue—and I admire people who struggle instead of just "giving in." He realizes his baby needs a father—that's right—and honoring obligations is what ennobles one's life.

If you're expecting a Toys R Us existence forever, you're going to have a meaningless life. If you expect that love is a feeling you're supposed to *get*, or that horniness is meaningful in a long-term relationship, you're wrong. Those feelings initially get people together in order to give them the opportunity to really bond.

Ultimately, you need to learn to make love, not sex. And that feels great too. There is no question that John could find a young thing to worship him. But, as Switch revealed, it is the responsibility to something and somebody else which really makes people happy.

John was at the crossroads—he had to ask himself which decision—marital responsibility or heart thumping—would help him die in peace. I was gratified to immediately receive his second fax:

> *I'm the 40's guy that you just read the fax from. I was getting my baby out of the car when I heard you reading my fax. Tears are now running down my cheeks. You told me the answer I knew in my heart. I guess I just needed to hear it from someone else. Thank you.*

Male Itch

The "excuses" for affairs take many forms:

- The Birth of a Child
  A listener, Steve, collapsed in front of that challenge:

> *After seven years of marriage we had our first little girl, after two miscarriages. But, it was during this time my wife stopped being my wife, and became our child's mother. I had a hard time dealing with this, because for seven years she was all mine. I didn't handle this normal event of adult male life well, and had an affair. My wife has forgiven me, but still, 18 years later, I can*

still see the hurt every time I have to go out of town without her. The real bad part is dealing with myself. I will never forget how bad I hurt my mate, and let myself down JUST FOR SEX!!!

To men with new children—believe me, it will be better if you support her, and honor her for undertaking the most thankless job in the world. Nobody teaches young men that brides turn into mothers, and mothers turn into wonderful life partners, if we only will support, love and honor their hard work.

- Unhappiness. Jim's letter underscores the truth in this area:

I began drinking at approximately age 14, and abused alcohol for the next 26 years and finally managed to quit when I was 40—13 years ago. After 12 years of marriage I began having an affair with my secretary who was always available and fantastic in bed. I continued to drink and commit adultery. I divorced my wife, married my secretary, divorced her and had yet a third marriage—rocky at best. After considerable time, and more than considerable patience on the therapist's part, I was able to begin to consider the unthinkable—that I played some role in the continuation of my unhappiness, depression, loneliness and turmoil. Facing the truth that I was a person whose own behavior I found despicable was heart wrenching. Admitting that I was a person who did intolerable things almost took more courage than I possessed. I began listening to your show—your insistence on taking responsibility, refusing to excuse aberrant and abusive behavior have been of invaluable service to me. I am attempting to be continually vigilant, monitor my behaviors and actions; constantly learning to apply appropriate remedy, and holding myself lovingly accountable for my mistakes.

- False Sense of Manhood

Jason, a twenty-three-year-old caller, has been married two years to a woman seven years older than he is with an eight-year-old son. Jason was "busted" for an affair two months ago. When I asked him why he did it, he said,

"For the excitement of it all." After I pursued that point, he admitted that the responsibility of marriage and stepfathering "started to be overpowering. My other friends were out having fun."

It's not unusual for young people to want to be "instant competent adults"—often "accomplished" via smoking, drugs, sex, and marriage. Jason married an "older woman," a parental figure he could "count on" to be the adult—as a cushion against the scariness of responsibility. Like most "adolescents," he rebelled against the very "authority" he hoped would protect and nurture him.

Also in this category are men who feel that they don't measure up in ways they assume others (their parents, their wives . . . themselves) value. To them, an affair becomes an interesting twist on the proclamation "Screw you!" and a very indirect reassurance of their worth.

- Fear of Death

Frank, a fifty-two-year-old caller, talked about wanting to "go back in time" to renew the "lost love" of his high school years. He's been married twenty-five years and seems to see "most of my life behind me." I left him thinking about disrespecting the commitment, love, and sacrifices his wife continues to make for him—reminding him that what was "behind him" was also "behind her." What is next is something to be discovered and created as a "team."

- Entitlement to Happiness

A terrible thing has happened to our culture. Growing in intensity since the 1960s, it is the supremacy of personal fulfillment and gratification over notions of obligation and commitment. The psychological community has "helped" with this degeneration of attitude about life's purpose by defending and promoting the rights and prerogatives of individuals to pursue their own satisfactions in spite of obligations. Consequently, "I want my happiness—I'm entitled to it!" has become, in so many minds, a justification for abandonment of family obligations.

My caller, Pat, married ten years with three children (eight, five, and two months!) has "fallen in love with the pediatrician" (female) and is agonizing over "what to do," because "I know what to do morally, I'm having fun sex and am entitled to my happiness, too."

This was a sad call for me—I couldn't make a dent in his determination to put self over what was right.

- Ego

Tim and Roberta called together. They're married four years and have no children. Tim had an affair for nine months, which ended thirty days ago because the "other woman" called Roberta. It seems that Tim, once out of shape, has been pumping iron and has a new hard body, to which Roberta gave little fanfare. "So, I got my strokes outside," Tim pouted. Roberta came back with, "Well, you still look like my husband to me."

While Roberta could have been more complimentary and supportive of Tim's efforts to look better, I brought to his attention that his wife accepted him when he was less "buff," because she loved *him*—while the honey was responding only to the "buff." "Which," I asked Tim, "really makes you feel more important and accepted?"

He was speechless.

- Proof of Masculinity

Some of you men define masculinity by protesting too much about femininity; so that to prove masculinity is to deny or demean women and your need for a woman's love. To accomplish this you "conquer lots of women" (therefore you pretend that you don't "need" them—you just "use" them), or never let one "control you" (i.e., monogamy is considered castration). All in all, this behavior is an indication of insecurities, fears, inadequacies, and problems which will never allow you to be loved and happy.

This fax from "T" summarizes the typical results of running away from interpersonal fears and difficulties with affairs:

I am writing you this letter because I did not follow my conscience or values—I engaged in inappropriate behavior, and I am suffering the consequences. Several years ago, in an effort to numb the pain of a difficult marriage, I had an affair. In my own eyes and perhaps in the eyes of the world I had all the right reasons (excuses) to cheat on my wife. At the time, of course, I was swept away with the illusion of romance that an illicit affair will bring. This act started a cycle, which became a lifestyle; this lifestyle very nearly destroyed me. My marriage ended in divorce; the last three years since my wife left have been the most difficult of my life. I lost everything I valued in life. I lost my wife, my family, the respect of my children, my parents and my friends. I lost my home, and nearly lost my business. I spent many nights, searching my soul, crying myself to sleep, and thankfully learning many lessons along the way.

I did come to understand that these "absolutes" are not here to harm us or restrict us, but to protect us and to save us from ourselves. I wish I had listened to your program, I wish I had listened to my conscience, I wish I had lived by the values my parents demonstrated.

I did learn and grow through these difficult years, and I have been blessed to have a second chance in life. Tomorrow I am getting married. My fiance and I have talked much about my quest, my mistakes, and more importantly, how to deal with difficulties that arise in marriage, and the value of "values." I hope someone can learn from my mistakes.

Food for the Eyes—Starvation for the Soul

Numerous female callers have complained about their men being swept away by pornography. One male listener challenged me with the following: "The opposite sex is appealing to the five senses, including sight. So how can you condemn one who actively pursues stimulation of the optic nerve.

Based upon the prolific dispersion of pornographic maga-zines, sexually stimulating advertisements and movies, it is clear that a large majority of people in this country are also voyeuristic. Do you really think this behavior is wrong?"

Let's be blunt here: it is more typically male than female to pursue sexual gratification as an end in itself—it is the bio-logical, male-animal side in a tug of war with the human-man's possibilities. But, more nameless, faceless, discon-nected sexual gratification does not lead to a greater desire or ability to be close, loving, bonded, and intimate. The more you exercise one muscle, the more the opposing muscle weakens and the more out of balance you become.

Occasional viewing or reading of "sexy" material often helps stimulate "sexy behavior" when stress, family, and work distractions might be stalling you in "neutral." So, as an aphrodisiac to help jump-start you and your wife—fine. As an alternative to relating on a real, meaningful, and recip-rocal way—not fine. Pornography is about "getting," love-making is about "giving and getting."

According to evolutionary psychologist Douglas Kenrick's research (*Time* magazine, 8/15/94), men who are shown pic-tures of *Playboy* models later describe themselves as less in love with their wives than do men shown other images. (Women shown pictures from *Playgirl* felt no such attitude adjustment toward spouses.) The following letter takes that revelation to its conclusion:

> One of the 10 things men do to screw up their lives (and that of their wives, kids, or girlfriends) is getting involved with pornography.
>
> As you know, reality is almost never up to the expectation of fantasy. Men lose the ability to have fulfilling and satisfying sexual relationships because of the unrealized expectations porn leads them to.
>
> I know this from personal experience. Even though I know in my mind that those fantasies are unreal and concocted, I still

cannot find any satisfaction in real sexual relations. NO one lives up to the fantasies—of course, no one could.

I have had to accept the sad fact that, for me, sex has become fun only to watch, exciting to think about, but completely unfulfilling to engage in.

Prostitution provides the same sort of emotional sinkhole: men who habitually go to prostitutes are incapable or avoiding of emotional intimacy or trust. Pornography and prostitution are attempts to have a "relationship" in which men can feel automatically and completely wonderful, acceptable, competent, masculine—without earning or deserving it! Pornography and prostitution are easy ways to feel like a "man"—in your own mind and in the fake behaviors of a hired sex partner.

In the end, inappropriate sexual expressions (promiscuity, affairs, porn, prostitutes) are paths to avoid becoming a fully functional, adult human man.

A Real Man

"Anonymous" wrote me this concluding fax:

I've been a pro-choice/pro abortion/sexually active guy for years. For the last several months I listened to you, I re-thought all my ideas, and I did something I never thought possible. I was at my girlfriend's apartment last weekend. We had not had intercourse yet, and things got a little hot and heavy. She offered to get a form of contraception out and I took a chance. I stopped everything and said, "If you got pregnant and had the baby I couldn't bear seeing my son or daughter put up for adoption. I would not want to live life knowing that the future of someone I created was to be determined by someone else. If you got pregnant and kept the baby, I would plan on being around for the next 20 years at least. Do you know me well enough to accept that now? If you got pregnant and had an abortion, you could risk future chance of having children, and I imagine that going through the abortion would be absolute hell for you anyway. I don't see how I can say that I love you and care about you and then be the one who has a part in putting you through hell!"

She started crying, and she said that she had never in her life met a guy who cared about her so much. Her eyes shone in a way that touched me very deeply, and since that day she has been treating me like a king. I thought that she would think I was weird, or out of touch, or unrealistic and stupid. At the very least I thought she would tell me I was being silly. Never in my life did I expect that she would become even more crazy about me. Thank you, Dr. Laura, for planting the seed (pun intended) that has brought me closer to a woman I love very much.

And thank you, Mr. "Anonymous" for being my poster boy for Smart Sexuality.

6

STUPID MATRIMONY

Marriage is like the midnight phone call.
First there is the ring.
Then you wake up.

GREG, 1996

"Marrying the Wrong Woman Can Ruin a Good Man's Life" is the headline of a 1997 newspaper article by June Brown, a Detroit journalist. "Many men don't perceive women as dangerous because they are often pretty, accommodating, and exciting to be around. Yet, the danger some pose is greater than most men can imagine." The article continues: "Men should set certain standards that the women in their lives must meet and men should refuse to associate with women who don't meet those standards. Never should a man look at the abundant supply of women and try to take as many samples as possible, because when physical attraction takes over, common sense goes on vacation, so that one night with the wrong woman can ruin the best of men."

Think that's an overstatement? Check out my listener Mike's fax:

Why did I marry my honey? I think the following is pretty accurate.

1. *I was looking for a better college roomie.*
2. *I was sloshing brim-full of hormones; either over-sexed or under-whoopied and something had to give. Back then you didn't often just shack-up with some willing (dumb) chick to solve such problems.*
3. *She had fun brothers.*
4. *She was willing.*
5. *She had a cute figure.*

Now, don't under-estimate #2 above! With that list, failure is a real probability, and so are the following:

6. *He'll be wrenched from his kids.*
7. *He'll be tossed out of his house.*
8. *Half or more of what he owns will be confiscated.*
9. *He'll be bound in involuntary servitude (through alimony, etc.) to a hostile master.*

And, I was! Even so, I think guys should marry, but given the above, I don't think it would be such a disaster if the male hormones weren't so up and the male wisdom/experience so down.

Contrast that marrying approach with another listener's approach:

I never dated anyone or spent much time worrying over girls that I knew I would never marry. Why waste the time or compromise my principles for someone that was not up to snuff! I kept searching till I found the best one, and I was not afraid to say no or be on my own.

I married on March 12, 1994. I know that I made the right decision and I have never looked back once or wished that I had made any other decision. She is the best and I burst with pride every time I think of her. She is why I work hard and strive to do my best—so she can be as proud of me as I am of her. She is my friend, my partner, and my lover.

Well, obviously a big difference in attitude and approach—and results. My caller Craig, thirty-two, phoned in about choosing between the two women in his life; ultimately, I believe, choosing between the two very different fates encountered above.

Craig's been dating woman #1 for three months. She wants to take him with her on a cross-country trip without any further commitment. He's been dating woman #2 for three weeks. Woman #2 will not tolerate his going on that trip with woman #1, and refuses to continue dating him if he keeps seeing her.

Craig's confused, poor thing, and wanted me to help him choose.

"So, Craig, one wants you to be serious, the other just wants you to be fun. Your choice will come from what you value."

"Well, the problem is that the second woman wants me to stop dating others and just focus in on the relationship—or she said not to call her back."

"At this age, when you find somebody you like and think is nice, you usually focus . . . unless, of course, all you want is action. So you have to decide if at this time in your life you're seriously looking for a life's partner."

"How long do you give yourself when you decide to commit?"

"Craig, commitment to me means marriage. Now getting serious usually entails focusing attention and energies in that one direction. This basically comes down to what you want for your life—whether or not either one of these women is appropriate. Do you want to be a family man or do you want to play?"

"Oh, without question, I want to be a family man."

"Does either one of these women seem like potential family material?"

"That's just the thing . . . neither."

"If neither one gives you the impression of being good

family material, then the answer to your original dilemma is to dump them both and move it on!"

Please, guys, don't let available sex and attention keep you from your appointed rounds; such sampling takes up time, energy, and resources, as well as building an ultimately useless familiarity which might beguile you into "thinking" it's more—or could be—or ought to be—or why not—or . . . ooops . . . she's pregnant. Pick your goals in life first, then pick the woman to match them.

You Like Me—You Really Like Me

Are you measuring your manly worth by the willingness of some woman to have sex with you? If you are, you may be letting yourself in for all kinds of trouble—mainly because measuring your "manly worth" by the activity of only six or so inches of you misses the point of your "human totality"; because your penis is as attached to you as your psyche and spirit, and when you're meaningless with your penis, you're being meaningless with your life; and because "women" are not a monolith of nice 'n' benign (remember the movie *Fatal Attraction*?).

One listener, James, confirmed that reality:

I met my first girlfriend in college and we became involved pretty much because she was there, throwing herself at me. After two or three weeks I couldn't stand her. So, in a roundabout way . . . that's my answer to why men choose the women they do . . . because they're there and initially you ignore all the stuff that's wrong with them because it's a great ego boost that this woman threw herself at you.

I know you fellas grew up hearing that girls are "sugar and spice and everything nice," but it just ain't universally true. I think you sometimes look at women through rose-colored Coke-bottle bottoms! Wise up! There are lots of women who are healthy, warm, creative, thoughtful, giving, open, fun, compassionate . . . and there are plenty who have mild to serious behavioral and emotional problems mixed in with that beguiling sugar and spice. In other words, being "wanted" by a female headhunter isn't a compliment—and it could be downright terminal!

Nonetheless, when you're feeling inadequate you don't always feel justified in being choosy. As Ken wrote:

> *I realize now that my own issues of "low self esteem" were the problem, i.e., lousy body image—even when I wasn't fat—caused me to be attracted to "needy women" because I felt like I wouldn't get judged. Only to realize now that the stupid things I did were to:*
>
> 1. *ignore incompatibilities in communications styles and attitudes about life*
> 2. *marry after only months of dating*
> 3. *fail to do the same level of research I would do when buying a car. My wife was on medication and therapeutic treatment. I was told by the counselor that she would be better within one year—I accepted that*
> 4. *marry because I was afraid of being an "old maid" at thirty*
> 5. *marry a "needy" woman, because it felt good that I was strong enough to take care of her . . . of course, she didn't do well whenever I was "needy"*
> 6. *go to bed not only before marriage, but before ring and a date. Boy, does that create pressure to follow through!*
>
> *I regret the divorce, but I am working on being the best ME I can, so I can find the best mate for the best me.*

And then there's Jeffrey:

> *Perhaps my excuse during those years was to hide the fact of my hearing-impairment. Who would want to go out with a hard-of-hearing person? I became involved with her because she took an interest in me—she was paying attention to me.*

Relief and gratitude motivate too many marriages, which usually end up in divorce because two people didn't really take the time to match up temperaments, ideals, goals, attitudes. The so-called commitment was really a mirage—the pairing up was mostly about gaining a sense of acceptance which, unfortunately, is not enough of a foundation to support a marriage facing the realities of life, simultaneously confronting the unsuspected, or ignored, realities of each other.

We're in the Dirt Together

On the other hand, such a marriage can be a perfect match— a match made in hell. Randy, a listener, wrote to me of his round-trip excursion into Hades:

> I was married for seven years before my wife left our family. I am 34 and I have custody of our two boys, 6 and 7. She was involved with drugs, gang members, and various loser sorts. I wanted a bed partner when we first got married—that's all—and she was not supposed to be able to have kids.
>
> When the kids came, I stopped drinking, drugs, smoking, carousing, etc., but she did not. She eventually got fed up with me and left.
>
> I am now taking full responsibility for the kids, and my family is helping me.

Randy's situation was more than an issue of acceptance; he initially rejected everything which was of universal value and found someone with whom to share that degenerate lifestyle. No challenges, no judgments, no effort required, that is, until the babies came. Randy took himself up and out of the muck for the babies' sakes, but no longer had a partner. A match made in hell isn't easily transformed into a marriage made in heaven.

Mommy . . . I Mean Honey, Hold My Hand

David, a listener, feels he has learned a great deal about himself and about relationships since his separation and divorce:

> *For one thing, my initial temptation was to blame the break up
> of the marriage solely on my wife because she had the affair.
> However, in looking back at it, I think that I married young
> because I was afraid of facing a new career and a new city alone.
> Also, my ex-wife was the first and remains the only woman that
> I have ever had sex with. In retrospect, I regret that we had sex
> so early in our relationship because my rationality about the
> seriousness of our bond was clouded by my hormones.*
>
> *Also, I am very obsessed with my music career at this stage in
> my life and was not around a lot at the time. She felt like she
> was secondary to my music and, in many ways, she was.*

I really appreciate such soul-searching honesty in the letters I receive from my listeners—especially the men, who
seem to be able to communicate more comfortably in print
than on air. Let's look at some of the points David brought
up. First, the desperate need to be married so as not to be
alone when facing a new, scary challenge. Second, his realization that once he had that security, the comfort of her companionship, he felt free to go on about his life as though he
were a free and clear single adult, charging after his dreams,
without another care or responsibility in the world.

This amounts to using your wife as a mom (remember
how good you felt just knowing that she was somewhere in
the house), and your marriage as an endpoint (I got one, now
I can get on with my life). Clearly, both predicaments could
be circumvented with life experience and maturity, which
doesn't often come in our early twenties.

The issue of sexual availability, which David brought up,
is an important one. Having an ongoing physical relationship
gives pleasure which is difficult to resist, as well as a sense of

permanence, which may not be warranted considering the other qualities of the woman—or yourself. Sex outside of a committed relationship gives marriage the momentum to send you crashing into a wall of reality down the road because, my friend, when you're sexually involved, you're no longer steering. Decisions made under the influence of an erection are not typically the best ones.

I Shacked Up with a Girl, Just Like the Girl That Shacked Up with Dear Old Dad

Let's be honest here, no matter what kind of erectile or hormonal frenzies might propel you toward inappropriate marriage, values and moral standards are always there to steer you right—something *else* to hold on to when the passions get you going. But, what happens when the morals and values you learned from your folks are substandard? You end up in chaos. That's what happened to Eric:

Why would I disregard all my values regarding the marital experience? For one, I never really had solid values. For two, I was scared—more about that later. My parents were divorced when I was 7. My father and mother remarried other people only after shacking up with a number of them. I did not have a male role model or a father for most of my youth (7–13). Nor, obviously, did I learn much value of commitment. I wonder if some of my messes could have been avoided with a solid two-parent family.

Now back to the "scared". I was moving back to a very insecure situation—no job, no place to live, no family to move in with during resettling. I didn't want all that instability as well as deal with the pain and loneliness of separating from a very attractive 26 year old, single woman from South Africa, whom I dated for 3 months and became very infatuated with. I was quickly emotionally invested in this woman by circumstances we shared (a hurricane, a very high pressure work scenario, both alone in a foreign country, and sexual needs being fulfilled). But

here's the catch: I figured if I married her, it would secure a
commitment in the relationship which would naturally work out
any problems that would come. We shacked up and it was all
downhill from that moment. Expectations were all messed up
with the roles of lover, house-mate, friend and fictitious spouse.
I was on an emotional roller coaster. The entire relationship? 1
year. No more listening to Mr. Penis.

Because of Eric's parents' divorce, shack-ups, and remarriages, he never had folks or a home he could count on when
in need, nor precedents set by his mom's and dad's committed behaviors. Hurricanes and sex are quite exciting, and
excitement fools the rational mind into thinking meaningfulness exists where it doesn't. At least Eric was able and willing
to pull himself out of the eye of that storm.

I Have a "Woman" Badge

Not all hysterical drives toward marriage have such profound reservoirs of boiling emotional dynamics. Some are
downright superficial. A listener, Dan, wrote me that for
seven years he only dated beauty queens. *"They were like*
trophies to display to family and friends."
Reggie expanded on this idea:

The bottom line, Dr. Laura, if a man wants a possession or
trophy he will go for the younger more attractive woman. If he
wants a companion on his level of intelligence, he will go for the
mature woman. As for myself, I'm still looking for a mature
woman with a young attractive body.
Seriously, I'm a very successful entrepreneur who has worked
very hard for everything I've attained. There is a reason some of
us men go for the young, pretty types:
1. nice, tight, young, hard, good looking body
2. easy to impress
3. not hardened from the war of the sexes (naïve)

4. *less chance of kids from previous marriage*
5. *less or no talk of ex-husband*
6. *not so negative towards men*
7. *makes man feel younger and more virile*
8. *makes other men envious*
9. *haven't "done it all" before (fewer comparisons)*
10. *see you as hero, no matter what you're like*

However, the big mistake that men make is in marrying these younger women, in spite of all the above pluses. A man shouldn't marry one of these women because:

1. *they have Cinderella mentality*
2. *they have nothing to talk about outside of bed*
3. *inexperienced in life*
4. *not intelligent*
5. *boring*
6. *useless as support*
7. *embarrassing in mature company*
8. *too dependent*
9. *too demanding*
10. *not useful for life's long haul*

Seeing a woman as a trophy ("Other men will think I'm cool") or sex toy ("Orgasm over? Move aside, little girl, I've got to get back to my life") is the mentality of an immature and ultimately lonely, empty kind of guy. I'm troubled by how many of my listener letters demonstrated a profound lack of understanding of the beauty and depth a loving relationship would bring. I wonder how many of those men came from homes where their fathers openly and lovingly expressed appreciation for wives and children.

Men Have a Biological Clock Also

Then there are those bachelor holdouts who suddenly "get religion" (maritally speaking) when middle age looms ahead.

University of Akron psychologist Charles A. Wachler

reported on the reasons these men decide to marry. "Either they [men] start to feel their mortality, and that makes them start to think that maybe I would like a partner; others achieve a certain level of success and want to share it with a partner. Others simply have grown up."

Brian wrote to me:

I felt a cultural imperative to get married. She was available and a pretty woman. I was also looking forward to sex, as much as I could handle, as we were both abstaining until marriage.

Kirk's religion was his imperative to get married:

At this point in my life, I felt I was ready to get married and was excited about the fact I had found somebody in church to marry. I was excited to think I could be close to settling down. In a matter of two months I had met, proposed to, and dumped a woman. I've thought a lot about what happened. As we had begun to date, I started to fall in love with the idea of being in love. I began to fall in love with the perspective of actually getting married. All my feelings and emotions were directed toward an idea, an ideal. This was my big chance to get married and fulfill the next stage of my progression. I was, and still am, committed to the concept of marriage. It took this one fiasco to realize the difference between focusing on an ideal and focusing on a person.

For whatever reasons the "time seems right," just any woman won't do (please reread this sentence eighty-two times before going on!). It's wonderful that you wish to share your life and grow and mature by your affiliation with love and obligation—but please, women are not readily exchangeable parts to this marriage machine . . . any more than you are. And that's the first secret: heal and/or mature thyself before even imagining you can make an appropriate choice, a good match in a marriage.

Matchmaker, Matchmaker, First Make Me Be Good for a Match

My listener Carl's innocence didn't produce bliss:

> *First, I'm 67, so I grew up in the 30's and 40's. I grew up thinking good relationships were the norm and that some kind of divine guidance had a hand in a boy and a girl getting together. For me, it was an era of naivete and simple trust. Despite three marriages, three divorces, and four other long term relationships, I am now much more positive about life and much happier than I have ever been. Despite decades of disappointment, for which I take full responsibility because of my passive manner, I am enjoying a relationship very much. The lesson I've learned is that love, trust, commitment and honesty are qualities that must be earned—not just assumed.*

Carl's story is important because it points out how destructive passivity ("any bus which stops here gets me") is when choosing a mate. Obviously, an active position requires your appreciating the importance of the choice to the quality of your life; you see marriage as an interactive experience, and you value the potential of a marital relationship as much as or more than any other part of your life. That's serious stuff—and it sounds more "girlish" than "boyish," doesn't it? Nonetheless, the marital state is too important to your sense of happiness, purpose, well-being, importance, and identity for you to make it the result of a casual decision.

Granted, this kind of maturity requires work and can be bolstered by religious affiliation. For example, my listener David's attitude about life and love changed dramatically when he decided to become an observant Jew:

> *Until I became religious, my life was only about chasing after all the inclinations my heart could desire. I saw "her" 3 years before in my Rabbi's house and didn't think much of her. After*

three years of my own growth and maturity, I ran into her
again. My eyes were then connected to my brain after my
heart—that was the difference.

And that's the simple key to a good choice: before you
begin to search, work to improve yourself spiritually, mentally, and physically. When you mature emotionally, your
goals and your needs mature as well; in fact, you may find
that for the first time in your life they are loftier and more
inherently meaningful than stimulation and gratification.
That's when you're at your peak of mate choosing.

I'm not claiming that growth and maturity are easy. My
listener Brad's childhood experiences being the brunt of jokes
and taunts was quite painful. It took time and life experience
for him to come to the place to be able to say:

I have concluded of late that my value and worth are decided by
me—not others (mean or nice)—and that nobody can take it
away. Since I started earning my own worth in my own eyes,
and therefore doing positive things in my life, my worth as a
man and human being grows stronger every day.

I have made some poor choices in relationships before I
learned this about myself. I had a great misunderstanding of
love. I didn't realize I had a choice in who and how I love. Love
is something I do (a verb) and not something I hope comes to
me (a noun). Instead of Cupid driving me around via remote
control—I do the driving now!

With all the popularized nonsense about how emotionally
impervious men are and how emotionally consumed women
are, both sexes haven't paid much attention to a man's inner
world. From all these male listener letters, it is obvious that,
because they haven't respected their own feelings and needs
for compatible intimacy, too many have ended up maritally
miserable. In addition to "fixing" your own psychological
problems (so that you don't select a woman on the basis of

your weakest self), men need to be clear as to what is important in their lives and select a woman based on that importance.

The hitch for so many of you men is seeing "relationships" as a "girl thing" (she'll take care of the relationship, you'll take care of slaying dragons), thinking girls are virtually interchangeable (as long as they're pretty/sexy you just need one for show and sex), and are basically afraid to show vulnerability and need (too reminiscent of needing Mommy?).

Because of those factors, men don't typically use wisdom in selecting a mate—they're too busy hiding their emotions. Nonetheless, as my listener Jim's letter reveals, the truth exists:

*Somewhere I read that men fall in love drastically more quickly than women. And, when you think about it, women always **do** seem to be more cautious about falling into a relationship. But we men are **so** desirous of affection (usually masquerading as sex) that we don't always question 1.—whether this relationship has all of the physical, mental, emotional, moral and spiritual dynamics we want, and 2.—whether we have pre-thought out what issues, attitudes and actions we are willing to lose a woman over. I wish I would have thought through the qualities in a woman I really didn't want to live without and held on to find her.*

Don't marry just because you finished school and have an established job or completed your tour of duty in the military *and so it's time!* Don't marry just because you can't imagine the sex being any better. Don't marry just because you're grateful that a woman likes you. Don't marry just because she's pouting about all her other girlfriends' wedding dates. Don't marry just because you've been dating her for a year. Don't marry just because your family is nagging you to do so. Don't marry just because. . . .

Don't marry until you've dated the woman for two years (to get past the infatuation stages), and only after determining you are compatible with respect to attitudes, interests, religion, goals about family life, feelings about children, comfortable relationships with each other's family, values, and morals. Don't marry anyone you can't trust or admire.

Don't marry anyone with lots of problems—until such time as she works them through. Don't marry anyone who can't handle problems with you—that's just a fair-weather wife.

While I can't possibly list all the danger signs of inappropriate marriage, many of my listeners have offered their experiences as a warning to you.

Women to Watch Out For

THE EMOTIONAL BAGGAGE QUEEN

Craig, a thirty-nine-year-old listener, has been in a tumultuous relationship for four years with a thirty-seven-year-old woman who has also never been married. If there were ever a red-flag beginning to a relationship, this was it:

When I met her she was very abusive toward me especially when she drank too much. Her parents are divorced (mine are still married). I sense a lot of emotional baggage in her from her childhood. She gets very emotional very fast and is quite blaming, accusing and critical of me—yet claims to love me (I believe her) and wants to spend the rest of her life with me.

Okay, men, here are some obvious no-no's in a choice of woman: a drinking problem, verbal and/or physical abuse, irrational and volatile emotions, and an inability to move past the "pain of childhood." It seems so obvious—so how come you guys get stuck in this neon quicksand? I think the answers are guilt, need, and an inappropriate sense of responsibility. When Craig says that he believes she loves him, his guilt for not accepting her "problems" is tweaked: after all, under all that dysfunction and abuse she loves him; how can he reject her? Craig, like any man, *needs* love, affection, and companionship—but because it isn't considered manly to admit to such need, he disguises it as helping her with her needs (which really are for intensive psychotherapy!). Also, he figures that if he is patient and understanding and giving enough, *then* he'll get his needs met.

Additionally, being a basic good-guy, Craig probably wonders what he can do to fix her (Mr. Tool time?). Watch out for women still percolating in historical misery (abusive relationships, molestations, rapes, etc.) who can't relate to you without:

- punishing you for their past hurts with anger and/or rejecting behaviors
- making their hurts from the past part of your current relationship by either constantly going over them or constantly making you tend to their undying pain
- making you feel you can't be "real" because that prospect is somehow threatening or upsetting—considering "what's happened" in her past
- making you feel guilty for having needs, wants, and desires—considering her delicate condition
- making you feel it's your responsibility to give her a perfect life now (no matter what is costs you personally) to make up for her past
- making you feel you have to be the more responsible partner in the relationship because she's still "healing"

Don't misunderstand. I'm not saying you shouldn't have compassion and caring for her problems and struggles. I am saying, however, that compassion and caring can be bestowed from the distance of "friendship." For a marriage to succeed, people must bring a healthy self to the table. You can support her as she "heals," but to think you could or should marry her and then perform a medical/emotional miracle is generally foolish. Don't get snared in the Damsel in Distress trap because you feel needed or useful. Women piled up with their own baggage have no hands, shoulders, or backs available to help you with the surprisingly heavy suitcases life tends to toss at us all.

THE LOOSE WOMAN

Dave, a listener, met his dream boat in church:

We "fell in love", have religion, home remodeling, walking, tennis and the symphony in common. We don't live together but we've had great sex almost daily. She's been married four times (12, 1 1/2, 2 and 4 years). She's been single less than a year between each of her last three marriages and had three intimate relationships since her last divorce 2 1/2 years ago. She is not too close to her mom, was distant with her deceased dad and she's distant with her five siblings. Last Friday night she told me she likes the idea of going out with other men, to have fun and new experiences. She says I'm the most compassionate, considerate, stable and loving man she's ever met—but she says she's confused and doesn't know what she wants. She wants me to be patient.

Am I being unrealistic? Jealous? I fear she hasn't learned from her previous experiences. Am I on the right track?

When I say "loose woman," I don't only mean one who is universally sexually available—I mean a woman for whom intimate ties have always been "loose." The significant point for Dave to focus on is whether *he* can learn something about his girlfriend from her past experiences! You guys' mentality tends to be black and white: sex is great and she says she loves me and that I'm wonderful—period; then you are flummoxed by additional contrary materials (like she's never had a successful relationship with anyone and she wants to keep her options and actions open—with you there as home base, of course). You men choose to look only at the white and think there must be something wrong with you when the black is bothersome.

A potential partner's history of stability, intimacy, warm

sustained friendships and family dynamics (or lack thereof) *is the rule*—so don't fool yourself into thinking somehow you will be the exception! This is true in spite of daily great sex . . . sorry, guys.

THE NOT SO MORAL MADAM

Robert, a listener, wrote to me after his marriage dissolved. He realized a little too late that issues of morality are really about dealing with life's challenges in noble ways:

Your assessment of the "moral situation" is absolutely correct. My ex-wife's life has been punctuated with selfish decisions of poor moral bases, that have devastated the lives of those around her. She is an "'honest" person, but believes that all there is to morality is honesty. Our only daughter was born at 26 weeks weighing only 2 pounds. The Doctors told me that my wife had an incompetent cervix due to damage from multiple abortions which she had before our relationship—multiple abortions about which she had failed to inform me (so much for honesty). That daughter has cerebral palsy. We tried to have another child now that the cervix problem was known. After two miscarriages my wife became pregnant. I was elated. In her seventeenth week, my wife decided to abort the child. There was nothing I could do about it. Now that we're divorced, she is shacking up with a new boyfriend.

My daughter will be 15 next month. A year ago she confided in me that someday she wants a husband, children, a home, etc. Now that her mother is shacking up, my daughter says that when she grows up that she will have a boyfriend to live with.

Of all my regrets in life, my greatest is that I didn't pay more attention to the moral signposts that flagged themselves before I married. The truth is that my ex-wife and I lived together before we married—I would have actually preferred not to but went along with her desires because it didn't seem to be hurting anything. I didn't recognize that our pre-marital shacking up was yet another indication of moral weakness and weakness of character that would ultimately destroy so many lives.

Perhaps this letter, and your on-air message, will help others avoid the pitfalls and unforeseen consequences of weak moral behavior.

Women historically set the limits of appropriate, permissible, and moral behavior. It was expected that a man might "offer" or "try" some things which came close to the line, but that he ultimately knew that the line would be set and enforced by the woman. I think many of you men, despite the sad loss of women's attention to social morality (thank you, feminists), still think it's okay if a woman says it's okay; in other words, what she will accept becomes acceptable.

Morality fundamentally protects against "unforeseen consequences" by guiding choice away from immediate gratification and toward the construction of something stable, longer lasting, and more profoundly gratifying.

You have to set your own standards and demand that others rise to them. If you live only for the moment, or live blindly, you will likely suffer disappointment and pain.

MS. TOO RADICALLY OPPOSITE

My caller Martin has been courting his twenty-seven-year-old lady for three years. They generally communicate well, only finances "seem to be the problem." Martin is very security oriented and prefers to budget and save, while she is more the "spend in the moment" type. He criticizes her flaky financial decisions, and she calls him controlling. What to do?

It is not unusual for folks who are quite self-controlled and unspontaneous to pair up with a free spirit. This way they can vicariously enjoy the freedom they deny themselves; also, the contrasting influence might serve to temper whatever rigidity is beyond necessity (i.e., the difference between being responsible and being constipated!). Unfortunately, it rarely works out that smoothly and positively, because as a rule each individual begins to protect and defend his own style and point of view.

"My girlfriend is a very independent person," Martin said, "who doesn't want anyone else to question what she does with her money and how she leads her life in that way. Some of the decisions she's made I've made commentary on, telling her that maybe it wasn't a very wise thing she did financially—I think that's caused some tension. She bounced fifty-four checks last year."

"Martin! This is worse than unwise. She's beyond a free spirit into the irresponsible and perhaps the illegal. I'm stunned at the way you presented this. This is not a philosophical issue of saving and investing versus enjoying the fruits of labors. This is somebody without self-control or responsibility to others, and who disdains authority. It's odd that such a contained, security-oriented kind of guy would put himself in the jaws of the dragon like this. Interesting."

Such extreme personality contrasts are about working out your personal inner dynamics through someone else. Take Martin, for example. If he is self-critical and concerned with control, what better way to get relief than to have to try to contain those impulses *in someone else;* then, the attention shifts away from his own anxieties—I mean, they're so bad, he looks good to himself . . . what a relief!

This technique of trying to control your own self-critical anxieties through a mate who is way in excess of your worst fantasy about yourself is not the only reason you may select an opposite. Opposites per se are not a problem, as long as you can appreciate and enjoy and allow yourself to benefit from the differences. If you're more quiet, for example, and you choose a more outgoing woman, but one who respects your personality and through whom you comfortably extend yourself past your old comfort zones—then something wonderful is happening.

However, opposites in such areas as values, goals, and religion should not be ignored or considered irrelevant simply because you're in love/lust. Marriage is more than advanced dating. Marriage requires a great degree of commonality in intention about the point of life and family. Without that deeper unity of spirit, there is no way you two will grow in your humanity, nor will you be able to successfully cope with life's challenges.

Problems will not work *themselves* out. You two have to have the skills and the commitment to work them out as a team. How can that be done if you see the world completely differently?

SHE'S FLORENCE NIGHTINGALE

You're going to have to be painfully honest with yourself here. Watch out for the woman who is willing to have you even if you're drinking, using drugs, promiscuous, out of control, unkind, abusive, etc. *A woman who wants you at your worst is probably not the woman who can handle a man at his best.* And, when the choices you make come from the weakest parts of your nature, they're not the ones that will carry you through growth to a healthier self.

THE DEMANDING PRINCESS

While I think it is supremely wonderful for a man to have a family to work for, giving his efforts meaning and direction, it is not so wonderful to have a wife who is a constantly withdrawing goalpost. Seth married a college girlfriend a year after graduation. She was an only child from a well-to-do family who grew up with resources around her daily; her parents followed her around making sure she was happy, so there was never a question about not getting whatever she wanted or needed.

Seth came from a broken home, put himself through college, and was entranced at the idea of becoming part of a family. However:

> *The only problem was that she was very, very critical of any person or action that didn't meet with her ideal picture of a husband, home, etc. I will admit that after about ten years of*

marriage I began to feel like I was on a treadmill that didn't stop. The work days really were becoming a grind, the more money our family made, the more ways we found to spend it. I became aware of the thought that "I wasn't happy." My observation is as follows: if you pamper and spoil an already pampered and spoiled woman early on in a marriage, you are expected to pamper and spoil her forever.

It's really a lack of reciprocity that is Seth's issue. It's wonderful when people sacrifice to bring pleasure to each other. It's not wonderful when only one individual's happiness is relevant. Seth, however, was a survivor, used to taking care of himself; he extended that to her, hoping that his actions could somehow create the loving family feelings he missed growing up.

Remember O. Henry's "The Gift of the Magi"? It is Christmas, and a poor but loving couple have no money to buy each other any gifts. So, she cuts her beautiful long hair and sells it to a wig maker in order to buy him a gold chain for his family heirloom gold watch. As it turns out, he has sold his gold watch to buy her a beautiful comb to decorate her hair. If you men don't experience mutual loving sacrifice like this while you're courting . . . forget it!

RAPUNZEL

A good marriage requires partnership. If the lady of your dreams has never been out on her own earning money, taking care of responsibilities, being independent, then she doesn't bring much understanding, experience, and competence to the partnership. So, if she's never moved out of her parents' home, or she has been shacking up with one guy after another . . . forget it. She needs to be competent and self-sufficient enough to get out of her own castle—or she won't be any good as your partner.

SUPER FEMINIST

David Klinghoffer, the literary editor of the *National Review*, wrote a column for the *Jewish Journal*'s "Single Life" section in which he said, "There is another barrier blocking the way to modern marriage. It is that I'm not sure modern women want families as much as men do. How can they get married, or, at any rate, how can they be mothers if they are pursuing careers as aggressively as their husbands? At the same time, an ambitious man would feel vaguely ashamed to marry a woman who is not similarly ambitious. . . . I want something impossible in my wife: a man's mind and a woman's soul."

Well, guys, don't be ashamed to look for a woman who is traditional; and don't be ashamed about wanting to temper your own career potential so you can be a more integral part of your wife and children's lives.

Beware the woman who thinks that the mere presence of a penis in the room is proof of some sexist plot; beware the woman who wants children but thinks it's in the kid's best interest to be more bonded to the hired help or an institutional child-care worker than a parent; beware the woman who believes in the "trickle-down theory" that as long as *she's* made herself happy, everyone else oughta be; beware the woman who thinks even marital sex is rape unless she is profoundly in the mood; beware the woman who seems to resent the blessing of femininity; beware the woman who always seems to argue about female victimization and oppression; beware the woman who sees life as a male-female war or competition; beware the woman who doesn't think that being a woman is exceptionally special.

None of this means that your partner can't be strong, talented, competent, and bright; in fact, such a partner will only add to you! Kent, my dentist listener, wrote about his "powerful" woman:

I think that a major reason I have been able to get what I want from life is that I have created an immense support system that makes accomplishments possible which alone I could never achieve. The more powerful the support system, the greater the possibilities. I owe much much to my wife, who is a powerful woman.

Don't be intimidated by a strong woman—her strength will provide you with a wonderful friend and helpmate, with support and encouragement, teamwork and cooperation—all of which makes her attractive because the attractiveness by definition becomes greater than the sum of her "parts."

When It's Right

A listener, Barry, wrote a wonderful letter to his children, clarifying for them what they should expect, demand, want, and settle for in a marriage. He realized that "attraction" is the typical basis for most relationships, and that there are four specific elements which folks usually ignore or are confused about: trust, respect, love, and commitment.

Trust: that you can share your honest feelings and expose vulnerability without fear of being manipulated or having weaknesses exploited.

Respect: requires that the respected person have morals, ethics, and principles which are held to be of universal value. Respect is something which must be earned. Honesty, integrity, compassion, and character are qualities of a respected person.

Love: putting the other person's needs, wants, desires, and well-being above our own. Using this criteria, "selflessness" becomes the definition of love.

Commitment: is a covenant, a pledge, a promise, an obligation that is not to be broken. It is the stabilizing force or glue that cements the relationship. In today's world there is little commitment to anything or anybody. The challenge becomes your responsibility to rise above society's ever-changing conventions and pledge yourself to never-changing values and truths.

It's fascinating that these four elements, when fulfilled, make a person infinitely more attractive than a hard body with pouty lips could ever provide. It's true! Don't believe me? Maybe you'll believe Mark:

At the beginning of our relationship, I found her attractive, but did not have the overwhelming sexual desire that was prevalent early in my previous relationships. Only now that I know what is in her heart and her mind, do I find myself overwhelmed with my desire for her. That desire is based on my deep respect for her intelligence, character, and values.

Wow, that's not a penis talking—that's a whole man talking! And the benefits of this awareness provide a wonderful life. Hear this bittersweet story from Bill:

I chose my wife because she was at least my intellectual equal, caring and compassionate. She and I had 33 years together in which we shared a committed love and raised four children. My wife was her kids' mom as I am my kids' dad. We built a family based on doing what was best for the kids. Janet suffered from Lou Gehrig's Disease for 12 years. This disease debilitated her to the point of complete dependence. I provided care for her in the home so she could remain an integral part of the family. The children throughout her illness learned to care for her and learned the compassion that she so freely gave.
　　I picked an angel, and although grieving, I am thankful that Janet came my way.

To be able to look back on a married life with such gratitude should be your goal when you think of marrying.

Before you propose, imagine yourself twenty-five years in the future, looking back at the decision you make today. Do you feel sufficient certainty that you are operating out of your strongest, most open, aware, and objective self? If you're not sure—forget it . . . maybe just for now, maybe permanently.

I think it should be illegal to marry unless you have six to nine months of premarital therapy. That counseling experience makes it virtually impossible for you to ignore realities, while giving you the opportunity to explore your mutual respect, trust, commitment, goals, dreams, values, and lifestyle. Sounds too pragmatic and not romantic? Good! We live in the pragmatic, motivated of course by love, commitment, and values—but pragmatic nonetheless.

One listener, Dave, highlighted the qualities he looked for, and got, in his wife of twenty-four years. Think about how important these qualities are to you:

> She is well-grounded in her religious faith.
> She is not materialistic—she appreciates what we have.
> She doesn't smoke, use drugs or abuse alcohol.
> She is polite in a world where politeness and consideration for others are becoming all too rare.
> She is able to make and keep a commitment.
> She loves me and supports me even when my own imperfection is showing.
> Does she sound too perfect? Actually, she does have some faults. I just can't think of 'em right now.

I hope you feel that this chapter has taken you on an expedition from your groin to your soul. Don't make picking a life partner a kind of accident of fate or lust or opportunity or circumstance. The family is not only the center of any society, it is also the center of your life, critical to your own welfare, as well as that of your children and the world.

I don't want to end without a mention of your obligation

and options when you've been stupid in picking a partner. Consider this letter from Deborah:

> My own Dad, rest his blessed soul, sacrificed for me and my sisters. He stayed in a loveless relationship with my mom who had mental health problems and truly made all our lives a living hell. As kids, my sisters and I would say to each other, "I wouldn't blame Dad if he left her," yet he hung in there and provided a stability that we otherwise would not have had. Here, he had kids that wouldn't have held it against him had he left, yet he honored his commitment. My dad wasn't perfect, he made mistakes and he took responsibility for them—even the mistake of marrying my mom.
>
> But I can say this, because of his noble and honorable sacrifice, I have been taught the option of such goodness, because he was there to model it for me. I'm in my forties now, and each and every day I bless my father's memory for not leaving us alone with my mom.

You see, men, when you do commit Stupid Matrimony, you still create obligations to be honored, which leave wonderful memories for those so honored.

Getting It Right

One day I challenged my male listeners to write an original wish list for the perfect woman, and then a revised one motivated by maturity and good sense. Here is one typical entry:

Original List:

1. gorgeous
2. sexy
3. cute
4. athletic body
5. plays musical instrument
6. loves sex

7. a great cook
8. dresses sexy
9. looks great and has minty breath when she first wakes up—all the way until bedtime
10. smart

Revised List:

1. intelligent
2. witty
3. sense of humor
4. loving
5. caring
6. loves kids
7. warm
8. accommodating
9. supportive
10. attractive

This contributor is clearly not walking down the aisle of Stupid Matrimony.

STUPID HUSBANDING

A man will focus his every waking moment to pursue a woman.
Then, once she is won over in marriage, he moves on to the next obsession.

JOHN, 1996

Let's get right to the "specifications" of a good marital relationship as clarified by my listener Dan's inspired parallel of a working relationship to a working car engine:

> A **relationship** is like a finely tuned **car engine**. The way it works better is by what you put into it (this is male talk). The better gas you put in, the better mileage you achieve. An engine takes careful maintenance with oils and filters and spark plugs. When there is a breakdown in one part of the engine it affects the whole performance.
>
> The **oil** represents the **communication** shared between the couple; there must be constant communication that entails all aspects of their lives. Couples must understand one another and enjoy their time together for them to grow. If the oil is

prevented from areas in the engine, that part will overheat and breakdown. When there is breakdown in communication, misunderstandings occur and we become uncertain and frustrated with our partner and finally explode into irrational behaviors.

*This is where the filters, which clean out the grime, crude and foreign materials from going into the running system, come in. The **filters** represent **forgiveness**. No matter how perfect your relationship may be, there will always be misunderstanding and frustration. If we carry our grudges we will end up embittered and depressed. To forgive is to forget and get on with life.*

*The **spark plugs**, which provide the fire and power which gets the engine started, represents the couple's **passion**. In order for a relationship to grow and develop there must be a passion and energy for one another. This spark is the sexuality, romance, and attraction.*

*Something must continually power the engine—that is the **gasoline**, which represents the **committed effort** couples must put into the relationship. As an engine will not run without gas, a relationship will not grow without attention and work. Both partners in the relationship must take responsibility for putting the gas back into their relationship. If the engine is kept in fine condition, there should be no problem when the gas tank is full.*

Now isn't that incredibly enlightened? Yup. It would seem, however, that for so many men, the leap from automotive to marital maintenance is a torturous, uphill struggle. Why is that? Why do so many of you feel anything from genuinely embarrassed to monumentally irritated at the notion of "doing the kinds of things you know she loves"—or of being "unabashedly romantic and attentive to the quality and growth of your relationship"?

Let's count the reasons you end up dumping shovelfuls of wet dirt on your marriage—rather than furrow the ground for your own emotional harvest of lifelong contentment.

Number 1: You don't see or believe that there is any harvest of contentment to be gotten from your marital relationship! Mostly, you imagine that "guy stuff" (typically seen as work, sports—either as a jock or beer-chugging voyeur—money, constantly available sex, and power games) is sufficient to sustain you and make you happy. There is no doubt that these enterprises and experiences are exhilarating. They are also high-risk ventures with unpredictable rates of success and failure. The ability to survive life's inevitable buffeting without desperately resorting to medicating yourself with promiscuity, drugs, alcohol, violence, depression, or anxiety ultimately requires a safe and stable base: your marriage and your family.

Number 2: You regard marriage as an "entitlement" program through which you "get goodies for life." This mentality stems from the unfortunate arrogance: seeing your so-called "guy stuff" as superior and more fundamentally necessary to humanity than what you perceive as being *only* "girl stuff" (relationships, family, children, community, home life, religion, volunteerism, charity, etc.). Therefore, since you're the man, and since you are braving the elements to bring home the bacon (in non-kosher homes, of course), nothing more should be required of you. Your sense of belonging and bonding to people other than those with whom you compete is so underdeveloped that when you hunger for attachment, support, and (God forbid!) nurturing, you turn to the bottle or a Twinkie (whether confection or "babe"). The trouble with that behavior is that you do not truly become a part of your own marriage or family—you virtually are nothing more than a visitor in your own home.

Number 3: You actually view marriage as a natural *conclusion* to your "conquest": you've chosen her, courted her, probably bedded her, engaged her, married her . . . it's done . . . now, you get on with your life while she's supposed to take care of herself and you, the neighbors, pets, and anyone else you're both genetically related to. Doesn't that sound all too familiar? For most animals, that's about it—you beat out other males for the largest number of prize females and keep your DNA in generational abundance—and now it's back to foraging and turf wars. Human male animals have (brace yourself for this one, guys) emotional requirements beyond DNA dissemination, acquisition, and pecking order: you have needs for understanding, support, tenderness, loving sex, acceptance, attachment . . . I could go on and on but I don't want to reduce you to tears this early in the chapter. Therefore, considering your woman "conquest" rather than "resource" is a great loss to your heart, soul, and being.

Number 4: You are fixated in a state of "advanced adolescence," where your mate becomes a "sexually available mommy" to take care of you (a kind of guilt-free incestual situation?). Whether or not your own mommy was your ever-obedient servant, your notion is that a wife is there to *take care of you,* and the fact that you're even there is, or ought to be, her reward. I suppose you justify this notion by believing your *work* is how you take care of her. Well, son, it just ain't so—work is what you'd be doing if you were single. A better way of looking at the situation is to realize that both husband and wife contribute *maintenance* work for basic survival and necessities; however, without what you two give to each other on a personal level, there is no humanity and meaning to the marriage.

Number 5: You regard being romantic, involved, and attentive as an embarrassing acquiescence to female domination or control. If the guys see you buying small, lovingly sentimental presents for your wife—and it's not to placate her "'cause you got her mad"—do they consider you pussy-whipped? Is it deemed "unmanly" to be deeply, profoundly, and sensitively in love with your wife so many years after the honeymoon? Do you let the envious, adolescent railings of your "buddies" determine your level of emotional involvement with your woman? Do you doubt your masculinity or maturity if you enjoy having your woman know how much you need, love, value, and depend on her? Is it true that a real man stands alone? No, it's not. A lonely man, with no true direction and purpose in his endeavors, or meaning in his life, that's who stands alone.

Number 6: Marriage to you is a necessary evil if you want to be seen as an adult, responsible, heterosexual male. You just can't believe that there really is anything for you in marriage—it's just something you're supposed to do at a certain age or folks will look at you as weird. I think this reaction comes only out of a personal sense of being "weird," and you therefore fear marriage as the "unveiling" of that possible truth. If you are this kind of man, you may seem strong or tough to the outside world, but are truly afraid of your inner self; the emotional isolation (evidenced by the denigration of marriage and/or the foolishness of women's desires for interaction and intimacy) is your chosen refuge. So, such a man as you might marry to "seem normal," but be emotionally uninvolved and inattentive to hide your vulnerability—typically at the same time putting down your mate's needs for involvement and attention. It's just the greatest charade going!

Number 7: You see marriage as a loss of masculine freedom to come and go and do as you please. Generally, when you're young, there is as yet no real point or purpose to your life. Youth's so-called spontaneity, the ability to do and go anywhere at any time for no particular reason other than you feel like it, stems from that purposelessness. You do "whatever" because it fills the void by providing stimulation, excitement, activity, entertainment. But this kind of existence really requires little of you, and what you "don't like," well, you just "don't do"—none of it means much to the flow of your life. And that is just my point. When you marry, your actions have a point and a purpose; they mean something to many others which automatically, and finally, make *you* significant to them. Perhaps that seems a scary burden; perhaps your protestations of a "lack of freedom" have to do with your fear of obligations and responsibility. Funny thing, it's always those endeavors posing the greatest threat and challenge which ultimately bring us the most satisfaction.

Number 8: To you, marriage is only a mere pit stop in your otherwise more important daily dealings? Do you see spending time with your wife and family as a drain on your otherwise productive time (you could, after all, be changing the oil on your Harley—right?)? It is terribly sad when men value their work above everything else in their lives—be it out of weakness and fears or arrogance and power tripping. Perhaps the part of the world you can control with threats of hostile takeovers is more satisfying than knowing whether your wife and your children care if you live or die.

Number 9: The marital relationship seems to you a "girl thing," which you tolerate in order to have readily available, safe, guilt-free sex. Chasing and seducing is such a hit-and-miss process; isn't it just better to have it at home when you want it? This way you can get your sexual relief without having to deplete yourself of such resources as money and time. It's just so annoying, isn't it, when your woman sees you as having the potential for a more profound existence than a quickie and off to work? I know that it is a standard male joke that what some uptight woman needs to set her straight is a good screw. I think that it should also become a standard understanding, that what every uptight (i.e., spiritually and emotionally lost) guy needs is a woman who wants him even *after* screwing.

Number 10: Home is a place where if you show up at all, aren't drunk, haven't screwed some other woman on the way home, and hand over your paycheck to your wife, you feel all which is reasonably expected of you has been done—and now you ought to be left in peace; after all, shouldn't a man's home be the one place in the world where he won't be nagged or bothered? If this profile fits you, you're one very depressed guy. You're a man who hates life and struggles to ensure you won't derive pleasure anywhere in order to maintain your victim image. You are a sad man who refuses to see the possibilities of joy and happiness.

If any of the prototypes on this list rings true for you, you're perpetrating Stupid Husbanding and missing out on many pleasurable, moving experiences which will make the difference between merely a life lived and a life worth living.

I'm Married . . . Now What?

For a lot of men on the list above, the parameters of manliness seem to be defined by the "stiffness" of an upper lip and/or a lower organ—certainly not by sweetness and gentleness—or so my listener Ken had thought . . . until:

My wife is a huge fan of your show—and she'd talk about something you'd said. I'd listen, but never took the time or the interest to tune into your show—until today. I was driving home when you spoke about having people fax into you something in their lives that changed their relationship.

I started to cry. And now as I type this, it's very hard for me to keep from crying because I love my wife so much that when we were first married I almost blew it and lost her.

We are both 42 now, but we got married at nineteen—not because we "had to", but because we loved each other.

In the beginning I was not affectionate, nor was I home and I moved my wife from her home of fifteen years and then I was so uncaring toward her that I would leave her alone while I spent time with my friends.

I never wore my wedding ring. I must admit that for some

unknown reason I never cheated on my wife and I know that she has not cheated on me. But for some reason the ring seemed to bind or control me—maybe take my freedom—I don't know.

My wife's mom told her to stick it out; that marriage was something that needed to be worked at—and because of this my wife stayed with me. She's such a beautiful person, inside and out, I wondered why she stayed with me.

I'm a total jock: martial arts, jogging, baseball—you name it, I'm it. And I've always wondered if that was the reason for my stupidity or stubbornness.

My fingers are actually shaking as I'm typing this. I've never done this before and as I write I can't help it—the tears are just streaming down my face—and I feel so ashamed.

The turning point for me was when our two children were young and they took up so much of our time that we just didn't have the precious time to spend with each other. Somewhere, we heard about taking showers together—so, we tried that at night after the kids were put to bed. If the phone or doorbell rang—so what?

It wasn't sexual—but sometimes it turned out that was. But it was a time when the two of us could talk and listen and really get to know each other. We'd wash each others' backs and feet and whole body. But most important, we got to know each other's real hopes and dreams and that the other was a major part in achieving those hopes and dreams.

And now I know why she takes by breath away: because I totally love her. She's my best friend and most important, I feel so good when I'm with her.

I think about her during the day and even though she's not beside me, she still makes me smile—if that's not love, I don't know what is.

If anyone is having communication problems with his spouse, turn off the tv, don't answer the phone, and take a shower together and be tender to each other and just open up your ears and listen—because the best thing in your life is standing right in front of you.

I'm sorry—but I can't take this anymore and I'm crying so hard that my head hurts. But I just wanted to let you know how I saved my marriage, through something as simple as a shower.

The intensity, candor, and spontaneity of Ken's letter deeply moved me. Judging from the many faxes and calls I get after I read a letter like this on the air, it's clear that this kind of shared experience has a huge impact because it says so simply, yet so passionately, what you men need and want to feel and experience. That's why these letters are here in this book—to catapult you *inward,* toward your own inner truths. Let's go on that pilgrimage together. We start with your honesty: isn't it true that you feel diminished if you're seen primarily as a *mere* "husband"?

To avoid a label Ken and so many other married men have joyously come to cherish, you make sure you

- don't say "I Love You" (maybe you resort to seemingly cute euphemisms like, "I muff you"? Yechh!)
- don't wear your wedding ring ("Oh, I hate jewelry," or "I don't need symbols to remind me," and other assorted lies)
- don't feel you shouldn't have to call home to say, "Hi!," or let her know you're going to be late ("I may be married, but I'm not castrated!" is your stupid freedom cry)
- don't ask how you can be helpful around the house ("I gave at the office")
- don't give up all your "single guy" or "buddy" activities ("A guy needs his space")
- don't involve her in major purchase decisions (your toys), but get angry when she wants the same privilege (her toys) ("Hey, who's in charge here? Who's the man of this house?")
- don't see "time spent with her" as productive or important ("I expect you to be here when I need you—not out wasting time and money with your ditsy friends")

- don't see listening to her day or thoughts or ideas as interesting or necessary (too threatening to you?)
- don't think of continuous courtship—you know, romantic stuff—as anything but annoyingly obligatory ("Women are just too childlike, dependent, and demanding")
- don't take care of your hygiene and appearance ("Hey, this is who I am. Take it or leave it")
- don't see anything wrong with watching TV or working in the garage all night ("This is my house—I can do whatever I like")

Well, guys, if any of this sounds like you, you may be feeling momentary swells of self-righteous power, control, or victory—but you will ultimately lose everything of value. My listener Alan discovered this in time—he considers himself very lucky:

Thank you for being my conscience. It has been approximately three years since while on my way to see my (as you would call) "honey", that I listened to you tell this guy who had said that he didn't love his wife anymore and that he was having an affair that he should expend the type of energy that he was willingly going to spend on his "honey" on his wife! I believe his response was, "How?" You replied, "Just love her."

These words have echoed through my head ever since. I think there are times in all of our lives that we all need a wake-up call. Mine came on that day. I have also learned that just saying, "I love you" to someone just doesn't cut it because this was the lie that I lived. All relationships are hard work. By this I mean we cannot take the other party for granted to try to think for them. We must communicate with each other and be prepared to sacrifice in order to make what is truly important to us work.

*Your down to earth moral thinking and ability helped to make me look at the real problems in my life from **inside** and not blame **others**.*

I have been blessed with two wonderful boys ages four and

two. I am also blessed with the opportunity to put my life back together with my wife. I cannot tell you how great a pleasure it is to have the special ones around you love and accept you in spite of your inadequacies—the thought of hiding from those inadequacies by leaving or hurting the ones who love you is stupid.

Not so hidden in Alan's letter is the unbelievably important concept of blaming others, especially your wife and family, for your emotional turmoil or for life's problems. I know that it is definitely more difficult for men than for women to appear weak, frightened, needy, worried, a failure, inadequate, confused, lost, or even sad. These are not among the most desired life experiences—yet they are definitely part of the human condition. When women display any one of those "difficult" states, men (and other women) rally to fix it! When men do it, they react by secretly attempting to "fix it," mixing in with other self-destructive actions; acknowledgment of need and reaching out for help are admittedly not typical male solutions to the very human problems which intermittently challenge everybody.

Sadly, so many women who protest men's lack of overt emotional display and discourse are the first to attack men when they do "open up"; that's because the women generally don't want their men to be blatantly sensitive about their own feelings (too much defensiveness and pressure on the women to be accountable to their upset men, as well as their loss of male as daddy/protector fantasy image); truthfully, the women want their men to be sensitive primarily to the *woman's feelings* and/or only want to hear his positive feelings with respect to her!

It is also true that by the time many of you men get around to being honest and open about your problems, you've already created such a mess by your desperate "fix it" attempts—actions geared to hiding feelings, and obnoxious behaviors motivated by frustration and self-defense (warranted or not)—that it becomes very difficult for your wife to settle down enough to give you what you need and should get in the way of caretaking. If this is what you typically do, don't blame her!

Let me go back to something else in Alan's letter: morality. It is the moral value we put in commitment which can make the difference between a life of behaviors aimed at "self-defense" (I'm doing these drugs, drinking, women, gambling, or whatever else, because . . . *now add some excuse*) and behaviors aimed at healthy survival, repair, and growth. My listener Art *finally* got it:

> *I have been married 8 times to 5 different women. Because of you I have finally got it right. You being so direct and to the point is what got my attention. My wife and I both listen to you—I am 60 and my wife is 63. This is her 4th marriage. The point I have always missed in all prior marriages was commitment. I always made a commitment to the woman. Then, when we were in disagreement, I could always quit. Through your program I have learned there was an area I had never committed to. That was the commitment to the marriage.*

This is a very profound understanding: since your feelings for the other person may wax and wane with gastrointestinal irregularity, your commitment to your marriage vows must override the moment. When that is so, you will always behave more lovingly and contribute to a growing, quality marriage. That means, for example, if you're miffed over some misunderstanding or irritation and you decide to get vengeance (even the score, teach her a lesson, let her experience the same pain) your overriding sense of commitment to marriage and family will help you bridge those troubled waters. Your actions will then follow your sense of what is right in the context of that commitment versus what you feel like doing in the context of a bad mood.

One of my listeners, mid-divorce, sent me the results of his three-month review of his Top 10 Screwups:

1. *Switching from overdrive romance to cruise control after the wedding*
2. *Listening only with one ear*
3. *Constantly watching cable TV sports*
4. *Forgetting (yeah, right) anniversaries*
5. *Criticizing personal habits (especially the ever-sacred bathroom time)*
6. *Only asking "what's wrong" once, when you already know what's wrong*
7. *Too much work and not enough play*
8. *Slipshod personal hygiene*
9. *Taking anything for granted*
10. *Not ever talking about anything important*
    Dr. Laura—thank you for being the band-aid on the bloody knees of my achin' broken heart.

Now, before I go on and on and on with the mistakes you guys make in not husbanding properly, I feel morally obligated to cut you some slack. While there are obviously basic standards of husband appropriate behavior (no affairs/addictions/abuse, good sex, conversation, mutual time spent, help around the house and with the kids—they are yours, you know—holidays with the relatives, and so on), the specifics are really not so clearly drawn because we women are—truthfully—changeable and complicated. This "list" off the Internet (author unknown) says it all:

The Rules

1. The female always makes the rules.
2. The rules are subject to change at any time without prior notification.
3. No male can possibly know all the rules.

4. If the female suspects the male knows all the rules, she must immediately change some or all of the rules.
5. The female is never wrong.
6. If the female is wrong, it is because of a flagrant misunderstanding which was a direct result of something the male did or said wrong.
7. If rule #6 applies, the male must apologize immediately for causing the misunderstanding.
8. The female can change her mind at any given point in time.
9. The male must never change his mind without express written consent from the female.
10. The female has every right to be angry or upset at any time.
11. The male must remain calm at all times, unless the female wants him to be angry or upset.
12. The female must under NO circumstances let the male know whether or not she wants him to be angry or upset.
13. Any attempt to document the rules could result in bodily harm.
14. If the female has PMS, the rules are null and void.

The only women who could find fault with this list are insanely radical contemporary feminists. Any other woman will admit this is all true! That's why I have come to love the television program *Home Improvement*. The marriage between Tim and his wife is an obviously good one. Tim has to deal with "The Rules," but he does so with the same acceptance, humor, and compassion that his wife does for him and his "Tool Guy" mentality. That's the key: acceptance, humor, and compassion—not frustration, anger, and resentment.

It takes time to "know your woman," and it takes time to mature into appreciating that, while you may never thoroughly understand or anticipate the female mind and behaviors, it is a journey worth taking.

Before I get back into the serious stuff, let me give you George's take on the Top 10 Things Not to Say to Your Wife:

1. *Not tonight, honey, I've got a headache, and besides, the game is on.*
2. *I only wish you were Cindy Crawford.*
3. *That dress makes you look 10 pounds heavier*
4. *Your mother reminds me of one of the Smurfs.*
5. *That dress would look better on me than you.*
6. *I was so sure that you wanted to have 6 kids at once.*
7. *Honey, I think that you have more gray hair than my grandmother.*
8. *Honey, from where did you say you lost that weight?*
9. *But honey, it doesn't matter, because I did not marry you for your looks.*
10. *I would never leave you for another man.*

Well, maybe not as profound as I like to think my lists are—but I'll agree, George, these are definitely best left *un*said. And that's the next point I think needs making: that the things you say can contribute to your woman's unease, and your wife can only give you her best when she feels safe.

Although it is the minority of marriages where physical safety is an issue, in almost all marriages there are those times when the emotional safety is threatened by criticism, sarcasm, blaming, and put-downs.

I think you men tend to be "defensive" (hiding faults, frailties, and vulnerabilities) and therefore use these disgusting means to try to improve your image or feeling of power. But, listen up: you are ultimately not going to get what you need and dream about from your marriage if you diminish your woman as your primary means of feeling whole and strong.

Additionally, threatening to leave as the "supreme control" technique is equally obnoxious. You have to deal with your anger and frustration in ways which don't give the impression that your wife must acquiesce (sell her soul) or be abandoned. You may get her to be quiet with that tactic, but you'll never get her to love you.

Can you see the underlying concept? You must not only "go to work and earn a living," you're responsible for "working on yourself" and should not expect to be accepted "as is" (What? Did she get you in a basement sale?) when "as is" isn't right. You're also responsible for seeing your wife as just as important to the universe as you are.

My listener Brent's 10 Rules for Stupid Husbanding apply here:

1. *Forget what we did to get the girl in the first place . . . and why.*
2. *Allow our minds the "indulgence" of so-called harmless thoughts/fantasies about other women . . . all get—no need to give.*
3. *Put ourselves in a position to meet the emotional needs of someone other than our wife in the name of "caring" . . . instant hero feelings.*
4. *Don't work hard enough to meet the needs of our wife.*
5. *Always make plans for improvement . . . starting tomorrow.*
6. *Don't humble ourselves—don't rely on the intuition and discernment of our wife.*
7. *Don't allow others to see the real us.*
8. *Forget the entire world doesn't revolve and hinge on what we happen to want at any given moment.*
9. *Have completely and utterly ridiculous double standards when it comes to our actions vs. our wife's actions.*
10. *Last and most important, believe that we have the inherent power within us to control, manipulate and guide our lives in accordance to our own will, instead of yielding to the divine, infallible direction of the Creator.*

So far I've been approaching the subject of *husbanding* from the negative, in other words, from what you shouldn't do and how you mess up. Let me change direction by introducing the "Pledge" which Chuck and Mary sent me. They made it part of their vows when they were married, and continue to live it every day.

Needless to say, Dr. Laura, our marriage is excellent. Enjoy:
1. *I will never make promises I can't/won't keep.*
2. *I will never lie to you to protect you or make it easier on you—if we can't face it together we have nothing.*
3. *I will always share my feelings openly and honestly—even if it hurts—because by sharing, we can ease the pain.*
4. *I will respect you as an individual, for as we grow as individuals, it will only make "us" stronger.*
5. *I will value your opinion, though it may be different than my own, and learn from you because of it.*
6. *I will cherish the love you give me, because there is no more precious gift than that, and if I lose it, it may never be found again.*
7. *I will never take our relationship for granted, for if I do, it will die.*
8. *I will always try to be a friend first, before a lover, because love is sometimes blind, and a true friend has nothing to fear.*
9. *I will be true to you and only you, in body and soul.*
10. *No matter what the future holds, I will be by your side.*

Yeah, But, What's My Motivation?

A lot of you guys are reading this book looking for lists of "to-do's," hoping that it's a simple instruction manual, that you'll mechanically know what you have to do to keep her off your back. That's not what this book is about and that's not what you need in your life. "Doing" is not nearly as important as "doing with the right attitude." Without the right attitude you won't be sincere, consistent, or as profoundly moved by the relationship with your wife as you could be—as you need to be in order to find your life worthwhile. Here are some examples of "motivation" and "the right attitude":

I wanted to write and tell you of a real turning-point in my marriage. I am one of the many tens of thousands of men who have attended a "Promise Keeper" event. The speaker was talking about husband, honoring their wives by serving them. I sat there quite smug at that statement because I DO a lot around our house: I provide a lot of care for our children, I cook, clean, do laundry and so on. But then he asked, "Why do you do the things you do for your wife and family?" And I realized that I did all the hard-working, helpful things I did because I wanted my wife to see that I was a great husband . . . a catch . . . and not because of my desire to show her my love and make her busy life easier. In fact, I realized that I would stand at the sink doing dishes—but my insides were wrenched with anger. I'm sure it showed because my wife was always apologizing for what I was doing.

My heart was changed that afternoon and I resolved to "do" around our home for the right reasons—and my whole outlook has changed. It is a joy to be able to serve my dear wife and children and it breaks my heart that there are so many men who miss out on the marriage-enhancing, child-shaping opportunities that dishes and dirty clothes provide.

I want you to know, that you as one man, change the history of the world for the better when your attitude toward your family is positive and your behavior unselfish and loving. How? By the message it gives your children: what it tells your daughter to demand in her man, and what it tells your son about how to be a man, a husband and a father. The influence on their lives and consequently through the generations changes the world!

Here's proof from my listener Keith:

*I'm writing this in response to your female caller whose boyfriend thought his micro-biology class was more important than her surgery. You told her there were better guys out there. I want to tell you about **my hero**, my **role model**.*

Just after I was born in 1961, my mother was diagnosed with rheumatoid arthritis. She has since had several surgeries including total hip replacement, both knees, artificial knuckles in her left hand, etc. I grew up in a house where my father cooked, cleaned, went to work, and loved my mother with all his heart. He used to say to my mom, "June, let's put the kids to bed and neck!"

Last year my grandmother (my mom's mom) started losing it mentally and my aunt said she could no longer take care of her. My father quit his job at the age of sixty-two, rented out his home, built an addition on to the back of grandma's house and moved eighty miles to take care of her. Grandma doesn't even recognize him or my mother. My father has found another job and now works and takes care of grandma and my mother.

If any man knows the definition of the words love and commitment to marriage—it's my father!!

With that vivid lesson, what do you think Keith's style of loving commitment will be in his marriage? I doubt that Keith's dad did what he did because he was consciously motivated by his need to be a good role model. No, I think that he simply did what he felt was right because that's what you do when you're in love and fate is demanding more of that love than anyone imagines or can anticipate.

It worries me that some of you men reading about Keith's dad might simply feel sorry for him and his "bum rap." Perhaps you'd be expressing reasonable compassion—or perhaps you'd be demonstrating your limited appreciation of what brings happiness. There's a lot more satisfaction to be gained in the nobility of making the best out of life's challenges, having compassion for those you love, and fulfilling loving obligations—a lot greater than the satisfaction provided by always having a tight-bodied honey at your side, demanding nothing of you more than jewelry and dinner out.

Does that sound like I'm talking about selfishness? Well, maybe so. But, there are two kinds of selfishness: the good kind and the bad kind. Here's an example of the good kind:

I have been married to a wonderful lady for 31 years and I am probably the most selfish man in the world. I say selfish because everything I do is because these things make me feel good and stroke me in the way I want. Let me give you an example.

I take my wife to lunch and/or dinner because of the great pleasure it gives me to sit across the table from this beautiful lady.

I open the car door for her because of the great pleasure I get from watching her slide in and out of the car. It is a beautiful sight seeing her legs swing out of the car and her foot touch the ground. What a surge of desire!

I take her coffee in the morning because of the joy and pleasure of seeing her open her beautiful blue eyes in the morning.

I telephone her from work each day because of the peace I receive from hearing her voice on the phone.

I kiss and hold her when I get home from work because just the feeling of her arms around me makes my day okay.

Well, you see that all I want to do is please myself—do you think there is help for me or not? It seems the longer I am married to this lady—the more selfish I get.

Here is a man open to the beauty of his love for his woman. He interprets all experiences with her as loving, sensual, and peaceful. Interpretations are constructed of attitude and choice. His continued sense of connection to his woman doesn't stem from her—it stems from him. That's good selfishness at its most elevated. And, if you're bored—that's also how you willed things to be seen and experienced.

My listener Brian confirms this:

I was listening to your show today when "Alan" called. He was 22 years old, married with two small children. During your conversation, you (very rightly) evaluated his situation as "boredom." I could not believe that he was so willing to toss his family out the window for that.

After the commercial break, you said that love is far more profound than the infatuation and lust that comes with a new relationship. On some levels I felt sorry for him—but then I realized that I too was 22 when my second daughter was born. I was married at 20, and now have 3 cherubs that I love past words. My first love, Kate, and I will be celebrating our 10th anniversary soon.

We've been through a lot, but I could not agree with you more about the definition of love. It is NOT just a feeling. IT IS a decision and a commitment. I also agree wholeheartedly with you about putting oneself back into the relationship.

I have found that when I've felt the overwhelm and the tedium of day-to-day, I start to overcome these feelings by taking small steps. First, to tell my bride about the situation. Talking really helps. And the next step is just to start putting myself back into the family. This includes doing something for myself to recharge.

There is such peace, comfort, and calm knowing that no matter what, my wife and I will always be, and I will always be my children's DAD.

Wow—it sounds so backward, doesn't it, voluntarily diving back into what you think is drowning you? But it is through that re-investment that you are re-charged, re-connected, and re-born into a higher level of relating to the realities of life with your wife.

Additionally, it becomes lite-beer clear that it wasn't the marriage and family dragging you down at all! It was your attitude and behaviors in response to all or some of the various circumstances of your life which you needed to approach differently—the family and wife were the scapegoats for your fears, worries, and general discomforts.

Don't Allow the Negatives to Assassinate the Positives

Attitude is important, mostly by its focus. If you're the type who is only relieved by, or generally inattentive and unappreciative of, the positives, then you probably have your antenna alerted to negatives. When she says or does something you don't like or want—it's war. When she says or does something you do like and want—it's what it's *supposed* to be? Ouch. There is no way to be happy with that perspective, since negatives are a persistent part of life.

No, fellas, the attitude you need to be happy is gratitude. Be grateful that the positive things are a blessing, a gift, and a joy as well as the insulation against destruction by the negative.

And remember—it isn't a *your* marriage, it is an *our* marriage. Neither the burdens nor the blessings are experienced or created by you alone. Anonymous from Pasadena pointed that out in this fax:

I've been married for 14 years to my wife and have three lovely boys. What's made our marriage successful is an easy and logical formula:
1. *trust is paramount between us*
2. *respect for each other's own being and intellect*
3. *sensitivity and attention to one another's needs*
4. *team work with household responsibilities*
5. *talk out our problem, not necessarily always agreeing—but keep open mind*
6. *team work with child rearing*
7. *constantly leave romantic messages for one another (romance games)*

WE share everything: money, trips, ideas, etc. Sounds ideal? We have our problems but we've always worked them out. Please share this with your audience.

See his attitude? It isn't "am I getting MY needs met," or "what have you done for ME lately." His whole attention is to the team, the marital unit, the WE, not just the ME. Anonymous's concern is with reciprocity, not counting only his pluses and minuses. He is primarily focused on what HE IS TO DO; since she too shares that focus, they are both well loved.

When Giving Is Too Threatening

One of the most obvious forms of giving is with a gift. When I was in private practice, a typical wifely complaint during marital counseling would be that the husband either forgot, refused, or messed up gift giving. It was rare that the woman was a greedy pain. It was more typical that the man was either threatened by the "meaning" behind the giving, or passive-aggressively frustrating and disappointing her—out of revenge for feelings he'd never have the guts to say straight out. Here's a letter from my listener Sherrie about such a man:

My boyfriend and I were discussing the roles of men and women in a marriage and I expressed how a woman needs to know she's important by having certain duties to perform, receiving cards and gifts from her husband, spending time together, being told she's loved, etc. He told me that the woman should not need those things to feel important—that just knowing that the husband made the commitment to her by making her his wife should communicate her importance.

He admittedly has a hard time expressing love whereas I tend to overdo it—although I know we both experience it intensely and deeply. My questions: #1 who is right? #2 how do I express

*my opinion without being a nag and how do I stop using
phrases such as, "but that hurts my feelings"?*

What's always fascinating in these predicaments is that the
very person negating the other's need for reassurance and
love is the needier of the two. By refusing to cater to his
woman's need for assurance and affection, Sherrie's guy is
really refusing to admit the depth of his own desperate need
for assurance and affection. Perhaps he thinks it unmasculine; perhaps he thinks his need should not be expressed, for
it shows his ultimate weakness; perhaps he is embarrassed by
what he thinks is excessive emotional dependency and neediness; perhaps he fears that if he admits to his emotional
needs, they won't be met (pain avoidance) or he'll be rejected
because of them.

Whatever your "perhaps," it can turn to cruelty, not only
by denying others what is reasonable in a love relationship,
but by denying that what they want is either possible or
healthy.

Contrast that to my listener Robert's experience with gift
giving:

> *My wife, Carol, and I have been married for over 30 years, and
> since we already have pretty much what we want, we agreed this
> year not to give each other a Christmas gift but rather to enjoy
> giving them to other family members. However, during one of
> your programs aired before Christmas, you were discussing the
> irrelevance of the cost of the gift, but that it was far more
> important that the thoughtfulness was evident. Immediately I
> thought of the large picture frame we've been meaning to fill for
> years—the kind with spaces to put a bunch of snapshots. So,
> stealing a few hours when Carol wasn't home, I looked through
> all our old snapshots and filled the frame with these memories. I
> wrapped it and, on Christmas day told her to open it. She
> looked at me suspiciously (had I violated our deal?) and then
> unwrapped it. Dr. Laura, I've given her many gifts over the*

years, but never have I seen her cry after opening one. THAT was her gift to ME. It meant so much to both of us, and it was FREE.

But What About the Problems?

While it is extremely important to have a grateful attitude, what about the problems that inevitably occur in any marriage and in general throughout life? First, don't ignore them out of fear or confusion. I can't tell you how many guys, mid-divorce, call my radio program insisting, "I thought everything was fine." I reply, "If you persist in this clueless point of view you lose your family. You have to be willing to look at what's wrong/bad/failed and work together with your wife to fix it."

At this point some of these male callers admit to problem drinking, a bad mouth, virtual uninvolvement with family, and more. A few stay stuck, proclaiming, "I honestly don't see anything wrong."

Well, guys, your attempt at seeming innocent will land you in solitary confinement once she moves out with the kids and the washer-dryer.

Cheryl's husband, Lou, was braver, and he gained everything back:

I found out that I had to have a hysterectomy. Lou is working 14–16 hours a day and our 5 year old is climbing back into bed with us. Lou sat down with me one night and said that we really need to talk and I could tell by his tone that this was going to be fairly serious. He said that he was really afraid of what was happening to our relationship and that we had lost all of the romance we used to have. Our lives were reduced to managing life, kids, work, activities, etc. He said that we really needed to get away and it would be sooner than later.

The first night of Hannukah, Lou handed me an envelope

and said, "This is the first of 8 clues for your Hannukah gift this year! The first night's clue was a certificate for a pedicure and manicure. The second night, a bathing suit. The next night a tape of Beach Boy Music and some tanning lotion . . . and so on. Well, he planned leaving the kids with mom and dad and flying to Paradise Island in the Bahamas for 4 days and 3 nights of romance.

Our love is stronger than it has ever been and the tough times have been the glue that has made our marriage work. The surgery went well and after the trip, we signed up for our first class together: ballroom dancing!

Instead of blaming his wife for the problems, Lou addressed the truths of the priorities that needed reordering—and he did something about them. Instead of ruing his "fate," he realized his contribution to the problem and bettered it!

There are, of course, times when YOU'VE righteously blown it. What then? Again, admit to screwing up—and fix it. This is much more productive than denial, blaming, rationalization, or annoying excuses. Just own up AND do something creative to repair the situation. Of course, sometimes it's too little and/or too late. This is Steve's case:

I'm 34 and my ex-wife is 31. We have two children ages 8 and 5. I had an affair, was caught, and am very sorry and guilty for my actions and the pain I've caused my family. I went for counseling and was diagnosed with depression and alcoholism and I'm in counseling and AA. The alcohol that I drank is my problem, and I realize that I'm the one who put it in my body. I just didn't see until now the damage I was doing. I want to restore the family.

Expecting your wife to tolerate indefinitely even one or some combination of the three A's (addictions, affairs, abuse) is obviously ridiculous—and only happens when she is just as disturbed or as weak as you. Obviously, the big losers are the children who are both exposed to these unacceptable behaviors and/or suffer the loss of a potentially loving, intact family.

Yes, you should do whatever it takes to bring your best self to the marriage for the sake of your children. If your sense of obligation to those innocent, powerless, dependent, sweet creatures isn't sufficient motivation for you to put your ego aside long enough to become more of a man (i.e., a better man), then the loss of happiness is too light a punishment for your crime.

Baby Shock

Speaking of children, it's a well-known marital phenomenon (and the subject of much sexual suffering) that sex and romance after babies becomes a definite challenge. Suddenly your sexy babe, your honey, your hot lover, turns into a *mother.* Most of her time, energy, and attention is directed to the small dependent creatures which you love . . . sometimes resent . . . and secretly envy for their special place on her breast. George, a listener who got through this torturous time, wrote:

> I heard on your show a call from a man who felt ignored by his wife and was considering having an affair. They had two small children and the man admitted that his wife had a lot of work to do. I have been where this man is, and I'd like to share my experience with that young pup.
>
> I'm a 40-year old guy, happily married for 16 years. We have two teenage boys. The unplanned pregnancy of the second one put their ages only 17 months apart.
>
> When our children were still pre-schoolers, I also felt ignored. Although I didn't seriously consider having an affair, because I really didn't have the time or energy for one. In my small minded way, I thought, "Well, if she's going to ignore

me, I'm going to ignore her, too!" This, of course, only made things worse. Then I heard a song on the radio where the singer implores men to find one hundred ways to show their women how much they are loved. "If violins she wants, let them play" goes one line. The singer promises a reward, "In your arms tonight, she'll reflect that she owes you the sweetest of debts."

So, I spent the next month finding things to do for my wife. I only did a few overt things, like leaving flowers on her pillow. Mostly, I did small things like making her favorite tea, giving foot rubs, making sure she had opportunities to go out with her girlfriends, increased my load of the household chores, warmed the cold sheets before she got into bed, rented romantic movies and cuddled a lot.

And I didn't once approach her sexually. After a month . . . I didn't have to. She came to me!

And it occurred to me afterwards that this is the same effort I would have put into seducing a woman into having an affair with me. And, I didn't have the associated guilt or other unpleasant side effects of an affair.

That was a long time ago, and I'm still finding One Hundred Ways, and I have no complaints in any department!

But What's It All About?

George found a way to get that lovin' feelin' back into his relationship, but is that all he learned? Too many of you men measure happiness in your marriage by how much sex or attention *you're* getting; sex and attention are an integral part of the process, but they really aren't the foundation of what you truly need and ought to expect. If you're not aware and appreciative of that reality, when your marriage goes into a slump, it'll be terminal. Mark, a listener, wrote to me of his marital "slump":

My wife and I encountered a slump in our "feelings". The "fire" seemed to fade in our marriage, and I had become too dependent on those kind of feelings. Within months I filed for divorce on the weight of the cry that I felt I was "married to my best friend and not my lover". Each of us still felt a deep respect and admiration for the person of the other, yet those "warm fuzzy feelings" had faded.

We were not in a financial position to separate, so I obtained P.O. Box in October of that year to begin establishing some form of separation. My wife, deciding that divorce was not the answer, set out on a campaign to rekindle the "feelings". Before long I began receiving letters to Santa Claus (Dr. Laura, tears are filling my eyes as I type this letter to you now). She would tell Santa how much she wanted her husband back for Christmas. Letter after letter came to my mail box; each chipped away at the stubbornness I harbored (one does not want to lose face by being wrong).

By late November I realized my foolishness (the foolishness that perceived friendship in a marriage as a problem, the foolishness that depended on passion to measure a relationship).

On Christmas I turned to her with a large red bow on my forehead, "You will get what you want for Christmas," I said. The tears flowed as we embraced.

This is what I learned in that growth experience. Love and romance are not just feelings. They are actions that embrace and create feelings. Love is other-serving, not self-serving. A solid marriage is built on respect for the character of one's partner, not "warm fuzzies". The fuzzies will be there, but they are not a foundation, they are a reward for depending on the true foundation: the actions of love, the honor of respect, and the awareness that a solid relationship requires effort, sensitivity, and permission to be wrong.

We are celebrating our 7th anniversary this weekend. Neither one of us can fathom life without the other. We have a delightful relationship that brings joy to our hearts daily. We are best friends—and more.

I'm just trying to imagine you guys reading this last letter and not being reduced to a puddle of tears—either of envy or shared emotion.

But Isn't This Love 'n' Cuddling Girl Stuff?

Many men have written me, shuddering at the term *cuddling*. That's because this word connotes soft, sensitive, feminine . . . yuchh, right? As my listener Tom wrote:

Can you imagine a guy working out at the club and being asked, "What did you and your wife do last night?" His ego could never allow the response to be, "We had some real quality cuddle time." Cuddle time just doesn't cut it. On the other hand, when asked, "What did you and your wife do last night?", a response of "We had some quality WOOPI time," would be greeted with lots of "thumbs up", whistles and hoots. "WOOPI time" is a masculine term, acceptable to the male ego. The acronym WOOPI has the exact same meaning as cuddle . . . it stands for WITH OUT ORGASMIC PENIS INVOLVEMENT. Can't we convert cuddle time to WOOPI time?

Fellas, if it works for you, it's okay with us!

Bear That Weight

All these examples seem too good to be true, don't they? What about when your wife is a real pain, when life seems so draining, and happiness seems perpetually out of reach?

One anonymous woman wrote me of the living hell she put her husband through, and wanted to share with my listeners what she learned from her MAN.

For almost twenty years of our twenty four year marriage, I was a real witch with a "B". Looking back on those years I can see the immaturity in my thoughts and deeds. I said and did things that I am still kicking myself for. Somehow I managed to raise three great kids—only because they have the world's greatest dad and two outstanding grandparents. I'm writing this to let you know what turned me around.

It was almost a nervous breakdown three years ago, in the midst of a very stressful job. I was diagnosed with severe depression and have been on meds ever since. Once I began thinking clearly and seeing things in a different light, I began to repent big time. I once asked my hubby how he could stand to live with me all these years. He graciously replied, "I loved you, but I didn't like you." Make sense? With his enormous amount of patience, a lot of prayers, and my kids' smiling faces and spirits, I have come a long way.

Mainly, I have come to truly appreciate what my sweetie has given to me and how he has set such a great example for me. He helped me to see how I needed to change things in my life, never forcing me into a mold or ideal person I should be. WE have grown so much closer in the last three years. Now I am more sensitive to my husband's needs and I've become much better at reading between the lines when he doesn't feel like talking. If it weren't for the courage, patience and endurance of my eternal mate, I wouldn't have a clue about the purpose of our mortal existence. He's a great guy, my best friend, and a wonderful dad to our three munchkins.

Marriage as a Religious Sacrament

Michael Medved's Commentary in the *Washington Times* (6/9/96) confirms this woman's assessment that there is a purpose to our mortal existence, and that we learn much of it through marriage and family. Mr. Medved writes, "If the only purpose of a marriage is for two persons to make each other happy, then that marriage is bound to fail. First of all, no one can give happiness as a gift to another, and no couple can experience unending and uninterrupted felicity. If, on the other hand, two persons are dedicated to common purposes beyond their own pleasure, they stand a far better chance of establishing a lasting relationship—as evidenced by the much lower rates of divorce for couples who share a religious commitment. Even the happiest, most romantic couples experience moments of misunderstanding and strain, and at those difficult junctures, it helps enormously to know that your union has significance beyond the walls of your own home."

I fear that the cultural evolution of the last thirty or forty years—with its combined impact of almost total focus on the "me," denigration of religious faith and observance, dismissal of universal values, diminution of the importance and value of family to the individual and society, the increased permissiveness of drugs, sex, and incivility, and the elevating of self-expression and self-fulfillment to the center of our consciousness—is robbing both men and women (and obviously our children) of what is special, warm, wonderful, meaningful, and ultimately satisfying because it is based in a sense of purpose beyond immediate and personal gratification.

When you deeply believe there is a point to what you do beyond immediate reality, there comes a commitment and joy which is not easy to explain until you've "been there, done that." That is, to a large part, what religion reminds us of and reassures us with.

A Note from Jan

Sometimes, though, you do and do and care and care and feel it's having no impact. Well, if you don't think that what you do for your wife or family is noticed or appreciated, here's welcome reassurance from the "other side," my caller Jan's perspective on her honey:

> You often mention one of the most important ingredients in a good marriage is "kindness". I can't agree more, and just last

evening my husband bestowed upon me a very loving act of kindness that brought tears to my eyes and filled my heart to over-flowing.

When I arrived home from a late night meeting, my husband told me to go and change and get comfortable—I thought it was kind of strange that he was so anxious for me to go change right away, but I did. On my bed was an envelope with my name on it, and inside was the most wonderful card I have ever received (there was no special occasion—just an act of kindness involved here). I wanted to share the verse from this card as it sounded like something you would like:

Someday, when we have been together for a very long time, we'll turn out the lights and slow dance on the porch in our bathrobes. I'll write you love notes in large print and tape them to the frige. We'll wonder where the time went. And each night, we'll roll to the middle of our old bed into one another's arms, where we'll kiss, and touch, and dream the secret dreams that only old lovers know.

So, what d'ya think, Dr. Laura, have I got a "keeper"?

Jan, in a word, "yes."

Last, But Not Least

A listener, Michael, wrote the following amusing letter, which will conclude this chapter because it wittily says it all about refusing to be a perpetrator of Stupid Husbanding:

Our friends are constantly complimenting my wife and myself on what a wonderful marriage we have and they wonder how we do it after thirteen years. Well, Dr. Laura, little do they know that inside the walls of our home there is actually a fierce competition going on! No matter how hard one or the other of us tries, we cannot out-do each other when it comes to "meeting needs".

I will fold a basket of clothes for her because she can't look at one more pair of underwear after a long day of doing laundry, so she will top me by cutting the lawn while I watch a basketball game on TV. Well—I couldn't let that go by unchallenged, so when she got a raise at work I bought her a card and a bouquet of flowers to tell her how proud I was of her. Well, being the fierce competitor that she is, when I was out of work for a few weeks, she would come home and tell me how nice I kept the house and caress and hold me and tell me how wonderful I was. Well, I just couldn't let that go unchallenged, so I decided one night that it would be the night of her fantasy in bed; the focus would be totally on her and her pleasure. Well, the next morning I woke up with memories of one of the most sensually satisfying nights of my life! Rats!!! She had one-upped me again.

*I fear that this competition will go on for **many, many** years to come, and neither of us seems to be willing to put an end to it.*

Dr. Laura, I don't know if I should tell our friends about our deep dark secret.

Shhhh, Michael, your secret is safe with us.

8

STUPID PARENTING

*I see the purpose of life
when I look into
my child's sweet face.*

MARK, 1995

I happened to come across a fabulous full-page advertisement for the National Fatherhood Initiative in *USA Today* (6/19/96)—which clarified the difference between (a) what it takes to be a father, and (b) what it takes to be a dad. There was only **one** inclusion for the "father column": a drawing of a single sperm! The "dad column," however, included:

- read to your children
- keep your promises
- go for walks together
- let your children help with household projects
- spend time one-on-one with each child
- tell your children about your own childhood
- go to the zoo, museums, ball games as a family
- set a good example

- use good manners
- help your children with their homework
- show your children lots of warmth and affection
- set clear, consistent limits
- consider how your decisions will affect your children
- listen to your children
- know your children's friends
- take your children to work
- open a savings account for college education
- resolve conflicts quickly
- take your children to your place of worship
- make a kite together
- fly a kite together
- *you get the idea . . . it takes a **man** to be a **dad***

As Mike Royko wrote in his syndicated column (6/25/95), "You can have the IQ of a frog and become a biological father. And why not? Frogs do!" And a quip from one male listener also highlights the difference between a sperm donor and a dad: "One of the ten stupid things that men do is to help make babies but don't help make them into adults."

Are men taking an undeserved bad rap for their apparent statistical and historical lack of profound concern about the *pregnant* consequences of unprotected, uncommitted sex, commonly known as a baby? No, of course not—and you know it. Of course there are biological influences at work, such as the male animal drive toward "seed" dispersal, or the lesser male sense of bonding, since the womb is a girl thing. Still, too much of our society's moral and cultural climate has been destructively remiss about fostering and maintaining a sense of male responsibility for investment, involvement, and commitment to children.

It may surprise you to consider one of the most insidious negative influences on our nationwide loss of responsible fathers is contemporary feminism—but it's blatantly and sadly true. Feminists have been pounding the notion of "choice" into our culture for several decades now, and results of "choice" on family life and men's responsibility for pregnancy are pathetic and disastrous.

According to Brad Stetson's comments in the *Orange County Register* (8/9/95): "The ethical imperative of 'my body, my choice' has meant that women can decide whether or not to give birth once they become pregnant. But this principle—that personal, bodily acts (like sexual intercourse) require one's moral commitments only if one wants them to—has not stayed confined to the narrow preserve of abortion rights. Its prominent repetition through the years has caused it to become installed in the public consciousness as an all-purpose ethical touchstone for determining what one's moral duties are. So, women choose whether to become mothers, or more accurately, whether to give birth to the children they conceive . . . women—through electing either to obtain or not to obtain an abortion—choose *for* men whether men will become fathers."

The problem then becomes clear: if women can *choose* motherhood, if motherhood is an option, if a child's continued existence in a woman's body is secondary to personal desires—then *why shouldn't men use that same elective yardstick in deciding fatherhood?*

An unmarried woman faced with an unwanted pregnancy has a number of options:

1. an abortion (chemical—RU–486 or morning-after pill—or surgical)
2. adoption
3. single motherhood

An unmarried man is confined to the choices the woman makes. Some male advocates, furious with this current reality, espouse the position that if the pregnancy is "unwanted," the man should have no obligation to the woman or the child. These types of advocates, who in my opinion can readily slide under pond scum, are obsessed (and thereby have much in common with the radical feminists) with making all male and female realities equal, even, and fair. Well, friends, *complementary biological reproductive differences between men and women* just naturally conspire to make equality impossible. And what kind of "fairness" extends to the potentially terminated or abandoned, defenseless, and dependent, completely innocent, human baby?

Nonetheless, some men have tried to legally absolve themselves of responsibility for their legitimate offspring—and lost. In November of 1996, Richard Sine reported in *Metro* that Frank Serpico (the police officer famous for exposing NYPD corruption) filed a suit in New York State family court stating that he should not have to pay support for a child that was admittedly his because the mother had deceived him into pregnancy by secretly not taking her birth control pills. The family court judge actually ruled in Serpico's favor, saying that "planned and intentional deceit barred her from financial benefit at the father's expense." But Serpico lost on an appeal, in which a judge more reasonably ruled that fraud charges were irrelevant when the only consideration was the *best interest of the child*.

It gets even more bizarre! An Arkansas Supreme Court rejected an appeal involving a gubernatorial candidate who also proclaimed his "rights" in not being socially or financially responsible for a child he said wasn't his. When the DNA tests showed a 99.65 percent chance that he was the father, his story got better: he said that *if* the child was his, it was conceived after the woman broke into his home, stole a used condom containing his sperm, and artificially inseminated herself. The child won financial support—but lost the opportunity for a decent, two-parents married, loving home.

Now, obviously it is not in the best interest of the child to have these kinds of folks as parents. When these errant men complain that parenthood should not be a punishment for sex (which supporters of abortion and welfare agree on), they don't seem to appreciate that the punishment is primarily borne by the unwanted child (death by abortion or the challenges and loss incurred in a single-parent household).

Sadly, "choice based upon immediate preference" has permeated so much of our thinking—for example, shacking up and having babies in so tenuous a situation, and divorces based upon such rickety grounds as "don't feel in love anymore" or "I'm not happy" (which also shatters children's lives) followed up by new sexual partners with an even higher rate of dissolution. Adult demands for perpetually changing "choices" are destroying the fabric of our society and, therefore, our children's lives.

The newest "choice" issue is *intentional* single motherhood. According to an Associated Press report (11/8/95), a Census Bureau researcher said that many unmarried women today "[are] older, their biological clock is ticking off, so they cannot wait to find a suitable man. So they are going ahead and they are having a baby even though it's out of wedlock." Let me try to understand this: if a woman gets knocked up by a one-night stand or a boyfriend, he's a bum if he doesn't pay up. But, if she uses his body to get pregnant because she's incompetent to be in an adult committed relationship, the guy is a hero for donating sperm and going off into the sunset. Duh?

The women who determine with intent that their children shall have no father, either by unplanned and uncommitted sex or planned single motherhood (straight or lesbian), are wrong—that's it, they're just wrong. They are robbing children of a father and an intact family.

But hear me, guys: **None of the stupid shenanigans of women, or any intellectualized arguments about rights, absolve you of your responsibility as a man to honor your obligation to your children. It is morally reprehensible for you to abandon the needs of your child (planned or oopsie) for any reason at all. Period.**

Interestingly, both legally and morally, your obligation is

not only to your DNA, but to your fatherly behaviors. In 1996 the Iowa Supreme Court ruled that a man who raised a boy as his own son must continue to pay support for the child—even though a genetic test established he wasn't the biological father. One justice wrote that "although [the man] wasn't biologically related to the boy, he had been for all practical reasons the boy's father for years and should maintain that relationship. She said it was in the child's best interest."

I shudder when any men's advocacy group comes down on the side of minimizing the importance of a father to children and the importance of fathering to men. Perhaps they should all read my listener Allen's letter:

> *Couldn't stop thinking about the fifty year old guy who called your show saying he got his young honey pregnant but doesn't want to be a parent. My son is twenty four years old and if I had done what I wanted to when he was conceived, he wouldn't be here. My girlfriend at the time wanted to keep "it". We had already aborted one and she couldn't do it again. To make a long story short, we did not marry but I lived only blocks away and fathered my son on a daily basis. I am so grateful that I did. I rose to the occasion and now I have a son who loves me and whom I love. We went through rough times: I couldn't afford private school and he had some difficult times as a teenager— but because I was there role-modeling values and love for him, he has come out on the other side. I wasn't perfect and I would never do it that way again. But, because I rose to the occasion I now have someone to visit me in the nursing home . . . even if I can't recognize him at that point. (ha ha). It's all worth it.*

No-Dad Disasters

While I've said and written a million times that "history is not destiny" with respect to the choices and actions of an adult life, I can't deny history's *influence* and *challenge*—not *omnipotent* influence, and not *insurmountable* challenge, but, in the case of an absentee daddy, sad, difficult, and unnecessary influence and challenge.

I can't help reflecting on the calls I've gotten from so many fatherless young women, searching for that daddy "feeling" in too many beds with too many manipulative men. Also, I think of the young men and women so afraid of suffering another monumental loss that they withdraw from friendships, love, and intimacy—and sometimes life itself (63 percent of youth suicides are from fatherless homes: Census Bureau). And then there are the young men, so confident on the surface, but inwardly surly and hostile, hyper-masculinizing their social behaviors to deny hurt and need; their exaggerated masculine persona a testimony to a lack of a proper role model.

According to facts and figures published in the *Kansas City Star* (10/2/96), children from a fatherless family home are

- 5 times more likely to commit suicide
- 32 times more likely to run away from home
- 20 times more likely to have behavioral disorders
- 14 times more likely to commit rape
- 9 times more likely to drop out of school
- 10 times more likely to abuse chemical substances
- 9 times more likely to end up in a state-operated institution
- 10 times more likely to end up in prison

Other studies produce even more darkness: In reviewing the lives of 25,000 children, researchers Sara McLanahan and Gary Sandefur found that, compared with children raised by both parents, those raised by one parent (nine times out of ten it's the mother) were twice as likely to drop out of high school and two and a half times more likely to be teen mothers. Dan Davenport reports in the June 1996 *Better Homes and Gardens* that, "According to NFI research (National Fatherhood Institute), a child's parents' marital status has more influence over that child's future success than any other factor, including race, income and educational level of the parents."

Why? Is it just having a second adult around to share and balance the input and responsibilities of child raising? Yes—in part. But there is something significant in particular about the *male* figure that some females, and feminists in particular, might like to ignore, avoid, or deny in their devotion to uni-sexuality (50 percent of mothers see no value in the father's continued contact with his children—see *Surviving the Breakup* by Joan Berlin Kelly).

My listener Terry (male) wrote the following summary of an article in the 1997 *Pulpit Helps* magazine entitled "Fathers, You Are Important":

Sons learn about male responsibility, achievement, suitable assertiveness and independence best from their fathers. A father's authority and discipline in rearing sons, particularly teenage sons, is difficult for a mother to achieve.

When a daughter enjoys her father, she experiences a healthier femininity, she feels worthy of love, and she is able to trust. Daughters who are able to trust men normally grow up and marry trustworthy men.

Fathers stress the survivor skills of competition, challenge, initiative, risk-taking and independence. In contrast, mothers emphasize social integration, relationships and personal well-being. Fathers focus on their children's long term development, while mothers focus on their children's immediate situation. Fathers set limits. Fathers stress justice, fairness, and duty (based on rules). Mothers stress sympathy, care and helping (based on relationships).

Fathers help children differentiate their gender roles. Gender-typed children grow up in homes where the sex roles between their parents are not blended but are differentiated. Children learn the healthy use of power from father and love from mother. Researchers Westley and Epstein (1970) said that only this kind of parenting "produces predominantly emotionally healthy children."

Fathers' involvement plays a unique and irreplaceable role in older children's intellectual, emotional, and social development. Children can expect improved verbal skills, problem solving ability, academic achievement, proficiency in math and reading. The most striking effect, particularly for sons, is a child's increase in empathy and compassion. Males who exhibit antisocial and criminal behaviors almost never had good relationships with their fathers.

But it's Terry's postscript that drives the point home:

I can attest to the validity of the above article. I didn't turn to criminality, but have suffered socially as a result. My parents were divorced over 20 years ago and I can see the major repercussions on my life and my sister's life as well. My father cheated on my mother and mom put up with it for 10 years because of us then decided to divorce. They both remarried and neither second marriage was great. I determined myself to break the cycle of divorce that exists in my family even though I never had a good set of role models to understand what a family really is.

Whoa! I bet that woke up some of you men who were lulling yourselves into innocent complacency by imagining that fathers were "gone" only because some "nasty bitch" tossed 'em out on a premenstrual whim! While I am indeed seeing more and more silly and selfish women doing just that in the name of "I'm not *fulfilled,* or *happy,*" most of the time you men **ask for removal** with attitude, affairs, addictions, and abuse. And, if it isn't removal, deserved or otherwise, your absence is made likely because you never bothered to have a relationship of any value, duration, or commitment with the woman—the mother of your child—before you started risking the sperm-egg conspiracy. And the curse for your actions falls upon the heads of your children.

Now that I've made it abundantly clear that you men are an absolute necessity in your child's life . . . how can you pull that off while also taking care of all the financial realities of life? Well, first be married to the mother of the children. It also helps not to have a string of children left in homes with ex-wives and/or ex-lovers and/or ex-quickies.

QUESTION:
"WHY ISN'T GREEN RIVER
OPEN WEEKENDS?"

ANSWER:
THE WORLD NEEDS DADDYS MORE THAN
IT NEEDS CHEFS.

GREEN RIVER
RESTAURANT
ESPRESSO BAR

Believe it or not, this ad was displayed proudly and repeatedly in the *Wilson Daily Times*, Wilson, North Carolina, by Paul Little, the owner and chef of the coffeehouse. Imagine actually advertising the fact that you're sacrificing business for family!

Just an isolated oddity? I think not. Consider this from my listener Janet:

My husband and I are our children's parents. When I was pregnant with our first child, my husband left his well paying job to become a commission based financial advisor. He did this not to increase his earning potential, but in order that he would have more time to be the kind of father he wanted to be for his family. At the end of one year of my maternity leave, my husband took over as primary caretaker. There has recently been a re-organization at my husband's company. Although my husband's earnings are solely commission based (if he doesn't produce, he doesn't get paid), the management has decided that everyone must produce—regardless. Follows is the letter of resignation that my husband has submitted to his current employer. Is it any wonder that I am in love with this man?:

On our meeting of XXXX, 1996, you spelled out some of your ideas and conditions under which a representative of our region office must perform and operate. Since then, I have seriously attempted to keep up with a business pace which could satisfy such conditions.

Unfortunately, such a pace has significantly disrupted the balance and quality of my children's life. In the last couple of weeks, I had to bounce my children among different baby-sitters and households at all hours of the day, all in the name of Investors Group and its performance based on sales and not quality of representatives servicing the clients.

Given this intolerance from you and XXXXX, for the sharing of my business life with my family requirements, I hereby give you notice of my resignation effective immediately. After all, not even the potential of $100,000 per year income is a decent substitute for quality parenting.

According to an article in the December 8, 1996, *Houston Chronicle*, "More Men Putting Family First": "U.S. Assistant Attorney General Deval Patrick is leaving his position in Washington to return to his wife and two daughters in Milton, Mass. . . . Patrick is not shy about saying he's tired of being a part-time dad. 'My children would like to see more of me,' he says. 'They want me home.'"

Add to that list one William Galston, senior domestic policy adviser to President Clinton ("announced that he had missed too many of his son's baseball games and was quitting") and Jeffrey Stiefler, who resigned as president of

American Express, and U.S. Labor Secretary Robert Reich, who made his decision to leave "after getting home late one night and having to wake up one of his teen-aged sons to say goodnight."

Is this truly a trend, or just some isolated malcontents getting PR mileage out of "family values"? It is true that some men have been forced back into the home by downsizing, early retirement, or corporate mergers. But, according to Kathleen Gerson, a professor of sociology at New York University, 30 percent of the 130 men she interviewed for her book *No Man's Land: Men's Changing Commitments to Family and Work* wanted to be more involved with child rearing but, fearful of being penalized at work, were reluctant to ask for more flexible hours or even mention that they were planning to leave early to see a baseball game or a child's play.

Some men just decide to accept that Daddy Track. It's called a "trade-off." The following was sent to me by a customer of a Mobile Tire Service. The "Tire Man" (I have edited out his name) sent this proclamation to all his valued customers and friends:

> *In the past 7 years, it has been my pleasure to work for each and every one of you on more than one occasion. In 1989, when I started in my old beat up truck, I only imagined being as successful as I have been. Just lucky, I guess. In this short amount of time I have managed to build a clientele of over 350 businesses. From truck independents, construction companies and motocross tracks to national carriers, I have worked for just about everyone around this valley at one time or another. I've seen a lot of your companies grow up as well as many of your kids. Many of you and I have struck friendships as well as business relationships. Most of you even know my kids by name and have watched them grow up. Remember? I started hauling them around with me when they were only 6 weeks old, bottles, diapers and all.*

I started this business with the aspirations of opening a family owned shop someday. Somewhere that my kids could possibly work at someday. Along the way, I have realized that you can't have a successful business like mine (I am sole employee) without putting many extra hours when others might be at home, church, camping or who know's where or doing what with their families or spouses. This is where "I" have run into a problem. My children are now both in public school. Kindergarten and first grade. Kelsey wants to learn gymnastics, Joshua wants to play soccer and baseball. My other half is a business professional in Newport Beach, leaving the house everyday about 6:45 am and getting home some evenings as late as 9 pm.

None of this is your problem, I know—I'm just trying to make you aware of my situation at this time. What I'm getting to is this: you all must have realized by now it's becoming more difficult to reach me at times and also my response time is not nearly as quick as it used to be. This has come about due to the fact that I truly am MR. MOM and that I have more business than I can handle on some occasions. Don't get me wrong—I'm not complaining. It is just that I have had to and you my customers will have to make some concessions and adjustments on occasion in order for me to rassle all of my commitments. I'm giving it my best shot, please try to work with me if you can.

My kids mean more to me than anything in this whole world!!! Possessions, money, cars, houses . . . they all mean nothing to me in comparison to my family. They are my NUMBER 1 PRIORITY!!

AT this time I am taking my son to school each day at 8 am and at 10:45 I take my daughter to school there also. Then, once again, at 2 pm I must return to pick them up. I have been privileged in one sense that I have been able to take my kids to work with me a lot over the years and spend time with them as they have been growing up. But now I must sacrifice the almighty $$$$$ to be a good parent and spend more time getting my children fed, bathed and homework done each *evening at a decent hour so they can grow up healthy both mentally and physically. **This is cramping my TIRE MAN style—but it is something I HAVE TO DO!!***

Bottom line: At this time my days don't start til 8:15 am. I've gotta get my boy to school. Then I have to play it by ear to get my daughter there by 10:45, playing it by ear again until I again must pick them up at 2 pm. When 5 pm rolls around, I apologize, but I am going to have to bring my kids home and take care of family type business.

This means no more night service. And like I said, I will be taking every other weekend off to spend time with my family.

As far as the weekends go, I will be working every other weekend to take care of your fleets and any other work that might be over flow from the previous week.

MANY OF YOU MAY NOT GIVE A DAMN ABOUT ANYTHING IN THIS LETTER, BUT I MUST SPILL MY GUTS AND LET EVERYONE KNOW WHERE I STAND. IT'S A FREE COUNTRY . . . YOU CAN TAKE IT OR LEAVE IT— THAT'S YOUR OPTION.

Once Again I must say, Thank you. I honestly care about all of your needs and will always try to help if I can. Please see if you can try to accommodate my special circumstances.

Yours truly, the Tire Man

P.S. Don't forget . . . your kids only grow up once. You only have one chance as a parent to do the right thing. If you have the chance, don't miss it. I won't.

Can you imagine the impact this letter had on the customers and their families? I can just hear the conversations in those households struggling with guilt, loss, shame, confusion, anger, frustration, gender roles, and more. The Tire Man did more than put his customers on notice about his schedule—he forced them to put themselves on notice with respect to their family obligations. . . . You've been told!

And, no, I didn't miss the part where the Tire Man's kids only see their mother as she drives away in the morning and (hopefully) on weekends (assuming this is still her schedule). This becomes virtually a single-parent household, with the family not communing together at dinnertime. While I applaud his enthusiastic commitment to his children, I deplore the loss of the mother to the household. A blending and sharing is more valuable to the children than one absentee parent, be it dad or mom!

I Am Not the Baby-Sitter!

It is amazing that in 1997, there are still so many women, much less men, who look upon a committed, involved father as an oddity or a wonder. This is just what my listener David's complaint was about:

> My wife and I have been married for 11 years and have four children. On occasion, my wife (a stay home mom) will go out with a girlfriend or to a PTA meeting or whatever, and naturally, I am on my own with the kids. This is to me doing my job. I enjoy this responsibility and take pride in my role as my kids' father—whether my wife is there or not.
>
> What gets under my skin is the comment I always hear from people who call for my wife on the phone or come by to pick her up, "Oh, you're baby-sitting. How nice." I suppose this is a compliment, but I deeply resent the term "baby-sit." Baby-sitters get paid to watch **other people's kids!** Not only that, once the parents show up, the baby sitter has done his or her time: they are off the hook. I am never off the hook. If my wife were not at home with them I would be doing all the same things, but because I am a man, it is assumed that I am being a good sport and that I am out of my element.
>
> Hey man, **this is** my element! Do these people think I had kids to keep my wife at home? Would these same people dare refer to my wife as a baby-sitter? We had kids because **we** love kids. We father and mother them, we do not baby-sit.
>
> I am not a baby-sitter! I am my kid's dad!

Just how do men come by this hands-on family involve-ment attitude? Is it built into the chromosomes? I think not. So how is it acquired? In 1994, a mother wrote to Dear Abby about her concerns for her small son, who preferred dolls to more masculine toys. Of course, the worry was that since the boy showed "nurturing" (i.e., female) interests, he couldn't possibly be heterosexual. That fear is so great that both mothers and fathers tend to push boys away from any-thing which isn't definitely masculine—robbing them of a healthy exposure to and education about babies, compas-sion, sensitivity, and deep interpersonal family involvement.

One response to Dear Abby's column was particularly enjoyable: "When my son was 2 1/2, I gave him a doll. He slapped it under his arm as he rode his tricycle up and down in front of the house, where I could easily monitor him through the kitchen window. One day I saw a rather disagreeable elderly neighbor woman bend over and say something to him, which caused him to run to our front door. When I opened it, he asked, 'Mommy, am I a little boy or a little girl?' Of course, I told him that he was a little boy, and since (even at 2 1/2) he spoke very clearly, I told him what to say if this neighbor—or anyone else—questioned him about his doll. This same neigh-bor asked my son again why he had a doll. I saw her startled face when he looked up at her with his big blue eyes, and said clearly, **'I'm developing my paternal instincts.'** Incidentally, Abby, both my sons have become wonderful fathers."

And then there are the men who've had to learn it all the hard, yet profound, way.

Morality and Maturity Matter

Rod wrote to me about the birth of his triplet girls, an event *"that was so exhilarating and so indelible that simple words cannot accurately describe its extreme power, its extraordi-nary beauty, and its deep, rich meaning."*

Rod's typical day in the hospital consisted of getting up at

7 A.M. and doing all of the feeding and diapering of the babies until the night nurses took over at 11 P.M., at which time his wife lovingly told him how proud she was of him because *"most men wouldn't do what you did today."*

> *In my mind, those simple and utterly necessary, if exhausting functions were the only imaginable things I could do. The way I saw it, there were no other options . . . none. From the first moment I heard our first baby cry, my role in life had changed completely and permanently. Thanks in large part to your direct, insightful advice, my wife and I both believe in the complete responsibility of parenting.*
>
> *Lest this sound like a too-healthy dose of self-congratulations, I must tell you why what my wife said was so profound: Ten years ago, there is no way I would have handled those parenting chores the same way I have these last three days. I could bore you with the details, but I have neither the inclination to dredge up recollections of an occasionally wretched past, nor the space to list those misdeeds. The bigger point is this: maturity and morality matter.*
>
> *Ten years ago, I was lacking in both. And although the same demons that haunt my past are still present today, they have been isolated and roundly ignored. The reason? In a word, God. While I don't intend to proselytize, I think it's safe to say that morality absent the full acknowledgment of a Higher Power is an empty shell. Your unapologetic support of religion has helped us to examine how important our still-growing faith in God is to raising a family.*

Practice Makes Perfect

My listener Joe wrote about how he "practiced" to be a more perfect dad. He was the uncle of twelve nieces and nephews and had done more than his share of baby-sitting. He had a great dad as a role model for the first twelve years of his life—until his father's death. He served as a Big Brother and had a rewarding five-year experience helping bring a boy to manhood. And he had found the woman of his dreams after a very long search; with her he developed a strong bond and a solid friendship.

> *Even all of this was not enough to prepare me for the relentless demands of being a parent that I have discovered since the birth of his children. I did genuinely feel guilt when I complained about the pressures of parenthood because it was something I wanted, planned for, waited for and enjoyed. I can't help but think of the men I know in the world who didn't have the preparation I had or the desire for fatherhood I had.*
>
> *I strongly feel that the majority of society's ills are caused more by poor fatherhood than motherhood as the majority of society's ills are caused by men. Boys are most influenced (good and bad) by their fathers or by the absence of fathers. Men need much more help to become good role models as the fathers of their families.*

After realizing he was wallowing in self-pity when talking to a friend about the sacrifices he had made for his two children, Joe also wrote the following poem. With Father's Day around the corner, he thought it would be appropriate to put some perspective on the notion of "being a dad":

When I became a father,
I gave up everything . . .
I gave up sleeping in on weekends . . .
now, we make our weekly early morning "pig adventure"
*   walk to*
get bagels, make cream cheese lips and find out how many
*   ways we*
can spill chocolate milk.
I gave up my beautiful sports car . . .
now, we pile into the van for a messy, cookie crumbled,
*   sticky-fingered,*

wet-bottomed, sandy-footed, laugh filled trip to and from the
    beach.
I gave up workouts at the club,
now, I hold my little girl on my lap on my home workout
    machine,
as we sing, "Row, Row, Row Your Boat."
I have given up sleeping through the night . . .
now, I get to wake up after an unsettling dream of attacking
    lobsters, chasing snakes or talking teddy bears wakes up
    my son, and I rock him to
sleep in my arms and feel his gentle breath on my neck.
I gave up quiet, candle-lit dinners with my wife . . .
now, I serve the umpteenth version of "Chicken Nuggets du
    Jour" and
try not to show a smile as milk squirts from the noses of the
    laughing faces gathered
around me at the table.
I gave up watching the nightly news . . .
now, I smile in amazed wonder as my kids and I laugh
    together at the
same "George of the Jungle" cartoons I watched 25 years ago.
I gave up having extra, expendable income . . .
now, I have treasures I cannot even begin to count.
When I gave up everything,
I became a Dad. . . .

Quality Time Is Bull

In the *Grand Rapids Press* (12/96) Charley Reese wrote
about the best gift for children from their parents. Was it a
great house in that impressive neighborhood? Nope. Was it
the hefty bank accounts guaranteeing future security? Nope.
Was it several terrific cars? Nope. "A friend of mine," Reese
writes, "once taught American history at an expensive private school to sixth graders. One day, during a discussion of

the Great Depression, she was startled when one of the children said he hoped the United States would have another depression. Several piped up in agreement. When she probed the children with questions, she found out why. At the time, *The Waltons,* a series about a Depression-era family, was on network television. 'If we had a depression,' the kids said, 'then perhaps our parents would spend more time with us, like they do on *The Waltons.*'"

Mr. Reese continued with, "Time is God's currency. One way to think of it is, that when we are born, God opens an account for us and credits us with a finite amount of time. We rarely know the 'account balance.' How we spend this time determines our life."

According to a December 1996 *New York Times* report, the number of new fathers older than sixty is less than 1 percent of all registered births, but they are primarily men with guilt over the lack of time they spent with their first families. The sixty-nine(!?)-year-old father of two-year-old twins said, "My hope is that—I've been pretty selfish about things that I do myself, because that's the way I've always lived—maybe this time around I'll be less selfish and spend more time with them than I would have ordinarily. And, it may be that I'll be compelled to do that by the fact that I'll not be able to spend more time with them."

Oh great, he *may* be less selfish, and whether he is successful or not in this endeavor, his child (the experiment or act of atonement) suffers losing a dad at a rather early age. Guys, how about less selfish . . . now?

Becoming Unselfish

My listener Ed came back from selfishness with a flourish:

After the birth of my first child, I persuaded my wife to return to work on a part-time basis. This decision was strictly made out of my selfishness. My wife did not strongly agree, but grudgingly went along. After about four months, my wife could no longer stand being a part-time mom, and she (we) decided that she would become a full-time mom.

This decision was one of the best decisions that we've ever made . . . no one can replace a mom or dad. We now have a second child, and both are at home full time with their mom. Financially, this is a burden, but in all other ways this is the best experience that both my wife and I have ever had.

Virtually everyday I receive a call from my wife describing wonderful and precious moments that cannot be replaced. I feel sad for parents who have not realized their selfishness and are missing the pleasure of their lives.

It Takes a Good Man to Be a Good Dad

For general male unselfishness to become the norm, it's going to take you men reminding each other of their obligations and missed opportunities in life. Richard, a physician, did just that:

I am so disgusted. My co-worker's wife just gave birth to a baby boy. She is not a strong woman and the baby was almost a month overdue. I asked him if he was going to take a few days off to help his wife? His reply? "She will take care of everything."

Dr. Laura, I worked in Pediatrics so I would have some knowledge of caring for children. Why doesn't he care about how difficult it is to take care of a baby or child? His wife must be exhausted.

It's going to take lots more male role models, teachers, and general nagging pressure to help turn more men into good dads.

Disappearing Divorced Dads

One of the most typical means of robbing a child of a father is divorce. In the December/January issue of *Parenting* magazine, *Parenting* Art Director Marcus Villaga reported having trouble staying in touch with his four-and-a-half-year-old daughter. He is seeking advice in the "Problem of the Month Column":

"Anais lives in Lawrence, Kansas with her mother. She's too young to fly alone to San Francisco, so our time together is limited. I visit her every two to three months and send her packages with books that I think she'll enjoy, and call her every few days. But I want to know how other parents stay in touch and continue to build a relationship with their kids when they're far away."

I never tune in next month for the selection of self-serving answers—so I'll give Mr. Villaga my own: **FORGET IT, BUSTER. YOU CAN'T BUILD A RELATIONSHIP WITH A KID WHEN YOU'RE FAR AWAY!**

As I've told innumerable men who have called me whining about the same problem—most of whom moved away on their own volition or didn't have court-mandated agreement on the geographical requirements of visitation—"Get off your butt and move back to your child." Many of these men moan about job, money, new honeys, emotional pain, and such, but my answer is still the same: "A long-distance parent becomes the visiting stranger."

I'll let my listener George drive this message home:

The primary purpose of this letter is to thank you for reinforcing what it means to be a parent for me, and reassuring me that what I do is the right thing to do. As a divorcee, it is more difficult to stay involved with one's children. But it's the right thing to do. I didn't divorce them, I divorced my wife. There is a distinction. Being a father means being a father. PERIOD. Helping with homework, hanging out, providing love, encouragement and discipline are all part of it. I've let go of more than a few potential relationships because someone wanted me to "put (her) first". I stay broke a lot so they can have. I have let jobs and promotions slip by because taking them would have taken me away from my kids.

People don't see kids as integral. What fools. You say, "I'm Dr. Laura, my kid's mom." I can say it equally. "I'm George, my kid's dad," and mean it. THANKS, I needed the encouragement.

My listener Kevin's twelve-year-old daughter wrote an essay for school about her feelings for her dad. Two years ago, Kevin, divorced, was faced with the decision of staying in Chicago and furthering a ten-year career with a Fortune 100 company, or starting all over in Northern California and being a real dad to his two adorable children. He's not proud to admit that the decision was a struggle—but he did what he knew he should do and moved back. This poem is his reward, and hopefully, your inspiration:

My name is XXXX. My dad's name is Kevin. He has two kids. There is me and my brother. I am twelve years old and my brother is eight years old. My dad lives in XXXX and my brother and I live in XXXX.

My dad is special for a lot of reasons, but one major reason is that he's there for me whenever I need him. My dad drives us as much as he can to our school and sports events. He listens to me and puts up with me when I'm in a bad mood. He makes sure my homework is done and that I am trying my hardest in school. He is also my coach in sports. He always does what is right for me and my brother, even if we don't know it. My dad spends as much time with us as he can. I love my dad very much. There are a lot more reasons that my dad is special, but, to sum it up, if I had a choice between all of the dads in the world, I will always pick my dad.

There are those men who fight for and win custody of their children after a divorce. Richard was divorced sixteen years ago when his children were fourteen and nine. His ex-wife moved back home with her parents and made virtually no effort to be with her children. After several summers of his taking them to see her, the children said, "No more."

His "children" are now thirty-two and twenty-eight.

My oldest son should be home some time this week for 30 days before moving to his next station. You better believe that when I see him, we will hug and kiss and tell each other how much we love each other and miss each other. My youngest son and I talk on the phone several times a week and see each other also several times during the week.

Both men have turned out great, own their own homes, nice cars, good friends, etc.

They do, however, have scars as I do, but before the scars there were serious hurts which healed.

Would I do it again? You're damned right I would! I cried a lot, lost a lot of sleep, turned down promotions so that I could be with them. Did not date until after they were finished with high school and in college or the army. I dedicated my life to my two sons. I gave them every thing they needed: love, understanding, guidance, compassion, help, hugs and even kisses. They wanted for nothing. No, I did not purchase everything for them. They wanted something, they earned it the hard way: sweat and hard work. I helped.

I am my sons' father and proud of it!

Dad Is Important

I'm amazed at the surprise so many men demonstrate, the welcome surprise, when they hear me rant and rave, defending fatherhood. My listener Carl wrote a bittersweet letter about his personal revelation. He'd been married three times, divorced twice, with children from the first two marriages (two sons from the first, a daughter from the second). He moved to take a job so that he could support these families in such a way as to maintain their *material standard of living.*

> *I really believed that keeping the house and maintaining the standard of living was more important than dad being around each day. I called them every day and spoke to each, flew them to see me on holidays and had them for six weeks every summer. Now I realize that I spent twelve years being depressed because I was separated from my children.*
>
> *Now I've leased a home 10 minutes away from my daughter (the boys are 21 and 26) and will be "home" next Monday. Don't have a job yet . . . but I'll work that out.*
>
> *Many dads for various reasons never had anyone tell them that being their children's dad is really important—so your message to dads is the most important message I have ever heard. The very first time I heard you, in late October of 1995, telling a father that his duty to his children over-rode any other issue in his life just stunned me. I really didn't value my contribution to my children that highly. What you helped me realize over the next few weeks is that dad's contribution is important.*
>
> *I'm so very emotional at this moment that I can't express the debt I owe you. Thank you for helping me make the best decision I've ever made. I am a convert and tell every dad at every chance I get how important they are and how much they and their children need each other.*

This All Goes for Never-Married Dads Too

Children don't split hairs about wedlock—they want and need their parents. According to a June 1996 article about Christopher Darden, one of the Simpson prosecutors, his number one 1 regret is not losing the O. J. Simpson trial. It's being a long-distance dad. The article reports that he has a

16-year-old daughter out of wedlock and Darden commented that "leaving (the child) was the worst mistake I ever made. I thought I was doing the right thing when I left. I'd have been better off living homeless under the freeway and still stopping by to see her twice a week."

Well, "dropping by" is a lot less than the intentional daily investment a child needs, but at least Darden is man enough to admit regret.

I suggest you guys don't wait until that long.

Men Who Change Diapers Change the World

That's the headline for the winter 1996/97 issue of *At-Home Dad*, a newsletter (e-mail to Athomedad@aol.com) aimed at dads who are the primary caretaker. According to an article in the July 1996 *Rocky Mountain News*, some 2 million men in America are stay-home dads. The number one reason fathers choose to stay at home: They don't want their kids in day care. That's the conclusion drawn from a Father's Day survey of 268 readers of *At-Home Dad* magazine.

This imperative to avoid institutionalized day care is supported by Wendell, a listener.

> I am a 25 year old single black male, and I started listening to your program about a year ago. I have to admit hearing your strong opinions and well-thought out advice concerning the best interest of children has prompted me to make a significant change that will affect my life in the future and that of my children.
>
> Being a product of day care, I was a very disillusioned young man that really thought the best interest of a child was stability and love. As long as there were two parents in a committed relationship who loved their child, I saw nothing wrong with day care centers. I was under the impression that this is a two-income society, and as long as each parent came home at night, everything else would be perfect.

I was wrong.

After 11 months of listening to your program, I am definitely a changed man. Not only will I not put my children in day care, but your program has inspired me to pursue being a stay-at-home Dad. I'm a journalist by profession and currently applying to graduate schools across the nation to increase my money-making potential. Eventually my goal is to be a freelance writer working out of my home. Thanks for all you do.

Of course there are some obstacles to this endeavor. Having what seems like a "role-reversal," where the wife is the primary breadwinner, can create tensions in the marriage itself. Given both biology and sociology, women still see the man as the "one the family is supposed to count on" even if she has a great job! Part of many women's resistance to stay-at-home dads is the fear and discomfort of having the financial needs of the family on her shoulders alone (stress); part of it is also her longing to be with the children; another part is her expectation that although she is an independent, liberated woman, she still expects him to be the source of ultimate protection and production; and last and not least is her guilty defensiveness that she's not home with the kids, which manifests in her denial that any parent is better than day care.

Another obvious source of tension is the lack of support for dads staying at home from other men, friends, and family. Dave, a listener, used to feel guilty that he wasn't going to work and that his children would grow up thinking less of him as a man because of it. He learned better:

The only real physical activity I can pursue is running. Jogging through the neighborhood one morning, I heard you say, something about doing something right if it was worth doing at all. That moment I decided to train for the Columbus marathon. I cannot tell you how many times I fell and picked myself up. But, every time I did, I heard you say, "If it is worth doing, do it right."

So, with all that said and done, we drove up to Columbus, and on a cold Sunday morning I ran the marathon. And the last three miles all I could hear was your voice saying over and over again, "If it is worth doing, do it right." That was the only voice in my head until I neared the finish line and heard one of my kids yell, "That's my dad!"

But my running the race is not the point. I am a forty year old, happily married man. A little more than a year ago, I had to quit work due to a degenerative eye disease which has left me legally blind. That's when I became a stay-home dad.

One of the best things I can do for my children is to be an example of discipline and dedication. You see, Doc, your words are true: if I am going to be an example to my children, it's worth doing right.

Daddy's Second Thoughts

Many men have serious second thoughts about the sacrifices they make in time, money, and status to care-take their children either part- or full-time. I remember an on-air conversation I had with just such a fellow. He was a musician who had doubts whether to "go on the road" or continue the caring for his children. He did think about the opportunities, the success, the money, the ego gratification, and the fame. He was struggling with the decision and wanted my opinion.

I simply asked him, "What will matter in fifty years?"

His response was simple. "End of conversation. Thank you."

Another stay-home dad wrote me the following:

It is very difficult for me to imagine missing the doing/guiding/teaching/learning of all this with our son. If I/we hadn't made this choice I wouldn't fully realize the impact of my absence—but what I now know I will never forget.

Fighting the Wicked Witch of the West

Let's face it, some of you made stupid choices in a woman and mother of your children. One anonymous letter writer probably enjoyed his woman's sexually free and creative lifestyle (ohh, baby), but when she wanted to carry it on after they were married and with child he felt stunned and help-less. Fortunately, he had called my program and I advised him to get a good attorney and fight for custody (no kid needs a slut for a mom any more than a bum for a father).

> By presenting the best parenting plan and keeping the child's best interest number one, the judge ruled that I should have the primary care of the child. She is now with me 80% of the time. Thank you so much for advising me to fight. It cost me a fortune, but it was worth it.

I am amazed at how many of you men roll over and play dead when your woman becomes ridiculous, unfair, illegal, or immoral. If more of you men would fight the good fight, your children would be far, far better off.

A Question for G-d

My listener David has two boys: Jonathan is five and a half, Nathan is four (July 1996). The following was inspired by a night when David, before going to bed, checked on his two sons who were asleep in their beds. Jonathan had fallen asleep on the floor, so David lifted him up and tucked him into his bed, kissing him good night. Nathan, upon being relocated, awoke slightly and asked Daddy for his teddy bear:

How many . . .
How many nights do I have, God?
How many nights do I have to tuck each of my boys into bed
   with their teddy bears?

How many times do I have left, God?
How many times do I have left to lift my boys up onto my
    shoulders before they are too big?
How many more kisses, God?
How many more kisses do I get to give my boys after I've
    tucked them in at night?
How many pushes, God?
How many pushes do I get to give my boys on a swing
    before they out-grow it?
How many days, God?
How many days of hot summer do I have left to run through
    the sprinklers with my boys?
How many more tears, God?
How many more tears of joy will I shed at the end of each
    day that my boys have grown through?
How many more times, God?
How many more times will I get to lift my boys back into
    bed once they have fallen out?
How many more years, God?
How many more years before they come and lift me from the
    floor after I have fallen?
How many, God?
How many?

The point of this chapter for present and future dads is
that G-d has left these answers up to you.

9

STUPID BOYISHNESS

*Men feel in love
when a woman provides
mother-like caring.*

RON, 1996

Okay, all you detective story fans, here's my sexy chapter opening:

> "It was one of those curiously still, dark, foggy evenings. You never know what to expect on that kind of night. The air reeked with tension—bringing a rush of excitement to that deep and special part of me.
>
> "And then it happened: 'he' walked in. He was tall, six two or so, and blond with a deep tan that made your heart kind of squeal with anticipation. He wore a blue blazer with gray slacks. Even from my cautiously chosen table in this quaint out-of-the-way bar, I could feel the erotic tension mount as I watched 'that walk,' no . . . more than just a walk, kind of a . . . oh, no . . . I can't forget what I'm here for.

"He got to the table and was quiet, almost devoid of expression. He eyed me unflinchingly.

"That's when he did it. He put the diamond solitaire ring on the table and looked up at me expectantly. Next to the ring he placed a picture of his mother: all white-haired and smiling. Yeah—but that sweet-ole-lady-smile stuff didn't melt me—nah, I knew better.

"I knew how relentless and ruthless the mind behind those soft blue kindly-seeming eyes could be. I'd seen it so many times before.

"I realized that when I picked up that ring, the die was cast—the deal was made—the 'contract hit' was consummated. But, I couldn't complain. The job had to be done by somebody, and, for sure, this tall, blond, gorgeous hunk of a guy obviously wasn't up to it. This was WOMAN'S WORK for sure!"

The Hit Lady Syndrome

The *Hit Lady Syndrome* is the name I gave to the behavior of the wife of the fellow who hasn't quite managed to cut the emotional and behavioral umbilical cord that ties him to his mother. For fear of not being a "good boy," he marries a woman with the will and personality to take his mother on in his behalf. As the two women in his life fight each other for his attention and loyalty, he remains in the middle, pathetically trying to appease them both. To his wife he is supportive . . . but . . . "She's my mother—and you just don't understand." To his mother he is loyal . . . but . . . "She's my wife—and you just don't understand."

However, when push comes to shove, this kind of man definitely won't suffer the guilt of disappointing or frustrating his mother in any direct way—such as deciding to have his wedding where and when he and his wife wants it. He'll make promises to both, but defer to the pressure of whichever woman is in the room, on the phone, or in his guilty head at the time. He uses each woman against the other in an attempt never to appear "bad" himself. His anger at each is thereby expressed passively by himself ("sorry . . . "), but actively through their competitiveness ("I know she's frustrating . . . ").

Some twenty years ago, while in private practice as a marriage and family therapist, I met "the mom" of this scenario. Right on time for her appointment, she was in her late fifties, slightly overweight, with a pleasant demeanor, and the most beautifully put together ensemble, perfectly coifed hair, and manicured nails. Trailing behind her to the couch was her current husband (number two, equally well presented, quiet, with a remarkable and obvious attitude of total deference to her; he watched carefully even to see how and where she would position herself on the couch before he thought to become comfortable himself).

I began the session as usual, inquiring, "Who would like to begin?" Somehow, I was not surprised when she began speaking first. The husband did not even inhale in consideration of speaking, nor did he even have to look at her, as many couples do, to decide who would begin talking. It was clear that she was in charge.

This woman was tearful and deeply hurt. She, lovingly and with emotional passion and nostalgia, spoke of her first husband and their only child, a son who was now a grown man in his middle thirties. She talked of their wonderful life together; the husband was wonderful; the son was wonderful.

Her current husband sat quietly, staring straight ahead.

When her first husband died, she and her grown son only had each other, and she sobbed, her son was always so thoughtful, attentive, helpful, companionable, loving . . . just so wonderful.

"**And then,**" she sputtered, uncharacteristically, "**he married that bitch! And now I don't see him or hear from him anymore. That bitch is keeping my son from me!**"

Whew! The switch from apple pie to street rage nearly hurled me back off my chair.

Now she began to rage with an incredible fury—all directed at the daughter-in-law, who, like a vampire, must have sucked the blood of her son just enough to mesmerize him away from his true place and liaison, his mother.

When I asked her to describe the daughter-in-law, she replied she was somewhat tall and skinny with kinky, curly, dark hair, very white skin, and rather pointed features (sounds very "witchlike," doesn't it?). She went on to recount that the girl was not very friendly to her, even though Mom had, in her words, "rolled out the red carpet to welcome her into the family." Her son's wife, she continued, was always sharp tongued and argumentative with just about every plan or idea or comment Mom ever made.

I asked her if her son ever got in the middle of this fray to defend or support either one of them. Mom said, "No."

I asked the current husband if Mom's rendition of all of these events seemed accurate to him. He quietly, succinctly, said, "Yes," with a brief, affirmative nod.

By the way, her son, wife, and new child now lived in Guam (a bit of a commute to Southern California, don't you think?).

Be clear about this: "Mom" was not a "bad" lady. She was a woman abandoned by death by her husband, who had formed an incredibly tight tie with her only child, and who really didn't understand how all that love and closeness could have resulted in not only no relationship with her son but the realization that he chose to sleep with her enemy. His leaving her home felt like an amputation of her body parts, like a living death.

The true role of a mother, according to Anna Freud, is "to be left." In the rest of the animal kingdom, where decisions are only extensions of instinct, mothers force their young toward autonomy—for survival's sake. However, our complex human balance of selfish needs and selfless purpose can get confused; and some parents cling to their children for their own emotional survival (identity and purpose).

This mom still wanted/needed to "mother" her boy, and was suffering horrible pain at the loss of him—and probably, not realizing or accepting her "un-motherly" demands for an adult son, displaced her own hurt as rage onto the daughter-in-law.

I began gently and supportively reviewing all those years of guidance, care, and worry she'd put into mothering her son when he was a child. I questioned whether the relationship with her husband, wonderful as it may have been in so many ways, lacked the kind of intense interactive bond she had wanted and needed—and was instead put into the relationship with her son even before the husband's death? I was guessing here—but she affirmed my suspicions as truth. I continued by suggesting that the intensity she put into her son—above and beyond what was necessary—may have taken time and energy from her own personal dreams and challenges. She didn't fight that one either. There is a thin line, sometimes, between sacrifice (giving up self-ful things for the "greater good" of family), and hiding (giving up self-ful things because you're just too darn scared to take risks).

I then dropped the "bomb": I told her that perhaps her son married a Hit Lady—that is, someone who could do the job he couldn't bear to do himself; someone who could make the effort and take the responsibility for breaking his too-tight ties with his mother (ties he felt too guilty and frightened to loosen up himself). He couldn't bring himself to say, for example, "Oh, gosh, Mom, you know I want to see you and spend time with you. It's not going to be possible because I've made important plans to . . ." This statement would imply he'd made a choice—and the choice wasn't Mom. He didn't have the stomach to face her hurt or angry response to the truth. Instead, it was freeing and safe for him to say, "Oh, gosh, Mom, you know I want to see you and spend time with you. It's just that *she won't let me!*"

Now the wife and mother "duke" it out while he stands on the sidelines, safe under the cover of "I'm trying to please everybody—what can I do?" He's free and clear and the two women of his life tie for "Bitch of the Year Award." Neat, huh?

At this point Mom's eyes opened wide with amazement. "Oh, my G-d," she said, "that makes sense. I never even for a moment thought that my son could be part of the problem!"

From then on, the session went smoothly. Mom was surprisingly accepting of the dynamic I'd presented. She understood that her relatively passive son was responsible—along with her—for the perpetual cycle of his apparent weakness (really his protectiveness of her) and her apparent overprotectiveness (really her dependency on him).

Since he felt responsible for Mom's happiness and welfare, he felt guilty asserting his right to a separate existence, even as an adult married man. Also, he must have experienced discomfort in giving up all the "catering to" which he got from his mom. So, he married an updated version of her in order to (1) have a hit lady to argue with Mom for him and to use as an excuse to pull away, and (2) provide the smothering mothering to which he had grown accustomed.

The problem with the "Hit Lady Syndrome," as with all other relationships based more on a solution to a problem than the merging of lovingly matched souls, is that there is a difficult price to pay for the service. Jim, thirty-four and married eight years, called about that heavy tariff.

"Dr. Laura, I want to talk about the relationships between my wife, Nicole, and other people, ahhh, including my mother. I realize now that for most of our marriage we avoided most all closeness. I was a workaholic, very self-centered, didn't really care about anything else in life. During the last two years, I started to realize things differently and we started to get closer. I feel like we're getting to the center of what the problems are. It's getting real sensitive now every time we approach something."

"Jim, what's the 'something'?"

"Okay, the last meeting we had with the marriage counselor, we talked about my wife and my mom. Most of the problem stems from that I never stood up to my mother. I've never gotten away from her. Finally, about a year ago I started to stand up for my wife and my family and my mother started to respect that and things started to get better. Then I said to my wife, 'Gee, hon, it's really important for you to sit down and talk to her and for you guys to get out some of the things between you.' She said she wouldn't do that and that my mother was my problem. We went to the counselor about it and I said that my wife never resolves a problem and we never keep a friend over a few months. Whenever anybody gets close, if my wife gets into an argument with them, she doesn't speak to 'em—she just goes away and that's it. My wife tells me it's my problem that I don't feel like we have friends. Then the counselor sided with her about me being responsible for my mother and not her. My wife and I are not doing so well anymore and I don't like this therapist."

"Jim, you know that you could deal more directly with your mother and put your own effort into making and keeping friends—so, how much of what your wife says is true?"

"Well, up to about a year ago I guess a lot of that was true. I'm going through learning that I have a very possessive mother, and I've gone through a lot of learning about how to let anybody else into my life."

"Jim, in what ways have you been using Nicole as a shield?"

"Well, for a long time I used her as a shield for all my relationships with anything that had to do with the world. I just worked and she took care of *everything* that had to do with anything: life, social, friends . . . anything."

"How are you using her now?"

"Okay, specifically, I've used her to get me away from my parents . . . my mother specifically."

"Your wife has been your Hit Lady!"

"Okay." He laughs. "Yes, I guess that's right. I probably haven't realized it."

"Jim, being a workaholic means that is where you are the most comfortable. With your work you feel confident, in control, and powerful. With interpersonal situations you don't have that same feeling. Not only do you leave it up to your wife to make and break relationships, you blame her for your relationship failures. I bet you complain to her about some disappointment or slight with a friend, and then she goes to war for you saying, 'Oh, my, I was just telling you what happened—I didn't expect you to go ballistic.' That's how you use her as your Hit Lady."

"Interesting . . . okay. I came from a family where my dad just worked all the time and life went on. People did not show emotion or love."

"Well, Jim, I realize that the emotional intensity, risks, and challenges of interpersonal dealings can be scary and uncomfortable, even for folks with more emotionally outgoing homes, but you have to start being more open, giving, and assertive or you're going to end up feeling more and more isolated, resenting everyone in your life for their 'power' over you."

"Yeah, and they really only have the power because I do nothing."

"Bingo."

My Son—The Surrogate Husband

Don, a listener, now fifty years old, wrote to me about the desperate consequences of the twisted predicament resulting from his mother's control over his life:

I was married to the woman chosen by my mother at age twenty three. When I was twenty eight, my father died. My mother made me her surrogate husband (no, not sexually) but we were very close as well as she was to my wife. As I began to want my distance from her net (of daily involvement), she became more and more attached to my wife, who, like my father, was an alcoholic!

My wife and I sought marital counseling with seventeen different counselors. Each time it got around to her drinking and drug abuse, we had to find another counselor—until I had enough. I took the coward's way out and had an affair which ended my marriage. Surprisingly, I was awarded custody of both sons (then aged fourteen and eleven), much to the chagrin of my mother who wanted the boys to stay with their mother so they would be close to her as she feared that I would leave town. In the hearing to determine custody, my mother testified against me! The judge awarded them to me anyway.

Even before her husband's death, Don's mother cemented their emotionally incestuous marriage by picking a wife for him just like her husband—therefore, someone she knew how to "control." That way, she'd be assured of her son's presence in her life. It didn't work, yet it wouldn't have been any less a tragedy if it had.

What is there about the mother-son relationship that lends itself to so much intensity? According to an Associated Press (1992) report, Peter Wish, director of the New England Institute of Family Relations in Framingham, Massachusetts, "When mothers-in-law cause problems, and they frequently do—the culprit is more often the *man's* mother."

Really? How can that be, especially when most of the jokes about mothers-in-law tend to come from men about their wife's mom? If you don't believe me, tune in any country music station.

Perhaps a hint comes from another Associated Press report (1992) which quoted Clinical Psychologist Roni Beth Tower, of Westport, Connecticut, who said that "most mothers relate to their daughters in a down-to-earth way, but they tend to idealize and even eroticize their sons. Giving them up to another woman is all the more difficult."

It is so rare for me to get a letter, fax, or on-air phone call from a man complaining about his father-in-law (and those rare times generally relate to the "results" of his abuse of the daughter, or, more typically, a "business" deal gone bad). Fathers of daughters don't seem to "live through" their daughters or compete with their sons-in-law for their daughter's attention or affection. If they are a pain in any way, it's by going off with the son-in-law to do "guy stuff," coming home too late after too many beers and too much story-telling (braggadocio).

Mommy, Mommy, Save Me!

Hey, don't get feeling all victimized by your mother's behavior. This overinvolvement is a two-way street of inappropriate social, emotional, and psychological benefits. An article in the *Wall Street Journal* (9/94) highlighted the fact that more males than females (I thought *women* were the weaker, defenseless, more dependent sex) go back to live at home as adults! "Two decades ago, the percentage of men and women who spent at least part of their 20s living at home was equal—about 40%. Today, some 45% of men in their 20s return to the nest, while only about 35% of women do."

Why are so many young men crowding back to their mother's womb? "Perhaps," the article continues, "because it is stress-free. Dads keep them on a loose leash and moms do their cleaning. Young men are increasingly more willing to forgo independence in exchange for extra cash and mom's doting."

Without having to pay rent, utilities, and food, the guy's got money for cars, clothes, and expensive toys and jaunts.

Basically, therefore, living at home is "cushy" for the men, while the young women seem to value freedom over possessions. So, it would seem that too many of you men have gotten both soft and greedy—sacrificing dignity and masculinity for boyish creature comforts and acquisition of things.

Not a good sign for our culture; not a good sign for a subsequent marriage. My listener Dave wrote about just that:

I think the most difficult things I've had to deal with as an adult result from my mother's insistence on being totally responsible for my happiness. It wasn't enough to provide me with food, shelter, clothing and parental support. I was prevented from suffering through my own decisions and facing the complete consequences—she was always there to make sure my suffering was minimized. For example, when I was about seven years old and made up my mind I wasn't going to go to Hebrew school any more, instead of telling me I had to finish (at least the current year), she surrendered to my yelling and screaming and I was off the hook—no more Hebrew School.

Boy, was I sorry when all my friends were being Bar-Mitzvah'd, but not me. There were many situations when she gave in to my tantrums and let me have my way just because it "hurt" her too much to see me suffering.

*In the end, I learned very little about how to be happy alone and how to deal with the consequences of a bad decision. **Could suffering be one of the most underrated learning experiences in life?** Now I have to be careful I don't go overboard with expectations for my own children (the other end of the spectrum from my mother's leniency). Thankfully, my wife and I together make a terrific team. We balance each other beautifully in many ways, especially when it comes to dealing with the kids.*

I'm now 31, my mother is 71, my father is 78, and my relationship with them grows stronger and more loving every day.

It's difficult to turn down or turn away from all that motherly pampering and "freedom." So, it is not too unusual for you guys to pick a woman who mothers, or to spend your time being helplessly demanding of her turning into your mother—albeit one you *can* have sex with!

Cameron faxed me this letter which highlights the downside of this expectation:

> *My fiance and I have been battling this problem about my mother for 6 years. She has the problem that I've been trying to change her into my mother by expecting her to react to me as my mother would when I was a **little boy**, and that she thinks that this is the reason none of my previous relationships have worked out—because that is why they left me. She always tells me that she wants a partner that is a **man** not a **boy**, or a man wanting a mother-child relationship. I don't know how many other men do the same thing—my guess is quite a few.*
>
> *My parents divorced when I was 12, and when I look back at my childhood, I wish I was raised by my dad. I do have a ton of resentment toward my mother which I know I transfer to my fiance, by doing all the things I do to piss her off.*
>
> *I do understand that the way I relate to women in many ways has to do with the relationship to my mother, for she is the first woman a man bonds to. Just because she is "MOTHER", she gets away with more just because of the title.*

The Curse of the Missing Father

Cameron's letter hit upon a very important point: the missing father. Whether he is absent through divorce, death or basic passivity, losing a strong role model for masculinity, independence, balanced autonomy with commitment is a disaster for boys. They need to learn how to love, honor, and respect their mothers without the benefit of an intact umbilical cord. Their fathers are supposed to teach them that by their own actions as a son and husband, and by an intensity of interaction with the son which balances the wonderful nurturing of mother with masculinity.

That is why the ideal condition for producing an emotionally healthy adult male is a home with both female and male components—that means a mother and father, who offer a diet of appropriate masculine and feminine nutrients. It is well documented that single-parent female households (in contrast to two-parent households) more often produce violent, emotionally isolated male children. The explanation is that these boys, in trying to develop their masculine identity, exaggerate those male animal qualities which contrast with "feminine" ones in order to become "men," virtually in the dark.

It is also true that many single-parent (female) households produce males afraid to develop their masculine identity separate from serving their mothers. Both of those outcomes occur not because the women are evil or bad mothers (although some might be), but because their homes do not provide complementary male and female role models.

Too Little of a Good Thing

The obvious problem is that not all two-parent households are manned and womanned by healthy specimens. And, the disappointments, frustrations, and difficulties in their own lives may result in some mothers' lack of fairness, love, and respect for their son's separate identity.

Debbie Reynolds came out of retirement in 1996 to make the movie *Mother*. In the film her older adult son, played by Albert Brooks, is trying to understand his relationship with her because he thinks it may be at the center of the reason he is having trouble with women. There appear to be two key issues: her aloofness and her seemingly flippant critical behavior toward him, especially with his writing career. After moving back in with her (to get "closer") he discovers unpublished manuscripts of her own in a closet. Apparently, she sacrificed a writing career to be a good wife and mother. Sadly, this sacrifice was not made with goodness in her heart, as she secretly blamed the children and husband for her lack of personal success and accomplishment. Additionally, she would be critically competitive with her older boy, coveting his success.

Supposedly, once he unlocks this "secret," he is relieved of guilt for her lack of "loving him"—understanding that it was her own weakness. The movie ends with her beginning to write again on a computer he provides, and he meets a new woman at the gas pump. Everyone will be "happily ever after."

Does this happen in real life? You bet. Here's a fax from Peggy which explains her husband's transition in understanding the same mother-son dynamic of rejection (the mother's) and desperate need (the son's).

> *Some years ago, after a psychiatrist told my husband that he did not really have a "mother", nor would she miraculously transform into one, and that he could get on with his life, he awakened me in the middle of the night to tell me that I no longer had to be his Mother, and that he never had one. It really shook me up, but my husband started to come out of his depression after that and has never returned to it. At the time I did not know that part of our marriage problems stemmed from the fact that he was using me as a wife **and** mother. When he was able to give up the hopeless desire to have a loving Mother, he became a great husband and father. Without that doctor our marriage would never have survived.*

Every human being, male or female, is a flesh and blood well, needing to be filled up with the best of Mom and the best of Dad. While it's not impossible to make a good life without the presence of one or the other, there is a good chance your perceptions of gender and life can become distorted, and the emptiness can obviously hurt your heart. Everybody's life has mountains to climb. Without the balanced input of two good parents, your mountain to climb may not be insurmountable, just rougher and steeper than it would otherwise have been.

Appeasing the Goddess

When women blame circumstance and others for their lack of personal fulfillment, frankly, they become dangerous to men, especially their sons, whom they often expect to cater to them with inappropriate levels of obedience, involvement, and loyalty. Some men end up rebelling, others acquiescing.

Kent's fax suggests that both responses also often occur:

My father was a Quaker minister and my mother was a "stay-at-home" mom. I was an only child for 11 years and so I received an extraordinary amount of attention from my mother. The manner in which she chose to give this attention was heavily tilted toward discipline and guided by constant attention to my behavior being a reflection of her attempt to be the perfect mother. I have the baby book which documents my progress as compared to the Better Homes and Gardens guidelines.

By the time I started first grade, I had mastered all of the skills that were being taught to the other first graders and the expectation for me to be at the top of my class never ceased. When I reflect on these times, I can see that I had already made my choice on how I was going to adapt to my environment. Since my father was gone most of the time leading the flock and my mother held the power to bring pain and misery down upon me, I had committed myself to compliance, hoping to somehow please her to the degree that eventually she would express pleasure, pride and approval of me as a "good boy."

I graduated at the top of my high school class. I was voted most likely to succeed, and gathered various awards for achievement. I also had ulcers by the time I was eighteen, and had to drop out of college for a semester to recover. When the doctor came into the examination room to tell me the diagnosis, he asked me what was bothering me. It was a revolutionary question. I had never considered that my being unhappy or disturbed was a matter that should be questioned. The only need that I had been aware of had been to please my mother and those other needs within me had been buried inside.

The approval that I sought from my mother never came, but as she lay dying at age 53 from cancer, we had a tearful moment when she asked my forgiveness for being so hard on me.

The rest of Kent's story has to do with his being terrified of the power that women seemed to have over him. After marrying someone who immediately *"started announcing her terms for being happy and I began to try to fulfill her wishes while wishing inside that a truck would run her over and rescue me from this 'fate'. If she had a daughter she would be happy, so she got pregnant and had a son she ignored. If we got a bigger house then she would finally be happy. But that didn't do it."*

Kent chose to "escape" into work, alcohol, toys, and a long line of staged suicide attempts. After fifteen years of this he filed for divorce and won custody of his son.

His letter ended with *"I think that there is hope that I may be ready for a relationship that doesn't have its foundation in my still trying to please my mother."*

Hey, Momma, What Do Women Want?

A boy's relationship with his mother teaches him early and well what women want, therefore, what to expect of himself in relationships. These lessons don't always turn out to be the best source of information for future healthy, successful relationships. Fred was born in 1942 to a father who worked six or seven days a week, at least twelve hours a day. His mother took a six-day-a-week wartime job and was away about ten hours a day. His grandmother was the primary caregiver until Fred was seven. However, Grandmother and Mother had strong opinions about the role of men:

Men were to be insightful of a woman's wants and needs, and solicitous in providing for them. Gratitude or what passed as affection was parceled out only when men actually read the mind of a woman and provided for the perceived need before the woman actually articulated that want or need. Failure to be perfect meant a cold shoulder and rejection. It was the role and job of men to provide financially for women, and they were failures if there ever occurred an unmet want in their women.

Dad had always been a rather timid person, withholding and stern in his demeanor, so I did not view any real affection in the family. Dad continued with long hours of work, sometimes being away from home on business trips for 3 or 4 weeks each month.

There it is: men just went away, physically and emotionally, and let the women rule. And rule they did, making sure that the men were the performance objects they were supposed to be. Attention was given to these two-legged objects for how they performed, not who they were, and what passed as affection was always conditional.

Until recently, I carried a large spiritual hole in me, not seeing or feeling any magnificence within, because who I was was not what was wanted by the women I was with (okay, okay . . . the one's I picked just like mom and grandma). I am still having a time discovering what does work. And, somewhere out there, is a potential life mate who sees in herself her own magnificence, and so can enjoy the true magnificence within me.

You see, it's not only the frustrated demands of his mother and grandma which caused stress, it was the absence of a functional man/father to balance perceptions, ideas, feelings, and behavioral styles. Fred's father may have been one of those types who lives only through appeasing difficult goddesses. So don't blame all Fred's struggles on the women—at least they were there!

The Road Back

For every sad story about difficult, distant, disturbed, or bad parents and the challenges they cause you, there is a parallel story of a challenge well met. Ultimately, no matter what the circumstances, you have the choice of how to behave, how to handle life and relationships. Now *feelings* are a different story. Feeling frightened, hurt, or resentful about your mother may be a perfectly reasonable response to a perfectly unreasonable woman. However, you can take the "easy way out" and keep marrying the same type in order to conquer the problem (familiar, although yucky, is safer, you know) or work toward something you intelligently know is healthier (unfamiliar, therefore really scary). You may not be sure of the tools or techniques—but you *will* learn (therefore mature and change) *only* if you force yourself to face the dragons and find out if they lurk everywhere, or just in your mind and heart.

I'm reminded of an episode of the classic original *Twilight Zone* series. A plane lands in an airfield which disappeared decades before. The men serving the airport are arguing about its meaning, when one argues about its existence. Now, they can all see it plain and clearly, but one fellow insists that their desire to have it be safe and present is actually creating it. To test his theory, he decides to walk into the spinning propellers. He is scared out of his mind (reasonable)—but certain that the object is not real. When he gets to within shredding distance of the propellers, the plane disappears.

Got the message?

Ex-Momma's Boys

Just how can an adult male withdraw from his mother's womb? Brett, a listener, faxed me his story:

I am 29 years old and the youngest of 4 children. I "was" a classic "mamma's boy". I have been married for 9 1/2 years to my wonderful bride. A good example of this mamma's boy problem is what began when I announced to my mother that I was getting married. Over-night, my mother became an even more very over protecting and controlling person with regard to me. I noticed that she used to speak so highly of my wife when she was my girlfriend, but now I was hearing from other family members that she didn't like her very much and she wasn't sure if she was "the one".

Well, things only got worse for the first two years of my marriage. My mother thought that she needed to be involved in every decision that we made and that if she wasn't, then we would make big, huge mistakes.

I soon began to understand that my mother could only control my life to the extent that I allowed her to. I started out my new revelation with the wrong approach. I would argue with my mother and try to tell her "not to control". This only upset her without results.

I then set up a face to face meeting with her and lovingly explained that when I got married, I left her to have a life with my wife and I told her how she had upset us by some of the ways she related to us. I then asked her to forgive me for allowing her to have unhealthy control of my life and this would not happen any longer.

She was furious and declared that I was no longer her son. After a few months, we began to talk again and now I would relate to her with love but without weakness and timidity. Now, years later, we all understand the rules to the relationships, and it is a wonderful thing. I am happy, my wife is happy, and my mother is happy.

Another listener Jim, like Brett, realized the potential for serious marital strife with his mother overly invested in influence and control. Jim's fax shows further creativity in solving the problem:

My wife and I early on recognized the possibilities of motherly control, talked about it, etc. I went out of my way to show mom that my wife came first. I would hug, or put my arms around my spouse in my mom's presence. That practice, plus some good smoochin' was good for our kids too, to let them know we were unified. My wonderful wife also went out of her way to become a "daughter" to my mom.

Thus, in the early part of our marriage, when we recognized the possibility of motherly control of her first born, we became unified and did something about it. Once my wife knew that she was numero uno, then doing things with mom didn't bother her. In fact, my wife encouraged me to spend more time with her—and our relationship was wonderful.

Stupid Boyishness

It ought to be abundantly clear by now that your drive for nurturing and your inappropriately guilty sense of responsibility for your mother's emotional well-being (identity and/or activities) can lead you to become a perpetual boy. To mature into a functional man, you must act on what you know to be good and healthy, instead of operating in "escape from difficult feelings" mode. Sometimes your mother will have been a terrible parent and person, so you missed the nurturing, mother-child bond. Sometimes your mother will have been a terrible parent and person, and you were overwhelmed by her disturbed, too intense mother-child bond. Sometimes your mother's energy and personality style didn't easily mesh with yours—but neither of you was terrible. Sometimes you just simply blame your mother for major faults in yourself and your life's choices, or your unwillingness to face life with gusto and guts.

Son, whatever it is . . . **get over it!**

Again, the key to "getting over it" is basically *behaving as though you were healthy*. If you don't know what that means, you're lying to avoid the traumatic vulnerability of trying and growing. If you feel too overwhelmed and frightened to permit yourself the new learning experiences, get some assistance from a licensed psychotherapist who just doesn't sit there and support you in your misery (a behavioral or cognitive therapist might be just the ticket!).

In the same way you "learned" a most self-destructive style of self-defense (all women are your mother . . . so . . . on guard!), you can learn to treat individual women as just that, individuals!

If you don't stretch in these ways, you will be as a gerbil in a cage, on one of those exercise cylinders which permit the animal only to run in place.

Ray, thirty-two, called my program complaining that his relationships don't go anywhere. It turns out that he has a lustful way of relating to women, overlooking qualities other than sexual attraction. After our lengthy discussion, I suggested that he may be afraid to combine sex and love because his mom was very critical. Since he generalized that criticism to all women, having acceptance through sex (and he was a virtual stud in performance) protected him from failures or rejections—because the relationship never got past the sex. Unfortunately, since he was aware that the "acceptance" was superficial and incomplete, he was always left with that same hungry, lonely feeling.

Another caller, Jerry, forty-five years old, had the repetitive pattern of selecting women with children. He would then point out to the mother how bad the kids were and he'd be dumped. As his call continued, it seemed clear that he was longing to be picked over the woman's children, to be the favored sibling; after all, as he was growing up, he was his mother's favorite even over Daddy!

Lynn, a fifty-one-year-old male, wrote to me about his "stupid boyishness":

Tonight on your program you had a 25 year old male caller who was having difficulty adjusting to a strong woman. He

wanted someone to love him "more". After some discussion,
you told him he wanted image without working for it. You also
told him he could spend the next 30 years in therapy and still
not achieve any goal if he weren't willing to "work at it"
himself.

Your final words to him were fantastic. I am a 51 year old
male, and I believe that what you said was so perfect about me,
and so frightening to me that I am intentionally avoiding
remembering your exact words.

I have a history of relationships and 2 marriages with
powerful and intelligent women whom I try to "live" through,
but then feel disappointed when they don't seem to have time
for me. Actually, some of them have had time for me but I had
no goal to show them or had nothing prepared to do with them
because I was depending on them for all aspects of my social life
and general well being.

I hope your 25 year old caller will change . . . I think it is
hopeless for me.

Change is very difficult to contemplate and expedite—no
question about that. And old habits die hard—but your soul
dies harder. Lynn's very admission of "forgetting my words,"
which he perhaps assumes will be the "key" to redemption,
is an example of how threatened you can feel even by the
suggestion, much less the action, of change; especially when
it means you'll be unsure. How can you pick miserable over
unsure?

Bob, forty years old, called about the lack of love in his
life. He keeps dating really young "girls" who are good looking. He went so far as to try to tell me that age meant nothing and that he felt a lot in common with these young
women. I suggested that they could truly only have a lot in
common if he were lacking in maturity! He described himself
as being the baby of the family:

"Mom mothered me. I had to escape my hometown to get
away from her."

"Bob, could it be that with 'girls' you are 'in charge,' but if you were with a woman, you would run the risk of being dominated by 'Mother'? Are you afraid of a woman's power, or your weakness?"

"What do you mean weakness?"

"Every man enjoys the maternal aspects of a woman. That's normal—not unhealthy. But perhaps in your case the nurturing was more stifling than lovingly attentive. If that is so, then you might hate your own natural need for female nurturing because it puts you at risk; therefore you reinterpret a healthy need for a weakness. Once you define it as weak—it is something to avoid. And with silly little girls, you avoid anything more than sex and hero-worship of yourself. You are connecting with 'females,' but not receiving from them what a mature woman has to offer. You've identified 'women' with 'threat.'"

Attempting to control what you've suffered from the "worst" in Mother through the women in your current life is terribly limiting to your growth—that's because you'd be dealing in otherwise "normal" situations with women, as though they were the "abnormal" interactions you had with your mother.

Marianne, a listener, wrote about her husband's efforts to do just that:

My husband is the oldest of ten children. His mother was very promiscuous, never married, and most of the kids have different fathers. He took care of the kids while she went out, got drunk, brought men home, etc. He kept the little ones while she got her jollies in the other room. He saw her getting beat up and thrown through a window. She cried on his shoulder when he was a little boy because she had been raped by three men she had been drinking with. You get the picture.

We have been married 25 years and have two children. How did his relationship with his mother affect us? I didn't think it did until our first child was born and he lost sexual interest in me. He showed his love for me in every other way, and apart from the almost total absence of a sex life, he was and is a wonderful husband, and there was never a better father.

For a long time I thought it was me—then I realized he was still thinking like a little boy, in either/or. "You can either be a good mother or have sex". And, he wanted his children to have a good mother. Since our marriage vows and the children were more important than my sexual needs, I learned to accept his love in the ways he could give it and be grateful that I had a good faithful husband and our children had two parents who loved each other and them.

I still miss sex, though. Anyway, that's how his relationship with his mother influenced his relationship with his wife.

It is obviously sad when a man mixes up Mom and wife in his mind—because he stays a boy and misses out on the pleasures and benefits of an adult man, spending his time running like a scared little boy.

Frank, a caller, realized that he was bugging the heck out of his wife but didn't know why. Whenever she even appeared upset at anything, whether it had to do with him or not, he literally went bonkers, pushing to get resolve on the problem right now! He only ended up driving her up the wall. He behaved as though he were five years old, and if he upset his mommy, she wouldn't love him and she might abandon him. Because of that irrational displacement of feelings about his mother onto his wife, he kept trying to fix everything so that his wife was always "happy"—if she was "happy," he felt safe. Truth was, he confronted problems with his wife, just tried to make her happy. She was missing out on an equal partner to work with and respect while he was bouncing back and forth from needy and frightened to damned resentful of the power she had over him: rejection.

Female Acceptance

It should come as no surprise that men are very dependent on the acceptance of women. They begin life in a woman's body, suck on her breasts for the food of life, are protected, loved, hugged, kissed, and fooled over by a female. Men's introduction to life, themselves, and relationships is through women. So there is nothing dysfunctional about needing and wanting women's closeness, nurturance, and approval. In fact, as a listener, Ron, wrote: *"men feel in love when a woman provides mother-like caring."*

So, if female nurturance and mothering is healthy—what makes for Stupid Boyishness? In a nutshell: when a man selects, labels, and reacts to all women in exactly the same way; when he cannot relate to his mother as an adult man (loving yet autonomous); when he fears in women what he can't face in his relationship with his mother—that's Stupid Boyishness.

To be a man, a guy doesn't have to ignore, abandon, or battle with his mother—even if she's not the "healthiest" maternal specimen. What he needs to do is multifold:

- Accept the "limitations" or "idiosyncrasies" of Mom's personality as uniquely "hers."
- Avoid taking responsibilities for Mom's unique moods and behaviors.
- Accept guilt for not being a respectful or honorable son— do not accept guilt for your mother's typical feelings or choices or actions or the consequences therein.
- Avoid expecting a woman to fill your heart for an absent or lacking mother.
- Accept that your mom will never be the perfect "mom," without giving up the good stuff you do get.
- Avoid making a woman responsible for the quality of the relationship you have with your mother.

- Accept that a woman can accept you and still reject some of your actions.
- Avoid avoiding women because you don't want to face your ambivalent feelings toward your mother.
- Accept that short of perfect can still be very rewarding in relationships.
- Avoid using women to compensate for your real or imagined gaps in wonderfulness.
- Accept that being a woman is just as difficult as being a man—so stop being so self-focused.
- Avoid avoiding feelings and problems; you don't end up any more competent or connected by doing so.
- Accept that needing and loving a woman is one of the signposts of a healthy, successful man.

The Dutiful Son

The following fax was not meant to help clarify the mom-son struggle for positioning:

> My mother asked me to fax you with the following comment.
> She believes that people who are in the public eye have an inordinate influence on popular culture, language, etc. They should, therefore, be careful about what they say and how they say it. Specifically, my mother was concerned about your use of the word "real" when you mean "very" and "hard" when you mean difficult.
> I did my job as a dutiful son who likes to keep the peace with his mother. You can do whatever you want with this input.

As *Star Trek*'s Spock would say, "Fascinating."

STUPID MACHISMO

Dear Dr. Laura,
   In Response to your comments last week about the difference between a male and a man, this exchange occurred between our oldest grandson and his mom. He is fourteen, soon to be fifteen. He informed our daughter that he has become a man! She took a big breath and calmly said, "Tell me about it." His response was, "you know, when I sweat now I really stink!"
   It was all she could do to keep from cracking up.

                                    BEV, 1996

Whatever it is that separates a man from a male,
it is a shame
that it takes such a long time
to figure it out.

                                RICHARD, 1996

I remember a time when the word *man* evoked images of husband and father, breadwinner, warrior, protector, and adventurer.

And now? Well, feminist hysteria and politically correct journalism project quite a different interpretation of *man:*

- *child abuser* (never mind that statistics for 1986–1993 reported by the National Center on Child Abuse Prevention Research, National Committee to Prevent Child Abuse demonstrate that 59 percent of persons causing children's death are female [!], and that 50 percent of persons found responsible for child abuse fatalities are natural mothers [!], whereas natural fathers account for only 23 percent, with boyfriends 10 percent)
- *child molester* (never mind the overwhelming evidence that divorcing mothers often use molestation as a surefire technique to punish the father and gain power in custody, and never mind that "recovered memories of childhood abuse" have been exposed as a largely shameful product of popular feminist psychology)
- *rapist* (never mind that the rape statistics were dropping until rape was redefined from a "violent *act* of penetration" to a "*feeling* of being forced," and never mind the new "date rape" pseudocrisis where passive, curious, resentful, drunk, or guilt-ridden women can claim "rape")
- *sexual harasser* (never mind the double standard of how much skin and pulchritude a woman can blatantly display—while a man must not even look or comment; and never mind how stupid it is to bring up an LAPD officer on sexual harassment charges for allegedly saying only "Hi, babe," without any pattern of disrespect or threats; also never mind the research that indicates the overwhelming majority of men retreat when the woman is direct in telling him to "buzz off")
- *violent* (never mind that males are the primary victims of all violent crimes except rape; and never mind the National Family Violence Survey's nationwide random sampling which reported that *wives* admitted they were

more likely to assault their husbands than their husbands were to assault them)

- *philanderer* (never mind the current female vogue of intentionally producing children with no fathers under the flag of "female reproductive rights")
- *noncommitter* (never mind the legion of women who, along with their minor children, shamelessly "shack up" with guys—and often make more babies without weddings; and never mind the women who are "sexually liberated," relying on abortions to remain "free")
- *absentee dad* (never mind the never married or divorced women who, for the sake of a new guy or life, think it's perfectly okay to relocate, thereby depriving him of his children geographically under the flag of female rights)

None of this is meant to minimize or forgive the "evil *that men do*." However, our cumulative awareness and understanding of both genders' ability to perpetrate "evil" or stupidity has been ignored, hidden, and lied about in the growing antimale climate, to which even some decent inappropriately compassionate men, in self-defense to the constant feminist rancor of self-proclaimed oppression and victimization, subscribe.

Indeed, even the mere mention of "male" or "masculine" *nature* is met with a cry for universal rehabilitation. For example, this 1994 letter to the editor of the *Wall Street Journal* in response to a previous article which evidently polled teens about their expectations concerning the family roles they will play as adults: "If I were raising a boy today, my main concern would be that he not grow up to be the kind of guy who joins a fraternity gang rape of a drunken young woman or who batters his wife."

If that isn't way overgeneralizing, incredibly negative, hysterical, man-loathing rhetoric, then I don't know what is. I certainly hope she never is the mother of sons if her "main concern" in raising one is *only the avoidance* of . . . whatever. I'm the mother of a son and my main concern in raising him has been to create a loving, respectful, spiritual environment, in which he'll learn responsibility, compassion, and charity so that he can contribute something important to his life and the world. Come to think of it—I'd have the same main concern were he a girl!

I don't see "male" as inherently degenerate or dangerous. The same passionate aggressiveness which can wield a sword to kill innocents can wield a sword to protect innocents. The same creativity which can manipulate nuclear energy into a bomb can manipulate nuclear energy into cancer-killing power. The "energy" is neither evil nor good—it is neutral until intent is imposed.

Let me give you a parallel. In Judaism it is said that each human being has two impulses, one for evil and one for good. That dual nature means that you are neither inherently good nor bad; and you are, or become, what you do. The so-called evil impulse is a powerful source of energy and, ironically, it is the source of vitality which may result in competitiveness, anger, lust, and greed, or energize you to struggle to create, rise up in righteous indignation against tyranny, commit to marriage and family, and achieve in areas which benefit many. Therefore, that *tendency* toward "evil" can result in despair and destruction or creativity and achievement—depending upon values, reason, and judgment which form the decision to override emotion and impulse for nobler intentions.

With that same line of thought, that which is "male" is not inherently bad and needful of repair. G. Pascal Zachary wrote in the *Wall Street Journal* (5/2/97) that "boy behavior" is being increasingly *diagnosed* as a disability or malady: "critics object to the phalanx of teachers, counselors, and administrators who insist on medical diagnoses or clinical classifications when boys refuse to nap, sit still, fail to fulfill their ill-defined potential, scrap with their peers or otherwise defy authority.

"In viewing these traits as disabilities, schools have 'pathologized what is simply normal for boys,' says Diane McGuinness, a University of South Florida psychology professor. Adds Michael Gurian, a therapist in Spokane, Wash., and the author of a book on the virtues of boys, 'The country is making the argument, without often realizing it, that boyhood is defective.'"

The bottom line is that *male* and *masculine* have become synonymous with all that is wrong and evil with society, and femininity is touted as *the* answer—never mind that for thousands of years, medicine, law, philosophy, science, government, and religion have been primarily male enterprises. Of course this can't be part of male intellectual and spiritual humanity; it must only be a product of sexist domination and oppression? Oh, please. It is because the "male" (evil?) impulse to challenge, conquer, adventure, competition, etc., can be channeled to create such substance, truth, and beauty.

I agree with most of what Richard, a listener, said in the following letter:

We have slowly but surely emasculated men in our society— made a mockery of "real men"—expunged all the old heroes. The results have been boys growing up to be men who do not know how to be men nor how to treat women—who have no respect for women—nor are they able to provide the strong male figure their sons need in their quest for manhood.

This "neutering" of the male is and has been due to an apparent unwillingness to accept the nature of the male. This nature is there whether we like it or not—and I strongly suspect it is there for a reason.

There is a natural "warrior" in all boys. A boy needs to learn that to be a good warrior, he must learn to control his aggressive nature. A boy needs to know that a brave warrior believes deeply in honesty and justice, has a strong feeling for God, and is able, in his own way, to love and show kindness, mercy and tenderness. If he does not learn this, it will be the women who will suffer most from lawless males. It is in a woman's interest that a boy grows up to be a good man, and if this is to happen, I might add, he must have male authority figures: his father, his minister/rabbi, and, yes, God.

In previous generations, boys often settled things, "out behind the barn" with their fists, and, if they were to be "manly" about it, they followed fairly well defined rules. That type of conduct has since been considered uncivilized— considered uncivilized by a generation that has produced a society which is far less civilized than the generations that preceded it—and it continues to produce much of the same.

When an attempt is made to strip a boy of those things that identify his natural maleness, he will either be left with an aggression he has never learned to control, or with nothing that identifies his innate maleness—he becomes an emotional eunuch—a "nice guy" perhaps, but an emotional eunuch nevertheless. And, Dr. Laura, emotional eunuchs do not protest evil at any level. They feel no commitment to do so.

When women set out to remold men into what their emotions suggest is a civilized human being—they turn them into women! These are the guys who sit by, leaving many of the problems they should be facing in the laps of their wives.

Feminist thinkers—male or female—see violence of any kind and for any reason as totally impermissible. It is most fortunate for them that thinking such as that did not dominate past generations. Good warriors have been a major influence in the civilization of nations. Civilization requires warriors—good warriors.

The disrespect men receive in our society leaves them not only broken and confused, but precludes attention to male-oriented issues of importance. For instance, more men die of prostate cancer than women of breast cancer—yet, the headlines scream with rage against the inattention to women's health issues, when the fact is that less monies go to prostate cancer research and treatment than to breast cancer. Who would dare to suggest donning blue ribbons in protest and awareness of prostate cancer? Who cares?

For all the harping on "poor oppressed girls," it's the boys who are in trouble. A December 4, 1994, *L.A. Times Magazine* article entitled "The Fragile Sex" reports that "emotionally disturbed boys outnumber girls nearly 4 to 1. For learning disabilities, the ratio is more than 2 to 1. The murder rate for teens—victims are almost all male—is up 194% from 20 years ago." The article further states that "altogether, the research suggests that today's boys—deeply distressed and tragically misunderstood—may be victims of their own biology and society's confusion about masculinity."

With respect to male aggression, the author quotes a researcher who concludes that "sometimes he (a boy) is just going through a difficult adolescence at a time when society looks askance at all male aggression. It is possible, that aggression and other masculine traits—including many that were once admired—have been so 'pathologized' that today Tom Sawyer would have been labeled disturbed."

David Blankenhorn, author of *Fatherless America*, claims that "males are now regarded as 'The Problem' and people look at boys as if their masculinity is something to be cured or overcome." He further argues that "schools are institutions run by women in which women and girls are seen as disadvantaged and boys are seen as a toxic problem."

The *L.A. Times* article further quoted Pricilla Vail, a New York educator and author of books on child development as saying, "Good feminism helps boys with feelings and relationships, but harsh views about boys being awful creatures and jokes about testosterone poisoning hurt rather than help. Bad feminism has eroded our willingness to respect differences in males and females."

And finally, Paul McHugh, chairman of the Psychiatry Department at Johns Hopkins Medical School in Baltimore, insists that "boys have a genetic influence to be aggressive. But if you raise them a certain way, that will assert itself as leadership or entrepreneurial skill. If he is raised in another environment, that is not as nurturing, he may become violent. That is why broken families have more of these problems."

I certainly haven't questioned the reality of a male/female biological polarity of aggression/nesting instinct. However, in both cases, without proper instruction in values, we have violent men and women dropping babies at fifteen; both of which we do see in ever increasing quantities since feminism took its anti-men/marriage/and child-care turn. Because of this, as the above letter from Richard pointed out so aptly, civilization is suffering.

It seems to be an obvious truth that both the male and female have characteristics specific to their gender and reproductive purposes. They also both have incredible brains which permit a degree of learning and creativity unknown in the rest of the animal kingdom. Male and female brains seem to have uniquely distinct wiring—being largely responsible, for example, for the female dominance in certain forms of communication and the male dominance in specific mathematics functions; the latter not being due to math phobia or anti-female math instructors or environment . . . oh please.

In order to make men out of biologic males, or women out of biologic females (the transition from animal to human), something has to happen—and this, for the men, is the subject of the rest of this chapter: Stupid Machismo is what occurs when this transition fails.

Benefiting from the large male audience for my radio program (national statistics indicate a 54/46 percent male/female audience ratio), I asked the questions, "How did you come to realize that you were finally a man, and not just a male?" and "What *is* a man?" Quite frankly, I was incredibly touched, moved, and impressed with the more than one thousand responses.

One of my first replies was from Tom, who wrote:

I firmly feel that the words "manhood" and "G-dliness" are synonymous. When G-d measures a man, He puts the tape around the heart instead of the head. Males try to become men of success, but those who want to be a man become men of value. Here are my findings of 15 years working with men. You can be a "male" by birth, but you can only be a "man" by choice.

Males	Man
1. Led by instincts (lust, anger, etc.)	1. Develops self-control
2. Concerned about self	2. Concerned about others
3. Flees responsibility (blame-shifts and denial are way of life)	3. Accepts responsibility
4. Constantly proves himself macho	4. Secure enough to be gentle
5. Loves conditionally (what's in it for me?)	5. Loves unconditionally
6. Independent, isolated (loner)	6. Team player
7. Seeks control—power	7. Leads fairly and justly
8. Empty talker—boastful	8. Man of action
9. Primarily a taker	9. Giver
10. Inconsistent in morals and ethics	10. Holds to a standard of conviction

Another early entry, written by Jack, was a more personal outline, which demonstrated an evolving awareness of the traits and factors which go into making a man out of a male:

I thought I became a man when I:
- *joined my high school football team*
- *at fourteen with my first sexual experience with a woman*
- *during my first fist fight*
- *at sixteen, when I got my driver's license*
- *when I graduated from high school*
- *the first time a younger guy called me, "Sir" (ouch!)*

- *when I started and then completed college*
- *got my first job*
- *with every young woman I had sex with*
- *when I got my tattoo/ear pierced*
- *at twenty when I got married and got my own place*
- *at twenty-three when I fathered my son*
- *when I got divorced at twenty-eight*
- *when I admitted to myself and others that I was bisexual*
- *during my first sexual encounter with a man*
- *with every guy I had sex with*
- *when I finally moved into my first apartment completely on my own*

I knew I wasn't a man when I:
- *deceived my ex-wife by not telling her the truth about my sexuality before we married*
- *when I got my first S.T.D.*
- *when my son (at five years old) asked me why I didn't live with him*
- *when I was too caught up in the pursuit of happiness to spend time with my son*
- *when my lies and cheating finally caught up with me*
- *when, after giving myself sexually to so many people, I realized I had very little else to give*
- *when I got the news that I was H.I.V. positive*
- *when I got into trouble with the law*
- *when I once conveniently forgot to pay child support*
- *when I moved in and shacked up with a few people in the name of love when it was really convenience*

I became a MAN when I:
- *started to own up to my responsibilities*
- *scaled down my busy life to spend more time with my son*
- *when I started being honest with myself and others*
- *when I sincerely apologized to the people I had hurt and deceived*

- *stopped blaming everyone else for my actions*
- *started to properly care for my health*
- *stopped having sex with everything that moved*
- *realized that long term gratification is a reward in itself*
- *realized that a committed, loving relationship with one person was worth waiting for*
- *when I realized that it was more important to have self-worth than a large ego*
- *when I acknowledged that actions are more important than words*
- *when I acknowledged that I wasn't the center of the Universe*
- *when I went for counseling*
- *when I realized that just because I was Gay did not mean that I was any different than anyone else, thus exempt from moral, ethical behavior (Thank you for that one)*
- *when I realized that a mind is a terrible thing to waste*
- *when I stopped talking about change, and started growing as a person through my actions*
- *and most important of all . . . when I realized that my actions were a legacy I was leaving for my son and started being the proper (living) example I had always dreamed of becoming*

The notion of developing "man-ness" on a continuum of both experience and self-discovery (often sidetracked with lapses into "male-ness") was shared by Jan:

At 13, Bar Mitzvah, I was called a man . . . I was still a child
   At 17, had sex for the first time . . . I was still a child
   At 26, had my first child . . . I was still a child
   At 30, got married to the mother of my child . . .
unfortunately, I was still a child
   At 31, got a great job and moved the family to
California . . . I was still a child, albeit a responsible one
   At 36, had my second child . . . I'm getting closer, but no cigar!
   At 38, submerged myself in my job . . . money, money, money . . . it didn't work . . . I was still a child

*At 43, lost the money because I was looking for a quick way
and almost lost my wife and kids . . . obviously—still a child*

*At 44, learned the meaning of love for my wife and
children and began putting money and work in their proper
perspective—hard lessons . . . I'm growing up*

*At 45, lost my great job—stood up as a man, started my own
business with the support of my wife and children—fell in love
with my wife and we became a team. By the way, that wussy
junk I used to do with my mom and other people in the family
no longer exists. I am responsible for my actions, emotions,
morals, ethics, the teaching of my children and the partnership
with my wife.*

*At 47, I enjoy being a man and I continue to learn . . . I can
still be like a child.*

One of the natural truths of life is that while we can and
ought to strive for perfection in our goals and ideals, the
striving is a continuous process, without a definitive endpoint. Being able to acknowledge and accept the perpetual
quest involved in bettering ourselves and the world is indeed
another sign of male maturity: manhood. Attaining manhood
is a never-ending experience.

However, all journeys have some starting point. And, for
males to become men, the best of all starting points is role-
modeling by good men—in general (heroes), and in specific
(your dad).

Women Give Birth to Boys, Men Give Birth to Men

Paul Ciotti wrote in the April 3, 1994, *L.A. Daily News,* that
"now with the possible exception of a few deeply bitter and
radical feminists, everyone understands that teen-age boys
need fathers. They need stable fathers, fathers with jobs,
fathers they can look up to and admire and fathers who will
physically kick their butts when they get out of line.

"Man is an animal and teen-age boys are more so than anyone. It may be repressive to force teen-age boys to toe the line, but the alternative is letting them raise themselves without any adult male guidance at all. And we've seen what that gives us—'Lord of the Flies in the Inner City,' accompanied by murder, rape and boys who beat other boys until their heads gush blood."

It is true that without constant, involved, and strong male role models, preferably biological fathers, many boys will overcompensate by exaggerating what they believe to be "male qualities," becoming overly aggressive, even violent, in order to forge a male identity. This is the source of problems for boys being brought up in female single-parent households—and why I think it is better that adolescent boys live with their dads, when by divorce or never-marriage, the appropriate two-parent family is not an option.

It's also bad for boys when their mothers are bitter about some man and generalize their attitude to all men—forgetting, ignoring, or not caring about the impact those negative sentiments have on their male children.

A good paternal role model helps boys to properly channel that inherent raw male energy into constructive activities and personality characteristics, while also instilling an appreciation for feelings, compassion, cooperation, values, and more. Which is exactly what the actor Dabney Coleman revealed in an interview for *Parade* magazine in August of 1996: "My problem growing up was not having a direct role model to emulate in becoming a man. I either didn't know a lot of the rules of manhood or else I didn't believe them. But now I've learned those things—unfortunately maybe too late to be the dad for my children that I would like to have been. But now I know a lot more about the rules. And I believe them."

The author queries Coleman as to what he meant by the "rules" that make a man. "Caring for others around you," he answered, "helping your kids, taking time to be alone with them. You have to show love. Another rule is loyalty. Giving. Fairness to people. Decency. Honesty."

As you can see, being a man has a lot to do with reconciling classical masculine ideals with so-called feminine (actually, deeply human) qualities that deal with the truth of one's human nature with respect to feelings. Because, without an awareness and acceptance of feelings, a male doesn't become a man, he becomes a male cartoon—the animation required for humanness *is feelings*.

Kelly, a listener, wrote about this very issue:

One way men tend to mess up their lives is to assume that to admit/own their feelings makes them less a man. I have run the gamet with this one. I am a recovered alcoholic of nine plus years. I had no male role model growing up and got my male ideals from such wonderful men as Zane Gray and Louis L'Amor (both of whom are authors of western stories). These were confirmed and solidified by the Giants: John Wayne and Clint Eastwood.

By the age of twelve I knew that REAL men don't cry and they do fight, swear, drink, smoke and take what they want. This learning took me to wonderful places: I spent from age 12 to 18 in reform school. I had no respect for myself or others. I soon found out that no one liked me and wondered why.

I began to believe that no one cared and became driven—the harder I tried to make people like me and pay attention to me, the more I got rejected.

I have come to realize that the things that drove me to my insane behavior was hurt, fear and shame.

Within 3 weeks of finding this out, I was able to start the healing process.

I am more a man today than any time in my past. I can communicate with my family without anger or violence. Being able to identify and express my feelings has been one of the most liberating experiences of my life. And all I had to do was be willing to feel the feelings and put a name to them. So simple . . . but not always easy.

Moms Count Too!

It's not that moms aren't valuable and necessary; I am the mother of an eleven-year-old boy and see every day how my affection, attention, discussions, reactions, participation, and expressed attitudes and behaviors are important to his life, soul, and psyche. Which is why I was particularly touched by this motherly contribution from a female listener, Becky, to this book:

> *Ten Bits of Advice from Your Loving Mother . . . Who promises Not to Nag You Any More*
> 1. *Do not date anyone who believes that you are perfect. Not only will you not be challenged and stimulated, but you should date people with more intelligence.*
> 2. *Separate whites and colors when doing hot wash.*
> 3. *An erection is NOT the primary reason to have sex.*
> 4. *Buy a cookbook. All food does not come with the instructions:*
>   *Remove from carton*
>   *Heat in microwave, 2–3 minutes on high*
>   *Serve.*
> 5. *Learn from the mistakes of others. You do not have time to make them all yourself.*
> 6. *Flush.*
> 7. *Phone your parents, even if you don't need money.*
> 8. *Remember, fear + action = courage.*
> 9. *Know that shortcuts do not build character.*
> 10. *Make your decisions with virtue and honor, and you will not have to shave with your eyes closed.*
>
> *Your perspective and wisdom, in this small corner of the world, help keep the inmates from taking over the asylum.*

It seems that the day I solicited input about this male-man transition, one man's wife challenged him to define what a

"man" was to him. He responded at first by calling manhood a "daunting task," but felt compelled to undertake it
anyway. He admitted that this analysis just scratched the surface—but I thought it was wonderful:

- *A man is an individual who worships the G-d in heaven,
  takes pride and ownership in his family and works hard to
  provide for their needs.*
- *A man does not use profanity*
- *A man is an individual who views his career not as the primary means of self-achievement, but merely as a means to
  provide for his family*
- *A man is an individual who respects and cherishes women,
  he is one who will put a lady's needs ahead of his own personal convenience. He will defend her honor. He will hold
  a door for her. He will relinquish his coat to her on a cold,
  windy day. He will look into her eyes when he is speaking
  or listening to her.*
- *A man is one who holds deeply held convictions, and high
  ideals of integrity. He is dedicated to these principles, willing to invest his life in them, and if necessary, give his life
  for them. It is his life, not his conversation, that serves as a
  quiet testament to his integrity.*
- *A man is an individual who keeps his commitments*
- *A man is an individual who does not measure success by
  material attainment, but by the legacy that he leaves
  behind.*

It is in those ideals and that legacy that we open the eyes
of the current and next generations as to what is expected of
them. Spencer realizes his participation in and responsibility
for that process:

> *I am very aware that my son, Reilly (almost 5) watches me very
> closely to see how a "man acts". I will have considered myself*

successful if, when my son is grown and on the verge of having his own family, he can say to himself, "I want to be a man and a great dad—just like my dad."

It is no accident that throughout the five Books of Moses, G-d condemns certain behaviors by "cursing" subsequent generations. I don't think it's because G-d is a "meanie"; it would seem we are being reminded of our responsibilities to all the world that is and will be, that what we do today not only has immediate impact, but will affect generations to come. That thought is at once awesome and humbling.

Sons suffer agonizing pain and loss when their fathers are either deceased, neglectful, absent, or rotten—as James can testify:

I always feared becoming like my father. We are not very much alike. He had a very quick temper and I am very slow to anger. He was a voracious womanizer. I believe in monogamous committed relationships. He would hit me at the slightest provocation. I never struck my two boys in their entire lives. I could go on and on—but it serves no purpose. I did not turn into my father.

I am 60 years old, and for the first time in my life I feel at peace with myself. I look at my life now as somewhat a success and feel good about many of the things I have done. I just know I did not turn into the worst part of my father. Although I don't remember many good things about him, I am sure he had many good qualities and I hope I am like him in these.

Of course, it is far better and far easier to develop as a man and as a person when the ingredients are correct—but even when they're not, you can still become a man of quality, character, and virtue. Perhaps . . . the journey is harder and longer with more potholes and detours—but it is still navigable. Some of those potholes and detours might be called:

Stupid Criteria for Male Status

Jerry sent in a contribution that belongs in this category:

> *I recall during my younger years conversing with a friend who told me he would turn his bar glass up side down in a tavern to indicate to anyone interested that he could whip anyone in the place. He explained that being able to whip anyone in the place meant he was a better man than anyone in the place.*
>
> *I told him that according to his own definition, that if a large gorilla were to come into that bar, that the gorilla would then be the best man in the place.*
>
> *Another told me that the sign of a man was how many times he could perform sexually. The queen bee in almost any hive would be a better man than any of us, or even the local male prostitute would be a better man than he.*
>
> *I believe what makes a real man is his willingness to accept responsibility for his own actions. Most are so busy blaming someone else for hot coffee on their crotch.*

ALL MEN ARE CREATED EGO

Adolescent-style contests of drinking, spitting, and belching as a sign of superior manhood or masculinity are obviously (I hope) stupid criteria of manhood; but so is the self-centered focus on ego gratification that drives men to show off, foolishly risk their lives, or push otherwise reasonable goals and activities to excess. A listener, Mike, wrote that this was his difficulty:

> *The second common denominator in the stupid things I've done, is impossible to eliminate, and that is ego. The male ego is a powerful motivating force that left unchecked and un-understood will run a man's life and be the driving force behind all decisions and actions. Everything I did was ego driven; from driving fast, succeeding in school, buying motorcycle, excelling in sports,*

dating, drinking to excess, being the best, taking the risk, etc. Dr. Laura, all motivation, good and bad, were ego driven. I had to be the best or die trying. That resulted in some very positive accomplishments for all the wrong reasons. The positive accomplishments covered or hid the driving ego, which was interpreted by friends and family as self-discipline and motivation. All the time it was the dangerously strong male ego.

The stupidest thing a man can do is to let his life be dominated by the male ego. Had my wife not walked out on me and caused me to explore myself, I may have gone through my entire life with this warped sense of how things ought to be. It would have been a terribly empty life with all the outside appearances of success and happiness.

What people would think determined my happiness or lack of it. I realized that I had this ego that when used properly was a powerful positive force, when not using it properly, letting it control me, would eventually destroy me.

For example, my wife wanted me to run with her. I resisted it because my ego said it wasn't the "manly" thing to do, and no woman was going to make me do something the guys may not approve of. She eventually left me and married her jogging partner.

Thank G-d I learned to channel that ego into the discipline needed to train for and complete a 26 mile run!

The "ego" in psychoanalytic terms is the conscious, rational component of the psyche that experiences and reacts to the outside world and mediates between the demands of the id (instincts which drive toward pleasure) and superego (conscience, standards, values). In everyday language, your ego is your sense of self, as distinct from others. So, if you are excessively focused on your "self" and what you have/how you look to others, you naturally become isolated from real shared intimacy (except for showing off and impressing functions) and become self-centered.

Something can be good (like salt in soup), but bad in

excess (like salty soup). Ego is a necessary component of a healthy psyche, but too much of it distracts you from growth, human connections, and therefore happiness.

Manhood As a Big Bang

Moving from the boyish immaturity of an ego-driven life to manhood seems to happen differently for each man—although there do seem to be some commonalities of experience. Many men report *events* which seemed to catapult them into a state of manhood. It is possible that the event was really not so precipitous—perhaps they were simply ready when the experience crystallized the concept of manhood for them. Here are some of the circumstances which men reported to me concerning their transition from "male" to "man":

Steve: *For me, there is an exact moment, and I can recall it as though it were yesterday. In the second trimester of my wife's first pregnancy, she had a sonogram which revealed abnormal measurements of the head of our fetus. The nurse at the HMO gave us this news with all the concern of a waitress taking a sandwich order at a deli. She basically said we'd have to simply wait and see and come back in a month for more tests. I said, "I don't think so. Call the doctor—I don't care where he is or what he is doing, find him and let's see what he will say or do." Fifteen minutes later an embarrassed nurse came back in and sent us directly to the hospital for more tests. Yes, there was trouble and my wife was ordered to quit her job that day and go home to complete bed rest. For the next several months, I cared for my wife and our baby-to-be with the help of my angel-in-law. It was at that moment in the office that I realized my DUTY and made the transition from male to man. By the way, our daughter is celebrating her sixth birthday tomorrow. She is perfectly healthy now, always running, skipping, or jumping wherever she goes!*

Michael: *The final part of becoming a man came this last year when my father died. For me it was the ultimate **PASSING OF THE TORCH OF RESPONSIBILITY**. That is when I became a man.*

Mike: *I became a man when my mother (who is now 82 years old) had a major stroke two and a half years ago, which required her to spend a month in the hospital, and has a permanent disability because of it. No matter what one owns or how old one gets, one tends to maintain a certain relationship with parents until such an event occurred. At that point I realized my parents were more dependent on me than I was on them. Ultimately, one becomes a man when the realization comes that the kid inside has **NO ONE TO RUN HOME TO ANYMORE**, and must accept full responsibility for all actions.*

Gary: *I am a 24 year old male; 6 years ago I was raped and infected with HIV. Before this event I was very immature, never really wanting to see any real beauty in life, just a boy who was happy being a boy and couldn't comprehend the difference between a man and a male. After receiving the news about the HIV I tried very hard not to slip into depression, although it was and still is hard. I started working with People Living With Aids (PLWA) and that opened up a whole new world for me of spirituality, true friendship, growth and love. I have had to find a lot of strength and courage to conquer the past 6 years. I'd like to think it has made me more on my way to "manhood". How can a male become a man without having **COURAGE, LOVE AND STRENGTH IN LIFE**?*

Richard: *At 18 I became a man. I was sitting in the right seat while my brother was driving. It was windy in Chicago, and the heater in the car had stopped pumping out hot air while the blower motor continued to run. After playing with the* *heater for a couple of minutes, my brother said we should stop, call my Dad, and ask him what to do. I responded that we would simply turn the blower off and continue on. I know that doesn't sound profound. I'm a year older than you, Dr. Laura, and it does not sound profound to me either. However, from that moment, **MAKING A DECISION ON MY OWN**, I ceased acting (and thinking) like a child.*

*Howard: It was when I was 18, dating a sexually active (with many guys) 16 year old girl. I thought I saw something more in her. One week after we met, she told me that she wanted to make love to me. Since I was a virgin, sex, and how to finally get some, was just about all that was on my mind. But for some reason, I knew sex between us just wouldn't be right. I called her mother—I was scared to death but knew it was the right thing to do. I told her mother of my concerns about the girl's emotional health. Her mother thanked me and put her back into therapy. She wouldn't talk to me again. I will always cherish the first moment I was confronted with an **ADULT DECISION, AND LET MY CHARACTER DECIDE.** My late father role modeled manhood for me, and showed me that being a man requires honor and integrity—which can only be demonstrated when "the right thing" is also "the difficult thing".*

John: I had been seeing a therapist because my marriage was on the rocks and we had a three year old daughter and I was on the verge of an affair, determined to get a divorce. The therapist said one thing that probably changed my life: "When you have children, there is no such thing as divorce." Of course, she was right—there would be custody battles, arguments over visitation and holidays, and the guilt inherent in leaving my daughter. At this point I looked into the abyss that I was about to make out of my life and, more importantly, the lives of my daughter and wife. I realized that no matter how hard things were with my wife and daughter, they would be infinitely worse for all concerned if I were to leave them. It took time for my wife to forgive me and regain her trust in me, but I believe that our mutual commitment is stronger now than it ever was. To use your words, Dr. Laura, I don't know if it was courage, **COMMITMENT,** *or character (or even fear) that led me to make my decision to stay with my family, but I know that when I look in the mirror I now see a man.*

Connor: *After serving in the Air Force as a bomber pilot, successfully practicing a profession for over thirty years, trying to change my wife into the perfect woman, and raising wonderful children in spite of ourselves, at about the age of sixty I finally realized that I couldn't "fix" anyone but myself. At that point I realized that it was my own attitudes which were the cause of most of my problems. My tendency to judge my wife and blame her for our marital difficulties was at the root of my dissatisfaction. My duty was to work on myself. Period. On that day of* **HUMILITY** *I became a man. I can't tell you what an improvement this realization has made in my life, and how much more at peace I am.*

John: *The defining moment of manhood came when together we watched a tiny life moving in my wife's womb via sonogram. We could watch our daughter respond as we spoke and sang to her, and as we cried for joy, I realized a* **NEW PURPOSE.** *I knew then that while any guy could make a baby, it takes a man to raise one.*

Michael: *I went from male to man when I changed my first born's diaper, fed him his bottle and rocked him to sleep. I had done all the macho male things but this* **NURTURING** *stuff was truly being a man.*

Kenny: *After a bad breakup I saw the first girlfriend I ever had. We had a terrible, terrible relationship, but nevertheless* had the best sex life ever. She is engaged and shacking up with her honey. Apparently he is wonderful to her. Only— last week she told me that her sex life is unsatisfying with this guy and that sex is better for her when it is with some- one she isn't supposed to be with . . . and she insinuated it to be me. I know that if I pursue it, we could have the same great sex we did before. But I thought about what kind of pig I would be if I did that, and what kind of person she would be too. It takes a man to **REJECT WHAT IS IN HIS MIND TO BE WRONG** no matter how good it may feel to accept it. Speaking from my own experience, this is the moment that answers the question on becoming a "man".

Jim: I became a man when I finally understood SELFLESS- NESS.

Scott: I became a man at the age of 19 when in Viet Nam in 1971, I began to realize that **MY ACTIONS HAD CONSE- QUENCES AND THAT I NEEDED TO BE RESPONSIBLE FOR THEM** and that I needed to think about what I did. It was very apparent there that to survive and to help my friends survive, I needed to think and act like life was important.

Terry: **BEING A MAN IS ACCEPTING AND GIVING LOVE.** Even to the day before my wedding, I was skeptical I was doing the right thing. I was a very poor example of a boyfriend and fiance for all the reasons that can be thought of, but will not be elaborated here. When I arrived and stood up on the altar, staring at my wife-to-be, I thought that she must really love me, considering all she had done to marry me, and thought, "Wow, not only do I owe it to my wife to be the best I can possibly be, but I owe it to all those that are here to witness this. I am proud to say that I have been the best I can be and strive every day to be an even better hus- band and father to my two daughters. You see, I am a stay- at-home dad!

Marinating into Manhood

For many men it wasn't a crisis or event which turned the manhood switch to "on"; instead, there was an ever-growing awareness, an attitude, a deepening understanding which seeped slowly into consciousness. Here are those descriptions:

Craig: *I would say becoming a man from a male was a matter of my state of mind and nothing else. The change in the state of my mind that I would say triggered the change and a change in my* **ATTITUDE TOWARD RESPONSIBILITY**: *when I felt I was the one responsible for my own well being, my own achievements, successes and failures, decisions (correct and incorrect) and the consequences thereof, and my own financial support, then that is when I became a man.*

Thomas: *Occasionally I go through my old papers and I read the citation that accompanied the Silver Star I received so long ago. It mentions my being an "inspiration" to my entire unit. How great it is to inspire my family. Decorations and medals don't make you a man.* **FACING DAILY STRUGGLES** *alongside your spouse and children—that's what gives a person character! I know what it is to become a man, and I found it out a long time after I returned from Viet Nam.*

John: *I didn't start growing up until I was 28. This is why I say that: I am a recovering alcoholic and addict. I put myself in a treatment program and ever since then I started* **TAKING ON THE WORLD SOBER.** *So that's when I became a man.*

Bill: *You're a man when you don't do these things—which did occur to me: do drugs to obliterate the reality of life, get tattooed, succumb to peer pressure for conquest sex, join gangs to feel wanted, disregard the need for education, abuse credit cards, don't listen to or learn from the experience of others, don't accept responsibility, don't listen to or under-stand the views of others, be selfish.*

Saul: *What made me a man is when I truly and sincerely came to not care about the following: how much money I made, what kind of car I drove, my social status, the look and location of my house. What made me a man is when I came to care about my relationships with my loved ones and friends. A man is a man when he is* **CONFIDENT WITH HIMSELF,** *his place in life and has the ability to be direct with himself and those around him. This, of course, has to be tempered with compassion and care in the way you communicate.*

Mark: *My passage into manhood, true manhood, came over a long weekend about two years ago. I attended a conference for men (Promise Keepers) which was aimed at getting men back on track with their families. Before that I was out being a "male" while my wife of 16 years was at home raising our children. She was the one who took care of the spiritual upbringing, the day to day care, the loves and kisses and all the bruised knees. I was too busy being a "male". I was so busy providing a "good life" for my family, I didn't see until it was almost too late that I was losing my family. Providing a good life for a family really comes down to* **GIVING THE LOVE AND SECURITY TO YOUR FAMILY** *which they deserve.*

John: *I don't really think there is a special moment that converts one into a man. But rather, a point in one's life when you* **DECIDE THAT BUILDING CHARACTER AND BEING HONORABLE** *not only to yourself but to the family around you, far outweighs any pleasurable experiences that a "male" can have.*

Walter: *I am 20 years old and currently going to college and helping with my family's Chinese restaurant business. I* believe the difference between a man and a male are the governing values that the person has. As you see, I did not say responsibility. To be a man is more than just paying bills. It is about commitment. I am **COMMITTED TO GOVERNING VALUES.** For example, I seek truth, I love my family, I love G-d, I have a positive attitude, and I have integrity.

Timothy: *I felt that I had become a man when I realized and embraced the concept that it is my job as a man to be a SERVANT TO MY FAMILY. I am not to seek my own comfort, but rather to nourish (time and affection), provide for (cash and fixits), and protect my family (against bad guys and TV). I anticipate that my own needs will be met, too, but as a secondary effect. My job is to do what is right, regardless of the consequences. I am depending on Christ's power within me to make progress toward this goal.*

Ron: *I would suggest that becoming a man is to a male what becoming civilized is to a heathen. This is the ABDICATION OF UNRESTRAINED FREEDOM for the greater good of the group.*

Jeffrey: *I became a man when I finally understood that my FAMILY, JOB, AND RESPONSIBILITIES WEREN'T AN OBLIGATION, THEY ARE THE REWARD.*

Mack: *I believe I came to this conclusion through the pain I have gone through and looked straight in the eye. The PAIN AND DEALING WITH IT has taught me how to care. When I was only a male, I didn't care.*

Manhood-o-Phobia

It is obvious from all these "testimonials" that the transition from male to manhood is rewarding and fulfilling. Yet, some males absolutely refuse, in the old style of "Hell no—I won't go!" Why? Well, listen to David:

1. *According to my father, I passed through the threshold of manhood on the day of my Bar Mitzvah. I quit Hebrew school the day following. My first "adult" decision.*
2. *According to my mother, my manhood is non-existent; at 36 she will not allow me out of the house with a wet head. For this reason, although I love my parents dearly, I live 400 miles away.*
3. *According to my older brother, my manhood is nonexistent; our sibling rivalry has never ceased. My brother is jealous of my successes and I am jealous of his intelligence and creativity.*
4. *According to my best friend's children, my godchildren, I am a man of the world who has lived an adventurous life with great stories to tell.*

   So, I am relatively successful, have gone back to Synagogue, own a home, pay my bills on time, etc. What have I committed myself to? A career? A lover? Friends? No.

   I am one of those "men" who is so scared of real responsibility, that I avoid it at every turn. *I have yet to cross that chasm, to care for something so strongly, to achieve something so great, to love something so deeply and to dream so recklessly, that it becomes my life's blood. To answer your question, "When did I become a man?" I guess my answer would have to be "tomorrow".*

This idea of emotional/intellectual/spiritual/behavioral **passion** does seem to be at the core of what most of the men have talked about. For them, it's the passion for family and children which seems to define manhood—the willingness to invest soul-deep in things which have a meaning past your own personal ego gratification or gain. Interestingly, the ego is most gratified when the goal is sacrifice and not its own sake.

While "maleness" is that part or stage (or both) of a man which centers on incredible dreams, ambitions, ideas, experiences, being a man seems to make most sense when the connection to others is most focal. It is through this connection that a man feels defined by his purpose. So, ultimately it is through your meaning to others that you are defined and redeemed.

Ron, a listener, wrote this poem, which summarizes the definition of manhood through purpose/service to others:

> The Good Man
> *Blessed is the one*
> *who can be trusted.*
> *The one who follows through.*
> *The one with ethical boundary.*
> *The task is assumed—then completed*
> *by the one known through his word*
> *which becomes his deed.*
> *All that can be said,*
> *understood in high esteem,*
> *is captured, with great compassion, in the phrase:*
> *"He is a good man."*

Offered in conclusion:

QUICK-TAKE
I think the transition from male to man requires that the big head, although amused with the little head's ideas, is the primary pilot of the human body. Anonymous

Need I say more?

EPILOGUE

In an April 1997 nationally syndicated cartoon strip, *Second Chances,* a woman and a man are in line to ask book locations of a clerk in a fictional bookstore called SuperBooks. The clerk says, while pointing, "The aisles go: Bargains, Best Sellers, History, Languages, Travel, Women-Good, *Men-Bad*"!

This joke is based on reality. I recently picked up a book about verbal abusiveness, commenting casually over my shoulder to my husband, "I'll bet the focus of this book is how bad men are." Sure enough—I was right on the money. Never mind the cutting, cruel, confusing, agitating, and nasty mouths we women are well capable of displaying. If men retaliate in kind, it's not considered self-defense, it's simply further proof of the oppressive, controlling, destructive brutes they've already been made out to be.

Part of the reason for this hostile negativity toward men is the fact that they're targeted by this neurotic brand of feminization rampant throughout academia and psychotherapy in particular, which has tried to explain away women's basic female nature, personality, and character weaknesses, personal failures, or stupid behaviors on the mere existence of the male animal. Our current victimization culture (not just about women, but many determined-to-be-miserable designer groups) requires a perpetrator—and it's men.

I was recently listening to a radio talk show broadcast

moderated by what I consider a radical and irrational, but very well known, women's rights attorney. She was going on about a new ruling by some college which demanded that men get clear consent from a woman before having sexual intercourse. I suppose this tactic is an attempt to avoid "date rape." (It's a stupid tactic, since how can he prove he didn't coerce the "little innocent virgin" into signing or saying yes?) A male caller challenged the host by asking her if she had ever had sex without giving explicit consent. She played around for a while, clearly uncomfortable, and finally answered that she had. So, the next question should be, "Isn't that rape?"

Another male caller wanted to know if a woman taking off her own panties is giving explicit consent. The host laughed that maybe the woman just needed aeration.

Obviously the feminist host's brain already benefits from excessive aeration.

The main problem with the contemporary feminist movement (in addition to their rejection of truth or fairness) is that they simply can't stand the truth: men and women are inherently different; that fact is not a value judgment, it's just an observation.

Jane E. Brody wrote "Sex and the Survival of the Fittest: Calamities Are a Disaster for Men" for the *New York Times* (4/24/96). This article reviewed the physiological and sociological factors resulting in the ultimate survival of a member of the infamous 1846 Donner party, traveling by covered wagon from Illinois to California. While in the Sierra Nevada, a blizzard struck which stranded eighty-seven people in the mountains for six months. These folks struggled to survive, even resorting to cannibalism, yet forty died.

A report published earlier in the journal *Evolutionary Anthropology* pointed out the expected: the oldest and the youngest members of the Donner party had the highest mortality rate.

"But," according to the article, "most striking was that nearly twice as many men as women died—57 percent of the fifty-three men as against 28 percent of the thirty-four women—and the men who died succumbed much more quickly than the women. Furthermore, of those who tried to walk out of the mountains on snow shoes, all the men died and all the women survived."

Why? Two main factors were at work to "protect" the women:

- Biology—"[Women] are smaller, with 17 percent less body mass on average than men, so they need less food to survive. They have nearly twice the percentage of body fat— roughly 27 percent whereas men have only 15 percent (therefore women are better insulated)."
- Sociology—"The men died because they were doing what they are biologically fit to do. Characteristically, men take greater risks and do heavier work. The men in both parties (there was a similar second disaster with 429 Mormons) did a lot of energy-requiring tasks: hunting, cutting down trees, etc., which depleted their energy stores and put them at risk of an early death. Men are more likely than women to take risks and to act aggressively, which puts them at a greater risk of injury and death. Women, on the other hand, are designed to have children, and what adapts them to have kids enables them to deal better with deprivation."

Neither men nor women are inherently bad. It diminishes the potential life of both to diminish either. The cornerstone of humanity, and our potential for greatness among all animals, is our ability to create stable and loving families in which to raise virtuous, capable, productive children. Without an appreciation for the inherent magnificence in each gender, with an awareness of our troublesome limitations, there is no hope for benevolent, holy, happy unions. If so . . . humanity is lost.

This book is my contribution to that hope.